TAKE
MY HEART,
O GOD

*Riches from the Greatest Christian
Women Writers of All Time*

 ZONDERVAN®   A WORTHY BOOK

Take My Heart, O God
Copyright © 2010 by Worthy Media, Inc.

This title is also available as a Zondervan ebook. Visit www.zondervan.com/ebooks.

This title is also available in a Zondervan audio edition. Visit www.zondervan.fm.

Requests for information should be addressed to:

Zondervan, *Grand Rapids, Michigan* 49530

Library of Congress Cataloging-in-Publication Data

Author LName, First.
      Take my heart, o God : riches from the greatest Christian women writers of all
         time. p. cm.
      ISBN 978-0-310-32747-9 (hardcover, padded)
      1. Christian women--Prayers and devotions. 2. Christian literature--Women
         authors. 3. Devotional calendars.
BV4844.T35 2010
242'.643--dc22
2010001868

All Scripture quotations, unless otherwise indicated, are taken from the Holy Bible,
New International Version®, NIV®. Copyright © 1973, 1978, 1984 by Biblica, Inc.™ Used by
permission of Zondervan. All rights reserved worldwide.

Any Internet addresses (websites, blogs, etc.) and telephone numbers printed in this
book are offered as a resource. They are not intended in any way to be or imply an
endorsement by Zondervan, nor does Zondervan vouch for the content of these sites
and numbers for the life of this book.

Packaged by Worthy Media. For subsidiary and foreign language rights contact info@
worthymedia.com

Produced with the assistance of The Livingstone Corporation (www.LivingstoneCorp.com).
Project staff includes Dave Veerman, Linda Taylor, Betsy Schmitt, Linda Washington, Larry
Taylor, Joel Bartlett, Ashley Taylor, Andy Culbertson.

Cover design: Christopher Tobias, Tobias Design
Cover photography: © Mella/photocase.com
Interior design: Larry Taylor and Christopher Tobias
Interior photography: Winter: © AndreasF/photocase.com; Summer: © suze/photocase.
com; Fall: © suze/photocase.com; Spring: © john krempl/photocase.com

Printed in China

---

10 11 12 13 14 • 20 19 18 17 16 15 14 13 12 11 10 9 8 7 6 5 4 3 2 1

WELCOME

A cross the centuries and around the world, remarkable Christian women have been writing. Whether by candlelight with a quill pen or on the latest-version laptop computer, women have shared comfort, inspiration, admonition, and biblical insight. Writing from their personal experiences and lessons learned from in-depth study, they offer their hearts to us with their enormous riches to share.

Take My Heart, O God is a collection of devotions inspired by little nuggets of wisdom gleaned from Christian women writers across the centuries. From the writings of godly women, we've chosen powerful, one- or two-sentence quotations that will provide a spark in your personal walk with God. Each seed quotation is followed by a longer devotional, a suggested Scripture reading, and a short prayer starter—one for each day of the year.

As you take a few minutes from your busy day to enjoy God's presence, may you be drawn closer to him and be able to say in humble submission, "Take my heart, o God."

—The Editors

CONTRIBUTORS

Cheryl Dunlop

Heather Pleier

Carol Fielding

Kathy Hardee

Peggy Billiard

Sue Rosenfeld

Judith Costello

Diane Markins

Michelle Van Loon

Brenda Nixon

Kathy Lay

Drenda Thomas Richards

Linda McGee

Pat Stockett Johnston

Mary Grace Birkhead

Sandra Stein

Gail Krahenbuhl

Debbie Simler-Goff

Linda Washington

Betsy Schmitt

Linda Taylor

JANUARY

Among all the names that reveal God, this, the "God of all comfort," seems to me one of the loveliest and the most absolutely comforting. The words all comfort *admit of no limitations and no deductions.*

—HANNAH WHITALL SMITH

GOD OF ALL COMFORT

We love seeing the word *all* if it points to something favorable for us. We love when *all* of the shoes at our favorite store are on sale, or *all* of the candies in the bowl are dark chocolate, or *all* of the bills are paid in full. However, when *all* aspects of life seem to crash down around us, that's a different matter. We find ourselves in desperate need of the "God of *all* comfort."

Consider the ramifications of that name. No problem or heartache is outside of God's range of comfort. He has unlimited resources—a vast wellspring—at his disposal. When we're hurting, truly the loveliest name of all describes God bringing us not *some* comfort, not comfort for *some* things, but *all* the comfort we need.

The God of all comfort waits today to comfort you. No limitations. No deductions.

Read 2 Corinthians 1:3–5.

GOD OF ALL COMFORT, I NEED YOUR COMFORT RIGHT NOW.

God has chosen you and me for the purpose of bearing much eternal fruit . . . fruit that is simply the character of God's Son coming out in us.

—ANNE GRAHAM LOTZ

MORE LIKE JESUS

As the new year begins, you may feel melancholy, looking back with some regret or ahead with fearful questions. Issues and anxiety don't leave much room for hope. Certainly you *want* to feel optimistic, even joyful, but how?

The answer comes not in trying, but knowing; not in doing, but resting. In Galatians 5, God promises joy as a "fruit" of his work in us. So instead of trying to manufacture a feeling of joy, look to your Father in heaven and remember his promise. He has already planted joy in your heart by his Spirit. So *feeling* joyful is not the issue. Rather, quietly sit before God and express to him your deepest hurts and concerns and ask him to grow in you his fruit of joy. Then, as Anne says, you will continue to bear fruit—eternal fruit—for him, becoming more and more like his Son.

Read Galatians 5:22–23.

LORD, HELP MY LIFE SHOW THE FRUIT OF THE
SPIRIT IN EVERYTHING I DO TODAY.

O faithful soul! The repose enjoyed in thyself is but a shadow of that which thou wilt find in God!

—MADAME GUYON

HUNGRY SOUL

Rest. Repose. Times of quiet when we can think—about God, about life, about what we are called to do. Such times grant us refreshment, a needed break, a time to refocus.

And yet, Madame Guyon would have us realize that those precious times are a mere shadow of the kind of rest that our soul can find in God.

Our soul thirsts; he alone can satisfy. We hunger to know the depths of God's love; he fills us to overflowing with nourishment from his Word. We face difficult times; he gives us the refreshment that keeps us moving forward. We struggle with guilt over sins we have committed; he alone grants us forgiveness that brings true peace and repose. We need rest from the storm; he invites us into his refuge and wraps his arms of protection around us.

Today let your soul find its best rest in him.

Read Psalm 62:5–8.

LORD JESUS, MY SOUL RESTS IN YOU.

My calling is to press my face into the shoulder blades of Jesus so that wherever he leads I will go.

—MARGARET FEINBERG

PRESSING IN

Hold on tight and don't let go. That's the picture Margaret Feinberg creates when she describes her calling as pressing her face into the shoulder blades of Jesus. When we hold on that tight, we show trust, we draw comfort, we give love.

When you hold onto Jesus like this, you draw in his scent of strength and purpose. You feel the radiant warmth of his love. And you're so intoxicated by it that you follow closely so as not to lose a single precious moment basking in his nearness. As you lean into him, the direction of your steps becomes almost irrelevant. Each cobblestone you traverse, each ditch you leap across, becomes a victory. You care less about where you're going and more about simply trusting where he's leading you.

Press in. Inhale deeply. And don't lag behind.

Read Psalm 73:23–26.

LORD, MAKE ME SO ENAMORED OF YOUR PRESENCE
THAT I PRESS IN FOR MORE.

Uncrowd my heart, O God, / until silence speaks, / in your still, small voice, / turn me . . . to listening, waiting, stillness, silence.

—ESTHER DEWAAL

IN THE FULLNESS OF SILENCE

When our hearts, our minds, and our souls are filled with worldly concerns, we leave no room for God.

Silence. This is the path to clearing clutter and countering pride. Release thoughts and worries. Free the mind. Let go of desires and expectations. Open a sacred space inside your heart. Then God will take up residence.

Elijah experienced demonstrations of God's great power, but he heard God speaking directly to him in a quiet whisper. He felt humbled before that soft voice and covered his face.

Deep prayer is not about using a wealth of flashy words or demanding great miracles. Instead, it is learning to be so still that God's words and his will can be distinguished over the insistent clamor of the world.

In stillness, our eyes see with wonder. Our hearts open and our minds surrender. And then we can hear God.

Read 1 Kings 19:11–13.

I WAIT FOR YOU, LORD. IN THE SILENCE
OF MY HEART, I TRUST IN YOU.

Nothing seems more miraculous, more difficult for us who insist on figuring things out, than this matter of grace.

—ELISABETH ELLIOT

AMAZING GRACE

John Newton, author of the hymn "Amazing Grace," said he had a habit of swearing that was as deeply rooted as a second nature. His last will and testament reads, "I was an apostate, a blasphemer, and an infidel." The former slave trader continued, "I was capable of anything; I had not the least fear of God before my eyes."

Yet God saved him. Why did God pour out his grace on such a violent man?

Because God loved him.

God loves you. Not because of who you are, not because of anything you've done, but just because he is the God of amazing grace. Nothing you've done is so bad that you are beyond the reach of his grace.

You won't be able to figure it out; it doesn't make sense. It's nothing short of miraculous, this matter of grace.

And it's a free gift given to you.

Read Ephesians 2:8–9.

LORD, THANK YOU FOR LOVING ME,
FOR SHOWING ME YOUR AMAZING GRACE.

Sometimes the greatest answers to prayer happen when you have no place to go but God.

—CAROL CYMBALA

BIG PROBLEMS, BIG ANSWERS

Bad report. Dreams crushed. Hope lost. The perfect time for God to do his work.

The impossibility of our situation means nothing to God. He delights in bringing answers when all we see are obstacles. He does some of his best work when there is no money, no time, no hope, no way out.

Are you at the point of giving up? Have you done everything humanly possible to solve the problem but you feel there's no answer? It's too big for you to fix, too overwhelming to handle, too much to bear.

Fall on your knees before God. You have nowhere else to turn. And that's just the time when God says to you, "Relax, my daughter. It isn't over until *I* say it's over." Big problems require big answers. And that's God's specialty.

Read Mark 10:27.

MY PROBLEM IS TOO BIG FOR ME, LORD. I NEED A BIG ANSWER.

It is far better to endure patiently a smart which nobody feels but yourself, than to commit a hasty action whose evil consequences will extend to all connected with you; and, besides, the Bible bids us to return good for evil.

—CHARLOTTE BRONTE

GOOD FOR EVIL

God's way is often topsy-turvy to what we see. He promises that he works all things (even bad things) for our good. He promises to be our defender and the judge of anyone who would show us injustice. So, with his promises in place, he also gives us strength to endure pain when we have no way to escape it. He even gives us ability to return good for evil to those who hurt us.

That's exactly what we should do. Charlotte Bronte advises that it is better to endure a hurt patiently than to commit a hasty action that will cause evil consequences to everyone around. Better to hurt a little oneself than to spread the hurt to others. And, beyond that, better to return good for evil.

Not easy, not comfortable, maybe not even fair. But God-honoring.

And that's what matters.

Read Genesis 50:14–21.

FATHER, THANK YOU THAT YOU ARE ABLE TO TURN EVIL INTO GOOD. HELP ME TO TRUST YOU.

The telephone rings—loud, jarring . . . dissolving my precious moment of stolen solitude. Then . . . I suddenly know . . . that God is in the ringing, that God is the interruption.

—EDWINA GATELEY

INTERRUPTIONS AS OPPORTUNITIES

Stolen solitude." How true it is that to find precious moments to talk with God, we need to steal the time from other tasks that beckon us. And even then, we cannot always get away. Interruptions dissolve those quiet moments and the silence is shattered.

Like a breaking dish, the fragility of silence is hard to repair. Instead, we usually set aside the pieces of what could have been and return to the world of ringing phones and demanding obligations.

But what if God's message is in the interruption? To see it that way changes everything. Instead of being unhappy or frustrated, seeing interruptions as God-given allows us to simply take God with us back into the demands of our day.

God speaks in many ways. We crave solitude—and we do need it at times. But when interruptions come, let God redeem them. He has a message for you.

Read Psalm 34:1.

LORD, HELP ME SEE YOU AND HEAR YOU IN ALL THE INTERRUPTIONS OF MY LIFE.

We need someone to show us that our pain can be redeemed and there is light ahead of us. And the ones who show this best are those who have lived deeply and have not sidestepped suffering.

—REBECCA MANLEY PIPPERT

SHARING THE PATH

She buried her teen son ten months ago and was deeply depressed. "The pain of losing a child is crushing," she said. "And it grows more suffocating with each passing day he's not here."

An acquaintance introduced her to a couple who'd lost their only son a few years earlier. They built a friendship that allowed them to grieve their losses together. The couple's transparency about the challenges of their journey offered her a bit of light for the dark, difficult path she was walking.

The path of pain is stony and rough. We want to know that our journey is worth something and that we will find light ahead. Sometimes it takes others who have walked the path to show us the way. And sometimes we will be the ones walking with others in pain. This is the body of Christ.

Read 2 Samuel 22:31–37.

LORD, WHO IN MY LIFE NEEDS LIGHT FOR THEIR PATH TODAY?

Work . . . it should be looked upon—not as a necessary drudgery . . . but as a way of life in which the nature of man should find its proper exercise and delight and so fulfill itself to the glory of God.

—DOROTHY SAYERS

THE DAILY "GRAND"

Work. The daily grind. The "necessary drudgery" in order to pay the bills, or keep the house clean, or care for the needs of others. It's work, it's hard, it's not always very rewarding.

What if we could find a way to rejoice in the tasks at hand? What if every job was seen as an opportunity to honor God? The house to clean is a great delight because of the gift of home. The papers to file are a joy because of serving others. The meeting to attend is a gift because of sharing ideas. The daily grind becomes the daily "grand." Our everyday toil, when we apply ourselves without complaining, glorifies God.

Each day we have an opportunity to glorify God in our work. By our example we either demonstrate faith or a lack of it. Today, tackle your tasks with delight!

Read Colossians 3:23–24.

CREATOR OF ALL, GIVE ME DELIGHT IN MY WORK
TODAY SO THAT IT WILL HONOR YOU.

The only way in which Satan can persecute or afflict God is through attacking the people of God. The only way we can have personal victory in the midst of these flying arrows . . . to call upon the Lord for help.

—EDITH SCHAEFFER

HE HURTS WITH US

Remember when you were little and fell and scraped your knee? You didn't need to be coaxed to seek out a parent. You ran to your mom or dad like a shot, desperately wanting him or her to make it all better. Back then you couldn't understand how much your parent hurt when you were hurting.

On a more infinite scale, our heavenly Parent hurts when we hurt. As Edith Schaeffer explains, this is the enemy's only ammunition against an indestructible God. He attacks God by attacking God's followers—us. But that ammunition proves ineffective if we call upon the Lord for help. Satan may persecute and afflict, he may send his arrows, but we are assured the victory. The Lord knows. He hurts with us. When our knees are scraped up by life, we can run to our Father. He promises to make it all better.

Read Psalm 91.

FATHER, I'M IN PAIN. HELP ME, LORD. BE MERCIFUL TO ME.

From heaven's perspective, trials looked extraordinarily different. When viewed from its own level, my paralysis seemed like a huge, impassable wall; but when viewed from above, the wall appeared as a thin line, something that could be overcome.

—JONI EARECKSON TADA

PROBLEMS AND PERSPECTIVES

Gazing down at the land from thirty thousand feet in an airplane, everything looks doll-house size. Trees that would dwarf you if you stood close by look as if they could fit in the palm of your hand. Rivers seem like ribbons.

Life. It's really all about perspective.

And so it is with life's problems. On this side of heaven, we feel dwarfed and discouraged by hurdles that seem insurmountable. We feel walled in and helpless. But from God's perspective, problems look like opportunities for us to trust him. He waits for us to lift the concerns that look large to us and place them into his infinitely larger hands. When we do this, our big problems become bearable. We know that with God on our side, the problems can be overcome.

Ask your heavenly Burden-bearer for his perspective today. Your problems are an opportunity to draw closer to him.

Read 2 Corinthians 4:7–9.

LORD, TODAY GIVE ME YOUR PERSPECTIVE
ON MY PROBLEMS. I TRUST YOU.

God is a God of order. We can tell that by looking at the universe. None of it is random or accidental. He doesn't want our lives to be either.

—STORMIE OMARTIAN

GETTING CHAOS UNDER CONTROL

As we go through our days at a breakneck pace, meeting each demand as it arises, we can easily become frazzled and frustrated. We put out one fire, only to find that three more have sparked into existence. Grabbing and aiming the fire extinguisher may keep life from erupting into an inferno, but God has a better way. He wants our lives to be orderly and intentional. Sometimes we might have to say *no* to an activity we'd love to do; other times we may have to disappoint people. But as we begin to follow the Lord's model, we will be more productive and effective.

Living in an orderly way pleases God more than striving to get more done. Just as peace seems to emanate from the starry sky (a sky that was perfectly designed), trusting God to help plan our lives will replace sparks of chaos with a pleasant and warm glow.

Read Psalm 8:3–5.

TEACH ME TO LIVE INTENTIONALLY. ASSURE ME THAT YOU
WILL TAKE CARE OF WHAT I DON'T ACCOMPLISH.

Labor, therefore, to increase the fire of your desire, and let not a moment pass without crying to Me with humble voice, or without continual prayers before Me for your neighbors.

—SAINT CATHERINE OF SIENA

AROUND THE BLOCK

The sixty-year-old woman is a familiar sight in her neighborhood. Even during long, cold Midwestern winters, she walks the same route every day. During her walk, she prays for salvation and spiritual growth for each household she passes, even if she hasn't met the family. She's seen God answer her prayers in surprising ways in the lives of the neighbors she does know. As a result, she expresses confidence that God is at work in the lives of those she has yet to meet.

Her intercession has had an impact on her own spiritual journey: "The longer I pray, the more I sense the depths of God's love for me, and for those around me." She understands St. Catherine's passion—the power of continual prayers for one's neighbors.

Your prayer time today is an opportunity to "increase the fire of your desire" and to bring those around you before your heavenly Father.

Read Ephesians 6:18.

LORD, I ASK THAT THOSE AROUND ME WILL EXPERIENCE AND RESPOND TO YOUR GREAT LOVE TODAY.

The capacity to discern and do the will of God arises out of friendship with God, cultivated through prayer, times of quiet listening and alert awareness.

—RUTH HALEY BARTON

GOD'S FRIEND

Close friends know each other's secrets. They know what brings laughter. They can anticipate one another's reactions and "read" each others' hearts. Spending time together bonds the friendship. If one person doesn't take time to nurture the friendship, the pair drift apart.

God knows all our secrets, all our hurts, and all our concerns. He knows when we will laugh and cry. He always waits for us to meet with him. God tells us if we seek him, we'll find him. When we search to know him from Scripture and spend "friendship time" with God, we discover his ways. Our prayers are our side of the many conversations. His leadings and promptings become clearer as we spend more time with him.

As with any dear friendship, choose to set aside time to be with God, your best friend. He's waiting. He has so much he wants to share with you!

Read Exodus 33:11.

DEAR FRIEND, I'M HERE. I WANT TO SPEND TIME WITH YOU.

At its best our age is an age of searchers and discoverers, and at its worst, an age that has domesticated despair and learned to live with it happily.

—FLANNERY O'CONNOR

WORTH THE WAIT

Waiting. Filling time while we wait for the phone to ring and deliver the good news or get the bad news over with. Standing in line. Preparing for an event. Or simply waiting "until things get better."

But what if the good news we wait for never comes? What if things just don't get better? What if the waiting is meaningless? Too many people abandon hope, abandon trust, and decide, despite the contradiction, to live happily with their despair.

Christ has something far better in mind. In him we find meaning in the waiting. While we watch our hopes fade, he is turning our eyes toward a truer hope. While he makes us wait, we learn to trust our future dreams to him. Waiting is hard, but waiting on God means the wait will be worth it.

Read Jeremiah 29:11.

FATHER, HELP ME TO TRUST YOU WHILE I'M IN LIFE'S WAITING ROOM.

God allows us to have disappointments, frustrations, or even worse because He wants us to see that our joy is not in such worldly pleasures . . . our joy is in the fact that we have a relationship with God.

—CATHERINE MARSHALL

THE POWER OF PRAISE

God alone holds the "big picture" of our existence. He alone can lift us up to transcend anxieties and problems. Ah! What a gift to have such help!

Many people wonder why, if they stay close to God, they still experience disappointments, frustrations, or worse. They want God to insulate them from the realities of life. They think, *If God loves me, then these things shouldn't happen.*

But God allows those bad things in life. As Catherine Marshall explains, "He wants us to see that our joy is not in such worldly pleasures." Instead, our joy should simply be in our relationship with God, not in what he does for us.

Step out of your difficulties for a moment. Look into the face of your heavenly Father who loves you so much. His love for you is all that really matters.

Read Habakkuk 3:17–19.

THANK YOU FOR LOVING ME, LORD. MY JOY IS IN YOU ALONE.

Our worship is based on truth, not emotion; it is based not on the fervency of our words, but on the faithfulness of our God. Emotion follows truth!

—KAY ARTHUR

STAND AND WORSHIP

Through the truth-flowing words of our songs, we worship our Lord. We center on him and open our hearts. We read Scripture and reflect on his attributes and faithfulness through the generations. Tears flow; we fall on our knees in humility. Words may come easily or not at all.

Our worship is based on the truth of who God is. He is worthy of every word of praise, every tear of thanks, every smile of joy. It is not the fervency of our words or emotions that make for truth; the truth already exists. Worship is simply our way of responding to God's love and faithfulness.

Emotions are evidence of your deep devotion to God. Listen for his still, small voice or his gentle touch on your heart. Soak in the wonder of God's love. Linger in worship until you are full to overflowing. Praise him. Thank him. He deserves it.

Read John 4:24.

LORD, I WORSHIP YOU BECAUSE OF WHO YOU ARE!

For most of us, the subtle encroachment of pride is more dangerous, and more likely to render us useless to God and others, than any other kind of failure.

—NANCY LEIGH DEMOSS

FAILING THROUGH SUCCESS

Failure is a sad word. We fear failure. We don't want to fail at anything. Yet how do we view success? God doesn't measure success by the amount in our bank account, the rung we've reached on the corporate ladder, or even the number of our friends on Facebook. Sometimes it seems that his measures are upside-down to ours. He treasures humility and hates pride.

Why? Because pride is dangerous. Nancy Leigh DeMoss warns that it can render us useless to God and others. How horrible to have great gifts and to be useless to God because of pride. But it happens slowly, subtly, almost without our noticing. Thinking a bit too highly of ourselves. Forging ahead without God's guidance. Doing good things without the humility of trust in God.

Want to succeed in God's eyes? Want to be useful to him? Serve with humility and love.

Read Proverbs 11:2.

> FATHER, I WANT TO BE USEFUL FOR YOU. KEEP ME FROM THE SUBTLE HOLD OF PRIDE.

What we call mundane is, in some very important ways, significant in God's school of preparation.

—LYSA TERKEURST

THE SMALL STUFF

Mundane. Boring. Unspectacular. Unnoticed. We want to do big things for God; the mundane is, well, mundane. But God says, "Right now, I've got tasks for you. Clean the church's toilets every week until I tell you to stop, and don't tell anyone what you're doing. See that single mom over there? Take her a home-cooked meal at least once a month, and don't tell others you're doing it. Mentor the worst hellion in the youth group. *Then* we'll talk about the next step."

Why does God make us prove ourselves in the small, unseen, mundane things before trusting us with more responsibility? Because integrity and character are born in the mundane places where no one sees but God.

God cares more about who you *are* than about what you do. The mundane tasks you do today are significant—both in how they serve others and in how God is preparing you.

Read Matthew 6:1–4.

THANK YOU FOR TRUSTING ME WITH THESE MUNDANE TASKS, LORD. HELP ME DO THEM WELL.

Because Jesus, the Gift, lives in the Christian, the gifts and fruits are present in our lives. They can radiate through us to a needy world.

—Leanne Payne

GIVE IT AWAY

Gifts are meant to be given. We love handing a specially chosen gift to a friend, knowing she will be thrilled to open it. We give because we love. It would make no sense to purchase a gift, wrap it in beautiful paper, tie a shiny ribbon round it, and then put it on the top shelf of our closet. That brings no joy. The joy comes in the sharing, the giving.

Jesus was God's ultimate Gift to us, sent to our needy world so that his Spirit could radiate through us. The gifts (1 Corinthians 12:1–7) and fruit (Galatians 5:22–23) of the Spirit are given to us for the blessing and benefit of those around us. The gifts are meant to be given. We find no joy in keeping for ourselves what God has given us.

Give your gifts away. A needy world is waiting.

Read 1 Peter 4:8–11.

PLEASE RADIATE THROUGH ME TO THE NEEDY WORLD AROUND ME, DEAR JESUS.

Sometimes in life we face incredibly complex situations—some created by our fools, some by our own lack of wisdom. All are allowed by God for a greater purpose in our lives.

—JAN SILVIOUS

HE WON'T WASTE THE PAIN

God is green. He lets no event go to waste in our lives. Whether it was a bad decision, a foolish action, or someone else's bad choice, at times incredibly complex situations arise and leave us wondering how we can ever recover. But in God's economy, nothing is ever wasted—not even the bad stuff. If we got ourselves into the mess, God's grace prevails. As we live with the consequences of choices made, God watches over us, willingly transforming the situation for a greater purpose in our lives.

So take heart, dear sister. Whatever complex situation is making your life difficult, be encouraged. God has not given up on you; don't give up on yourself. He has a greater purpose in and through this situation. You may not be able to see it, but trust the promise. God won't waste the pain.

Read Psalm 30:5–12.

LORD, I TRUST THAT YOU WILL TURN THIS
SITUATION AROUND FOR YOUR GLORY.

"This earthly life is a battle," said Ma. "If it isn't one thing to contend with, it's another. . . . The sooner you make up your mind to that, the better off you are, and the more thankful for your pleasures."

—LAURA INGALLS WILDER

TRIALS AND PLEASURES

God has given us many good things to enjoy, and yet this world is cursed by the results of sin. Both parts of that equation remain true for our entire lives. If we expect "happily ever after" in this world, we'll be disappointed. On the other hand, if we look only at the bad things of life, our joy and gratitude can be stifled.

Life is full of suffering, sorrow, betrayals, financial hardships, and everyday trials. Even the best moments carry hints of imperfection, and they end all too soon. But God truly does bring good out of bad. He uses suffering to teach us his sustaining power; he uses storms to bring rainbows. We can take Ma's advice and refuse to be surprised when we contend with difficulty. Once we make up our minds to do that, we'll be so much more thankful for the pleasures God has given.

Read 1 Peter 1:3–7.

FATHER, THANK YOU THAT YOU ARE GOOD
EVEN WHEN CIRCUMSTANCES AREN'T.

As we cope with the real world, it helps to keep an eternal perspective, not one that can see no farther than today's pain.

—BARBARA JOHNSON

LONGING FOR HOME

Sometimes it's hard to keep an eternal perspective, isn't it? It's difficult to see past today's pain. Grief can be overwhelming. Sorrow can be devastating. Difficulties can seem insurmountable. If this life is all there is, then we would have little reason to hope.

Barbara Johnson challenges us to keep an eternal perspective, a focus on the promises of God for our forever home. We don't know exactly what it will look like, how it will feel, what we will do, but it's enough to know that God promises a place with no more death or mourning or crying or pain. Eternity in heaven with him will be more wonderful than our minds can even begin to imagine.

As we struggle here on earth, it helps to remember we won't be staying long. We're just passing through. We're on our way home.

Read 2 Corinthians 4:16–18.

LORD GOD, PLEASE OPEN MY EYES TO WONDERFUL
REALITIES OF MY HEAVENLY HOME.

Like waifs clustered around a blazing fire, we gathered around it [the Bible], holding out our hearts to its warmth and light. The blacker the night around us grew, the brighter and truer . . . burned the word of God.

—CORRIE TEN BOOM

LIGHT IN THE DARKNESS

Corrie ten Boom gives witness to the power of the Word inside a Nazi concentration camp. In the midst of overwhelming horror, she read aloud from a smuggled Bible to the other women huddled in the barracks—their only home. They clustered around her to hear the reassuring words of hope in a place that teemed with hopelessness. And the Word stirred up a blazing hope and the fire of God's certain presence.

At this very moment God is waiting to speak to you too. He reveals his great love for you in the Bible. Whenever life's circumstances seem black, do not despair. In the pages of the Holy Book, God holds out light and warmth like a blazing fire. Let the Word of God warm you, guide you, and bring you light in the darkness.

Read Isaiah 42:16.

> *LET YOUR PRECIOUS WORD BRING ME LIGHT*
> *AND WARMTH TODAY, LORD.*

After a person encounters God, she should be changed. It is not enough for us to talk about what we have experienced. We should be living it out flamboyantly.

—PRISCILLA SHIRER

WRESTLING WITH GOD

Talk is cheap. Experiences may make for nice stories, but true change comes from an encounter that touches our heart and erupts into freedom.

We can't have an encounter with God and walk away unscathed. This isn't goose bumps and gold dust. This is going toe-to-toe with God and wrestling out our questions, discussing our hurt feelings, and dealing with our unforgiveness, pride, jealousy, addictions, or other besetting problems. Our heavenly Father loves us enough to confront us. He tells us the truth in love. We listen. We think. We challenge. We learn. We experience the only One who can change us from the inside out.

Such an encounter is more than just a good story to tell; it must cause you to live differently, to live in flamboyant joy! You are loved, so live like it!

Read Genesis 32:24–30.

LORD, I WANT A REAL ENCOUNTER WITH YOU.
I WANT TO BE TRANSFORMED.

If a person neither considers to Whom he is addressing himself, what he asks, nor what he is who ventures to speak to God, although his lips may utter many words, I do not call it prayer.

—TERESA OF AVILA

TOUCHING THE HEART OF GOD

Prayer is not about saying words. Jesus told the story of two men who came to the temple to pray. The first man, a religious expert, offered a prayer that was little more than an eloquent list of his good works and a declaration of his superior morality. The other man, a tax collector, couldn't utter more than a few words to God: a confession of his own sinfulness and a gut-wrenching plea for God's mercy. Jesus told his followers that it was this "sinner's" few words and poverty of heart that were rich with the holy reality of God's presence.

True prayer is a conversation where we must consider to whom we are speaking, what we ask, and who we are as we venture to speak to God. Only then are we conversing. Only then are we touching the heart of God.

Read Luke 18:9–14.

LORD, I COME TO YOU AS MY KING, MY LORD, MY FRIEND.

*I don't know anything about politics, but I can read my Bible;
and there I see that I must feed the hungry, clothe the naked,
and comfort the desolate; and that Bible I mean to follow.*

—HARRIET BEECHER STOW

TRUE RELIGION

Sometimes the simplest truths are the most important. Caring for others is a great theme in all of Scripture, and it doesn't take much research to understand that God calls on us—his hands and feet here on this planet—to take care of those in need. And need comes in a variety of colors. Maybe it's hunger. Maybe it's a lack of clothing or shelter. Maybe it's financial assistance. Maybe it's just a shoulder to cry on or a few words of comfort.

Jesus said that unbelievers will know we are Christians by our love. His ministry was largely known for the way he treated the outcasts—touching and healing lepers, teaching women, accepting repentant sinners.

If we mean to follow our Bibles, then we mean to reach out to those in need in whatever way we can. It means touching, caring, giving, sharing, loving. After all, Jesus set the example.

Read Matthew 25:31–40.

FATHER, HELP ME CARE FOR THOSE IN NEED AS JESUS DID.

Each person has a spiritual obligation before God to learn how to live well, to live fully, as opposed to knowing only how to live comfortably.

—LUCI SWINDOLL

LIVE TO THE FULLEST

Ah, comfort. Who doesn't want to live a comfortable life? We yearn for moments when we can wrap ourselves in a soft comforter, grasp a mug of hot tea in our hands, and listen to the warm crackling of a fire in the fireplace. Or maybe your picture of comfort has to do with exotic climes and a hammock stretched between tall palm trees.

When God provides such times of comfort, we can thank him for that gift. But when days come that are far from comfortable, we can then take comfort in the fact that God is teaching us to live well, to live fully. He has more for us in life than just to live comfortably. He may call us to take uncomfortable risks, or forego some of what is good in order to have what is best. Above all, it means having Jesus, who came to give us life to the fullest.

Read John 10:10.

SHOW ME YOUR DEFINITION OF LIFE "TO THE FULL," LORD. HELP ME LIVE YOUR WAY.

Pray for your enemies—even if you have to do it with gritted teeth.

—MICHELLE MEDLOCK ADAMS

GIVING GRACE

Harsh words hit us like a fist. Our mouths fall open in disbelief when people take advantage of us, cheat us, make us feel like a punching bag. We can't imagine how such people can look at themselves in the mirror. But we *can* imagine how we'd like to get our own brand of justice.

What do we do with the hurt? The answer, as always, is to take it to Jesus. We turn over to him what we cannot understand. We ask him to give us grace to pray for those who hurt us—our enemies—for it may be true that those who inflict such pain have experienced deep hurts themselves. Maybe God wants to reach that person through us. Maybe our loving reaction will help soften a hardened heart.

But first, pray, gritted teeth and all. God will give you the grace you need.

Read Matthew 5:44–47.

LORD, HELP ME TO BE GRACIOUS WHEN I HAVE BEEN WRONGED.

FEBRUARY

Every believer needs second chances. Some of us need lots of them.

—BETH MOORE

SECOND CHANCES

Second chances. We all want them, but in the reality of this harsh world, second chances don't come easy. When unkind words are spoken in anger once too often, friendships are ruined. When trust is broken over and over, marriages are shattered. The end comes. We don't want to be hurt again. No more second chances.

But not so with God.

God sees your heart; he understands your weaknesses; he knows that you fail. You need second chances because you are not perfect. But God who is perfect sees the real you and by his grace and mercy gives you the second chances that the world wouldn't. It's in his unfailing love that God offers his outstretched hand to those who humble themselves, knowing they can't do it alone.

God has lots of second chances. Take them. Don't give up, for he doesn't give up on you.

Read John 21:15–17.

LORD, I HAVE FAILED MANY TIMES BUT, IN YOUR LOVE, I WANT TO KEEP TRYING.

It is a great truth, wonderful as it is undeniable, that all our happiness—temporal, spiritual and eternal—consists in one thing; namely, in resigning ourselves to God, and in leaving ourselves with Him.

—MADAME GUYON

COMPLETE SURRENDER

An infant has no choice in the matter of surrender. The loving parent lifts the child and carries her, providing what's best. We, too, should submit—to the Father's outstretched arms—but we *can* choose.

How foolish to resist his care, to insist on living apart from him. With a love deep beyond our imagining, God wants only the best for his children. Thus, giving ourselves to him brings true happiness. Choosing an alternate way would be foolish indeed. But often our will and actions move that direction, seeking what we feel we deserve, what makes us feel good. "Resigning" ourselves to him means admitting that he sees the bigger picture and can be trusted.

Your heavenly Father loves you totally and completely, and wants to give you deep, abiding joy that is full and overflowing and lasting. Let him enfold you and carry you in his loving arms.

Read Psalm 62:1–2.

I GIVE MYSELF TO YOU TODAY, FATHER. I REST IN YOU.

The most important exchange of all takes place when God takes our guilt and replaces it with His forgiveness, His cleansing.

—EVELYN CHRISTENSON

TRADING UP!

As children we learn about trading: a peanut butter sandwich for tuna, or a better spot in line at recess for a saved seat on the bus. This important skill helps us as we grow up and begin making purchases or considering career changes. The rule of thumb: always trade *up*. Let go of one thing for something of greater value to you. In a fair trade, each person is happy with the result.

When we trade the guilt and shame of past mistakes for forgiveness, everyone wins. We feel cleansed, set free, joyful. At the same time, God delights in our willingness to give up the burden he wants to carry for us anyway. His Son died to make it possible. He wants us to trade up!

While it may seem to us that we get the better end of this deal, the Lord is very pleased with the exchange.

Read 2 Corinthians 5:21.

LORD, I WILLINGLY OFFER MY BURDEN OF GUILT TO YOU IN EXCHANGE FOR YOUR SWEET FORGIVENESS.

For we have this moment to hold in our hands and to touch
as it slips through our fingers like sand; yesterday's gone, and
tomorrow may never come, but we have this moment—today!

—GLORIA GAITHER

FLEETING MOMENTS

Y ou are holding a moment in your hands. What does it
feel like? Is it a soft, silky rose—a moment to be cherished and enjoyed? Or is it a scruffy, scratchy shrub—a moment
that is uncomfortable, a moment you'd like to forget? No
matter how it feels, it will soon be gone like sand through your
fingers. Time moves on. Time slips by.

Yesterday you cannot change. The future you cannot guarantee.
Today have. Embrace it. Cup your hands around it. Look
for the blessing in it, the hope in it, the joy in it. Focus on God
and serve others even as the grains of time run through your
fingers to be scattered in the wind. He longs for you to offer
this moment back to him, even as it slips away.

Today is yours. What will you do with this moment in your
hands?

Read James 4:13–17.

IN TODAY'S HOURS AND MINUTES, LORD, HELP ME
LOOK TO YOU AND CHERISH THE MOMENT.

*I knew that I had a choice. I could give in to my resentment
. . . or I could choose to believe what God's Word says to be true
whether I felt it was or not.*

—GRACIA BURNHAM

CAPTIVE HEARTS

When Gracia Burnham penned these words, she didn't mean them lightly. She had been held captive in a jungle by terrorists for over a year—on the brink of starvation, without modern conveniences, stripped of all freedom and privacy. She recognized that she was held doubly captive—physically and emotionally—if she allowed herself to become angry and to resent her captors. She chose to trust God, knowing that even this horrible circumstance was in his good and perfect plan for her life. She chose to let God work in her rather than putting up walls of bitterness.

What is it, beloved, that is causing you hurt, bitterness, resentment? You have a choice. You can give in to those feelings or, like Gracia, you can choose to believe that what God's Word says is true, whether it feels like it or not.

One choice leads to captivity, the other to freedom.

Read John 17:13–17.

---

*GOD, HELP ME TO GIVE UP MY RESENTMENT
AND BITTERNESS. I WANT TO BE FREE.*

He said not "Thou shalt not be tempested, thou shalt not be travailed, thou shalt not be dis-eased"; but he said, "Thou shalt not be overcome."

—JULIAN OF NORWICH

TROUBLE IN THIS WORLD

God never promised to make life easy.

Julian of Norwich understood that God never said that his followers would be excused from the storms of life, or the travail of difficulties, or the sorrows of disease and discomfort. But God *did* say that we would not be overcome.

Many people want it to be different. They don't want to believe in a God who would allow storms and sorrows and suffering. Yet God is preparing a perfect place for his followers—it's called heaven. For now, however, we are in the world—called to trust no matter what, called to stand strong. We have the word of the One who has overcome, the One who makes all things right, the One who has the power to bring good from evil.

Take your tempests and trials to the One who has overcome the world. He will take care of you.

Read John 16:33.

HEAVENLY FATHER, WHEN I'M OVERWHELMED, IT'S A BLESSING TO KNOW THAT I'M NOT OVERCOME.

Crisis has happened. What will come of this? . . . We have a choice to be conformed to the ordinary, the expected, the easier path. Or we can choose to let this event transform us.

—MIRIAM NEFF

DEFINING MOMENTS

When tragedy strikes, the pain can knock us off our feet. We face the tempestuous emotions of anger, denial, grief, and even depression. We fear for the future, wondering what can possibly come of this situation. What good can God bring from this crisis?

In those moments, we have a choice. We can choose the path that lets our emotions take over and leads us into resentment and bitterness. Or we can choose the less-expected path of allowing ourselves to be transformed by God. We can choose to let him work in us to do his will. When the world sees an out-of-the-ordinary response to crises in life, it sits up and takes notice.

You can come out of the crisis on the other side—stronger and more dependent on God. He doesn't want tragedies to destroy you or define you. He wants to transform you.

It's your choice.

Read James 1:2–4.

> LORD, PLEASE DON'T LET THIS CRISIS BE WASTED
> ON ME. I WANT TO BE TRANSFORMED.

It was kind of like a cave-in—this great big peace just kind of dumped in on me, washed in on me like a wave . . . "It's God," I said.

—JAN KARON

TRUE PEACE

We long for peace. A few moments of quiet when the world doesn't intrude in our thoughts. A respite from battles with folks who hurt us or disagree with us. We'd even like to see world peace. We want something that goes deep, that lasts, that penetrates into our very souls.

Jesus brings that kind of peace. When we find Jesus, we find peace that passes understanding, peace that does not go away, peace that gives rest to our fears and our troubled hearts. Jesus' kind of peace dumps on us like a cave-in, washes over us like a wave—inescapable, strong, overwhelming. His peace doesn't change or disappear.

What are you facing today? Is your world less than peaceful? Jesus promises peace, a gift freely given to you. Let it dump on you, overwhelm you, and wash over you. Today, walk in peace.

Read John 14:26–27.

FATHER, I THANK YOU FOR THE PRESENCE AND
GUIDANCE OF YOUR HOLY SPIRIT.

When we view God as just a source of information . . . we forget that God's words are not merely words, but life to be ingested.

—MARGARET FEINBERG

BREAD OF LIFE

For what do you hunger? What do you need to fill and fulfill you? Maybe you're not sure what's causing those pangs of emptiness and, therefore, nothing satisfies.

Consider your approach to God's Word. Are you reading because it's on your to-do list? Do you want to learn more about God? Are you seeking his will? If spending time in the Word leaves you feeling empty, perhaps it's time to put aside merely reading for head knowledge in exchange for fully engaging your heart.

To ingest the Word means to consume it and to let it fill the void, empty places. Read God's Word not just for information but as life-giving words that sustain you and become a part of you. Crave his every word, ingest it, be satisfied by it, and let it nourish your soul and your life.

Read John 6:26–35.

PUT A CRAVING IN ME, LORD, THAT IS ONLY
SATISFIED BY INGESTING YOUR WORD.

But how shall I speak of the glories I have since discovered in the Bible? For years I have read it with an ever-broadening sense of joy and inspiration; and I love it as I love no other book.

—HELEN KELLER

TREASURE CHEST

A special room in a New York City high-rise holds Helen Keller's Bible—several books were needed to bind the thick, Braille-filled pages, touched lovingly by the fingertips of the blind and deaf woman. From those pages joy and inspiration flooded her dark and silent world. She loved it as no other book.

Open your Bible. Run your hand over the pages. Each leaf is a love letter. You are an ancient mariner opening a treasure chest. You are an explorer following a treasure map. You are a child discovering the wonders of your grandmother's jewelry box.

Sent special delivery through the hearts of many servants, the Bible was packaged once all God's love letters arrived. Though it has no special bow, it's the best gift—full of endless love. Read it with joy and inspiration. Hold it tightly. Love it as no other book.

Read Romans 15:4.

THANK YOU FOR THE GIFT OF THE BIBLE,
YOUR LOVE LETTER TO ME.

Oh what a happy soul am I although I cannot see, I am resolved that contented I shall be. How many blessings I enjoy. To weep and sigh because I'm blind? I cannot and I won't.

—FANNY CROSBY

CHOOSE CONTENTMENT

We must resolve to be content; it is an act of our will. Contentment is a choice, not a result of a job completed or of perfect life circumstances. If we connect contentment to a work or expectation, then contentment will only come to those who finish the job. If we connect contentment with perfect life circumstances, well—we will probably never find it.

Life is filled with unfinished and interrupted work, yet contentment is available. Or, as with Fanny Crosby, life may deal us difficult circumstances beyond our control. We can weep and sigh, or we can decide that we cannot and won't do so. Instead we can choose to focus on the blessings we can enjoy.

Choose today to find contentment, to focus on the blessings in your life. Grab those blessings and don't let go. Focus on thankfulness and, like Fanny, you will find true contentment.

Read Philippians 4:11–13.

JESUS, I CHOOSE TODAY TO FOCUS ON THE BLESSINGS YOU HAVE SO GENEROUSLY GIVEN ME.

If I take offence easily; if I am content to continue in cold unfriendliness, though friendship be possible, then I know nothing of Calvary's love.

—AMY CARMICHAEL

CALVARY'S LOVE

Our feelings get hurt easily when we forget about God's big love for us. When others' sins and offenses become our focus, we have lost our correct focus as believers. As daughters of God, our attention is to be on him and what he has done for us, not on others and how they hurt us. We must remember that when we did not deserve it, Christ chose not only to forgive us of all our sin but also to declare us righteous.

Amy Carmichael points out that we know nothing of Calvary's love if we accept the forgiveness of Christ but then refuse to forgive others. When our cups are full of Christ's forgiveness, we are able to spill that grace onto the people in our lives. As we become full of God's great grace for us, we can overflow with unconditional love for others.

Read Ephesians 4:32.

LORD, KEEP MY EYES ON YOU AND WHAT YOU HAVE DONE, NOT ON OTHERS AND WHAT THEY HAVE DONE TO ME.

If you do the works of love before the emotions match up, the feelings of love will eventually follow along.

—JILL BRISCOE

THE HARD WORK OF LOVE

Movies make love look easy—romance is something you "fall into." But real love often involves more of a commitment than a good feeling. Sometimes we have to *do* love even when we don't *feel* love.

At times it's just plain hard to love. Those closest to us can hurt us the most. We don't *feel* like loving the husband who is acting insensitive, or the child who is being rebellious, or the parent who is overbearing, or the friend who is demanding. We can even justify why we shouldn't have to show any love whatsoever!

But love is more than just a feeling; instead, it is a choice. We do the works of love and let the emotions catch up later. As Jill Briscoe says, eventually the feelings will follow along. We may not always *feel* like loving, but God can give us the grace to love even the unlovely.

Read 1 Corinthians 13:1–7.

GOD, HELP ME TO LOVE IN WORD AND IN WORKS,
EVEN WHEN OTHERS ARE UNLOVELY.

This wild God of mine . . . loves me . . . not in the way we usually translate when we hear, "God loves us." Which usually sounds like "because he has to" or meaning "he tolerates you." No. He loves me as a Lover loves.

—STASI ELDREDGE

LET HIM LOVE YOU

Love." The word speaks to the soul, the emotions, the heart. A child cuddled by Mom or Dad. A toddler toddling toward outstretched arms. Friends reunited with bear hugs. An engaged couple walking hand-in-hand, then gazing into each other's eyes. Newlyweds driving from the reception, beginning life together.

Whatever feelings the word *love* evokes, multiply them by thousands to gain a glimpse of God's love for you. God's love goes beyond any kind of human love we can experience. It is perfect love—he loves us not because he *has* to, not because he *tolerates* us, but because he is wildly *in love* with us. Such love is almost unimaginable—but it is true, it is real, it is yours.

Let that thought, that picture, those emotions wash over you, cleansing you of any hesitancy or fear in your relationship with him. He loves you as a *lover* loves.

Read Ephesians 3:14–19.

THANK YOU, GOD, FOR LOVING ME SO MUCH.

Could I have been in Heaven without the Love of God, it would have been a Hell to me; for, in Truth, it is the absence and presence of God that makes Heaven or Hell.

—ANNE BRADSTREET

HEAVENLY EMBRACE

What is heaven anyway? We know that the images of sitting on clouds playing the harp all day aren't true, but what *is* true? Heaven is a perfect place, yes, but there has to be more. There must be more than streets of gold and pearly gates to make it so appealing.

What Anne Bradstreet longed for over three hundred years ago is exactly what we desire as well: A relationship. Being near the One who loves us more than life itself. Finally meeting the God who was willing to sacrifice his own Son so that we could be with him. Being looked at by Someone who knows how imperfect we are, how often we've messed up, and still sees us as beautiful and loves us with an everlasting love.

That's heaven. Seeing your Savior, your Lover, your Friend— and being held in his embrace forever.

Read 1 Thessalonians 4:16–17.

FATHER GOD, I WANT TO BE NEAR YOU. I LOOK FORWARD TO BEING WITH YOU FOREVER.

*This practice of listening to God has increased my intimacy
with Him more than any other spiritual discipline.*

—SARAH YOUNG

REAL LISTENING

Sit for a minute and just listen. What do you hear? The
gurgle of the coffee maker. The sizzle of food simmering
on the stove. Snatches of your daughter's phone conversation
down the hall. The deep pulse of the bass from a cranked-up
stereo in a passing car.

Our world is filled with sounds, both pleasant and unpleasant.
It is not an easy task to hear God's voice amidst all the other
noises. As Sarah Young says, it takes practice and discipline. That
means it's going to take a little work on our part. It may mean
finding that quiet place with few distractions. It means opening
the Bible and reading God's Word. It means intentionally
listening for God's voice.

Such intimacy with God! How wonderful that God would
choose to speak to us if we would only hear. Close your eyes
and listen. What is God saying to you today?

Read Deuteronomy 30:19–20.

LORD, HELP ME TO TALK LESS AND LISTEN
MORE. I WANT TO KNOW YOU BETTER.

*If I am a princess in rags and tatters, I can be a princess inside.
. . . It is a great deal more of a triumph to be one all the time
when no one knows it.*

—FRANCES HODGSON BURNETT

DAUGHTER OF THE KING

You are a daughter of the King.

Perhaps it's hard to believe that. You buy some of your clothes at yard sales. Your "chariot" has quite a few miles on it. Your house doesn't look like a castle and it needs remodeling. But you're in temporary quarters now. If Jesus is your Savior, your Father is King of the whole universe—imagine it! And someday you will live with him.

In the meantime, he calls you to be a princess on the *inside*. Sure, maybe it's a little more of a challenge because no one sees, no one knows, no one necessarily expects you to act like the King's daughter. But that is the best triumph of all—to live like the princess you are when no one else knows, to live like Jesus even when it's not expected.

Live for your King, your Highness. You are his princess.

Read Matthew 5:3–10.

MY KING, THANK YOU FOR CALLING ME YOUR
OWN DAUGHTER. I LOVE YOU.

We need to find God, and He cannot be found in noise and restlessness. God is the friend of silence.

—MOTHER TERESA

SIT AND PRAY

Prayer can be confusing, intimidating, and misunderstood. But it wasn't that way for Mother Teresa. For her, it was a matter of just sitting silently before her loving heavenly Father.

We too are invited to sit in an intimate place of stillness. God knows our fear and pain as he gazes on us. We know his power and love as we gaze back at him. Nothing has changed, yet everything has changed.

Most have never experienced prayer that way. We dash into God's presence with a gigantic list of needs and wants. By spending that time being seen and known, we are able to lay down the stuff we carried in and leave knowing it is being handled. We may choose to pick it up later, but that will be our choice. Today, gaze at your Savior. Rest all of your cares with the One who gazes back at you.

Read Psalm 27:4.

FATHER, I NEED TO FIND REST IN YOU. HELP
ME TO COME BOLDLY AND SIT.

God wants us to seek Him not merely for the functions He performs but just for the sheer joy of relationship with Him.

—MARY DEMUTH

THE BEST GIFT

Recall your very favorite birthday present as a child. Maybe it was a special doll, a hand-made sweater, or a favorite book or musical selection. While the gift may have been memorable, it's likely that your memory of the giver is even more poignant. Watching her face mirror yours as she saw your delighted expression, the awareness of how well she knew you in order to choose this particular gift, the generosity and sacrifice of buying or making this gift for you—they all said one thing, *I know you and I love you.*

Our lives are brimming with lovely gifts from God. It's so important that we don't forget for a moment to seek to know and love the Giver more than the gifts. He alone is the best gift we could ever receive.

Smile with sheer joy! You have a relationship with the God who knows you best!

Read James 1:17.

> *LORD, I HAVE SHEER JOY IN THE FACT THAT YOU KNOW ME AND LOVE ME.*

Love and Pain go together, for a time at least. If you would know Love, you must know pain too.

—HANNAH HURNARD

TO KNOW LOVE

We were made for a perfect world, but we do not live in one. In this life, love and pain come paired; one does not exist without the other. For now, the consolations of love come tinged with grief, misunderstanding, and even loss.

Yet Hannah Hurnard describes pain as a pathway to understanding love—the kind of all-encompassing love God has for us. To get to the heights, we must go through the valley. To understand love, we must be willing to experience pain—for true love calls for giving, for sacrifice, for facing hurt and loss.

Jesus himself showed the ultimate love by his willingness to sacrifice his life for us. His love for us was worth whatever pain it took to bring us to himself. If we want to truly love, we must willingly follow his example.

Read 1 John 3:16.

HELP ME TO UNDERSTAND THAT PAIN TEACHES ME MORE ABOUT YOUR LOVE, DEAR LORD.

Love is the only thing that we can carry with us when we go, and it makes the end so easy.

—LOUISA MAY ALCOTT

LOVE LASTS

Can the pain of death really be eased? In *Little Women*, as Beth neared the end of her life, she knew that love would go with her; love would make her final days easier to bear.

We don't like to think about life's end. With sorrow we grieve the loss of those who leave us through death. To contemplate our own passing is hardly a way we'd want to spend an afternoon.

Yet we must think about it. We must know both of our eternal destiny and of our duty to fulfill our God-appointed tasks in this life. Above all, we must love. Love those close to us with a love that looks past wrongs and hurts and endures anyway. Love those far away with a love that causes us to care, to serve, to give where we can.

Love will go with us into eternity. Love alone will last.

Read 1 Corinthians 13:13.

LORD, HELP ME TO CARRY YOUR LOVE WITH
ME WHEREVER I GO TODAY.

What Christ asks of us is a roomy workshop, for when He comes into the soul, He comes as a craftsman and brings His tools with Him.

—EVELYN UNDERHILL

THE WORKSHOP

Jesus wants to move into our souls. He needs a workshop, a place to lay out the tools he will use as he crafts his purposes in our lives. He needs room to do his work.

So we first clear out the clutter taking up space—the clutter of a desire for wealth, prestige, or the accumulation of stuff, or a craving to be noticed and appreciated. In order to give Christ his workshop, make some space. Spiritual housecleaning is a process of letting go of these desires and freeing ourselves from worldly attachments.

Invite Jesus into the workshop of your life. You may need his help to clean it up, but he willingly does it. He is the Master Craftsman and he has a plan more beautiful than you can imagine. Stop in. Take a look. See what he's working on in you today.

Read 1 John 2:15–17.

HOLY SPIRIT, I GIVE YOU ROOM TODAY TO DO YOUR WORK IN ME.

Just as the hemorrhaging woman crept up behind Jesus, so do we try to keep our "stuff" secret, hoping no one will notice our spiritual anemia, the eternal emotional bloodletting.

—JANE RUBIETTA

JUST A TOUCH

She kept her head bowed low and clutched her scarf tightly around her head. She shuffled through the crowd. If anyone knew who she was and the illness she had, they'd be panic-stricken because she was touching everyone—not really able to help it in the crush of the crowd. She had been bleeding for twelve years and this made her ritually unclean. No one should touch her; she should touch no one.

But her mission was worth the risk of detection. She had a plan. Jesus had come to town, Jesus the healer. She would simply get close enough to reach out, touch his robe, and receive healing.

We keep our heads low to try to hide our pain. We put on a happy face. We want to remain undetected so that no one sees our "spiritual anemia."

Jesus invites you to come close. Just a touch will heal you.

Read Mark 5:25–32.

I DON'T WANT TO HIDE ANYMORE, LORD. PLEASE
TOUCH ME AND MAKE ME WHOLE.

Perfection is attained through the active and positive effort to wrench a real good out of a real evil.

—DOROTHY SAYERS

FINDING THE "REAL GOOD"

How do we picture perfection? A scenic and restful holiday? A perfectly shaped body? A spotless home? Striving for perfection in those areas is nothing short of frustrating—for we can always find someone with a more exotic holiday or a leaner body or a more finely decorated house. We are fighting a losing battle.

Dorothy Sayers has another take on perfection. She asks us to live our lives wrenching real good out of real evil, living as Jesus lived during his time on this planet. When our evil world threatens to close in, we live as light in the darkness bringing hope and joy to those around us. We do not sugarcoat evil, but we put our trust in God, knowing that he alone can bring good from evil.

You will find God's brand of perfection as you bring light to your dark world.

Read Hebrews 10:14–17.

FATHER, HELP ME TO BRING LIGHT TO MY WORLD TODAY.

There is nothing sadder than an unfulfilled life. . . . Dreams don't come with expiration dates.

—MARTHA BOLTON

WE'VE ONLY JUST BEGUN

Deep inside each of us God has placed desires. We have gifts, talents, dreams of what we want to do. Years pass. We continue to live our lives, but we keep looking for that fulfillment. At times, we find ourselves delayed or sidetracked by life's unexpected circumstances.

Maybe you don't feel like you're living your dream—but you see, dreams don't come with expiration dates. Taking a circuitous route to your dream doesn't mean you won't get there. Life's unexpected circumstances come as no surprise to God. Instead, you may find that God is moving you toward a dream perfected for you—better than you have imagined. The life you live and the wisdom you gain will make your dream that much sweeter. Maybe that will prove to be the purpose of the delay all along.

Be patient. God is not finished with you—or your dreams—yet.

Read Joshua 14:6–13.

HELP ME TO SEE THE POSSIBILITIES AND OPPORTUNITIES YOU HAVE FOR ME, LORD.

The last and foundational part of my perseverance is born out of my faith. When all those other things . . . run out or fall short, my faith is the thing that enables me to just show up and take one more step.

—MICHELLE AKERS

ONE MORE STEP

It's tough to keep going. When our strength is gone, when that next step takes such tremendous effort, when our body screams in protest and our brain has called in sick—what can motivate us to keep moving forward? What reason can trump our tired mind and limbs?

There's only one: Jesus. Perseverance is born out of faith in him.

Everything else will run out. Our own determination, desires, or dreams may not be enough to keep us going. But faith in the One who calmed the raging sea, healed the sick, raised the dead, and gave sight to the blind—that will keep us showing up and taking one more step.

Whatever you've been called to do, know this: he will provide strength and energy for the work to do it. No matter how tired you are today, faith will help you persevere. Take that next step. Your faith will sustain you.

Read Isaiah 40:30–31.

LORD, I'M TIRED. GIVE ME STRENGTH TO TAKE
THE NEXT STEP AND FOLLOW YOU.

Being alert to the possibility that God may bring a person across our path will change our attitude toward first meetings.

—DEE BRESTIN

FIRST MEETINGS AND UNEXPECTED BLESSINGS

We have many first meetings. Some blossom into lifelong relationships, others last only a few minutes. But that first "hello" becomes important when we consider the possibility that God wants us to minister to that person, if for only a moment.

Haven't we all received a smile from a stranger just when we needed one? Or a helping hand? When we've been encouraged out of the blue in that way, we praise God for the unexpected blessing.

You never know whom you might meet today. Your smile may light up the day for a woman who is hurting. Your kind offer of help may rebuild someone's trust in the human race. Even if you're dealing with sorrow, perhaps you'll meet someone who's been there and she can have the joy of ministering to you.

Be alert to your first meetings today. See what surprises God may have in store!

Read 2 Thessalonians 1:11.

LORD, HELP ME TO SEE MY FIRST MEETINGS THROUGH YOUR EYES.

*That's what God says when he looks upon you, dear one.
"Ta-da! I did it! She's perfect, she's finished, and she's all
mine." You are gorgeous to God simply because you're covered
in the blood of His Son.*

—LIZ CURTIS HIGGS

IN GOD'S EYES

D o you hurry past the full-length mirror in the hallway?
You know if you stop, you'll be disappointed. That
reflection doesn't resemble the *you* inside. What you see doesn't
seem to reflect what *is*. You move forward to look at the details,
mainly wrinkles, and wonder if the product you saw on TV
really would tighten up your eyes. You step back and admit that
bikini days are over. The sequined dress in the back corner of
your closet will probably never fit again. No one will be chasing you down for a photo for their magazine cover.

But you know what? God says you're just right. Age has
made you a richer person inside, a wiser woman, a more
compassionate woman, a stronger woman. Jesus has made you
beautiful.

The magazine cover photos are always touched up, but you?
You're gorgeous! So give that reflection a great big smile!

Read 1 John 1:7.

*LORD, HELP ME SEE MYSELF THE WAY YOU DO.
THANK YOU FOR MAKING ME JUST RIGHT!*

MARCH

How shall we fix our eyes on things unseen? There is no answer but faith, faith in the character of God Himself. That and no other is the anchor for our souls.

—ELISABETH ELLIOT

ANCHORED IN GOD

The anchor of a great ship seems small compared to the vessel itself. Yet when dropped to the ocean floor, it holds even the largest vessel in place.

Faith in our God is the anchor of our souls, holding us safe. When questions don't have answers, faith means we know that God does. When circumstances don't make sense, faith means we know that God has the big picture. When we need something to hold us safely in the harbor when the storms come, faith means we know that God will not fail us. Faith means trusting in the character of God himself.

Gaze not on what life appears to be; instead, anchor your soul in who God is. He is able to hold you steady. No matter what is happening in your life today, have faith. God is still God— good, sovereign, omniscient, omnipotent, wise, faithful, and unchanging.

Read 2 Corinthians 5:7.

ANCHOR MY SOUL TODAY, GOD—IN YOU.

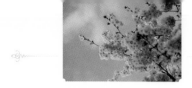

When God gives a command or a vision of truth, it is never a question of what He will do, but what we will do.

—HENRIETTA MEARS

I WILL OBEY

God is doing great things all around us. He is opening doors and changing hearts. Like Aslan in Narnia, he is on the move—warming hearts toward him, seeking the lost, bringing his loving touch to those who hurt. So the issue is, as Henrietta Mears explained, what *we* are going to do.

In other words, will we join him? Are we willing to engage in his unseen plans? We can look at the world around us and get angry. We can be apathetic and decide the situation is hopeless. We can hunker down and avoid contact. Or . . . we can decide we will join God in his work, doing whatever he calls us to do to spread his truth in a needy world.

Are you in?

Read Matthew 4:19.

LORD, I'M IN. WHAT CAN I DO TO SERVE YOU TODAY?

The more homelike heaven becomes, the more you feel like an alien or stranger on earth.

—JONI EARECKSON TADA

TRUE HOME

Home. The word evokes thoughts of the place where you rest your head and satisfy your hunger. Home is a refuge from the craziness of life—everything you need is there. Best of all, home is where everyone knows you and loves you anyway.

For the Christian, heaven is home. It is the only place where you won't have any need. Everyone will know and love you, but even more reassuring, everyone will know and love the Lord. Earthly life is confusing, full of dilemmas, pitfalls, and unpleasant surprises. Life in our eternal, heavenly home will be a ceaseless series of certainties, with times of joy and praise that will fill us with everlasting peace.

It's no surprise we feel uneasy here, like aliens in a strange world. We were created to walk with God. Heaven is our true home.

Read John 17:11.

I LOOK FORWARD TO MY TRUE HOME WITH YOU IN HEAVEN, LORD.

One thing is certain; namely, that never is the soul so perfect that it does not need the continual help of God, even though it be transformed in him.

—SAINT CATHERINE OF GENOA

HIS CONTINUAL HELP

It would be wonderful if we could just be perfect. Why doesn't God just make that change in us the minute we receive him? Why not just flip a switch for "perfection" and be done with it? He would have so much less trouble with us.

But, you see, that's not the point. God is not afraid of a little trouble. Instead, he's in the business of full transformation which—like an acorn growing into an oak tree—takes time but builds strength to withstand the storms. We have been made perfect in God's eyes, even as we are growing more and more perfect every day as we walk with him. Sometimes we trip up, sometimes we take a couple of steps backward, but always we are moving forward. And in that process, we continually seek God's help, drawing ever closer to him.

And *that's* the point.

Read Philippians 3:10–14.

I NEED YOUR CONTINUAL HELP TODAY TO WALK FORWARD—WITH YOU.

God calls them just the way they are, then He empowers them to get their act together!

—BETH MOORE

HE IS CALLING

God often touches our hearts to do something for him, but we feel unsure of ourselves, inadequate, unqualified. Many women called by God may have felt that way as well, but they didn't make excuses:

Mary didn't say, "I'm too young."

Rahab didn't say, "I have a business to run."

Esther didn't say, "I could be killed!"

Deborah didn't say, "A woman judge?"

Phoebe didn't say, "I don't travel alone."

After the call, God equipped these women to do what he needed, but they first had to be willing.

He *is* calling you today for an important job, a job he knows you can do because—well—he's going to work through you.

He just needs you to say, "Yes, Lord!"

Read Isaiah 6:7–8.

YES, LORD. SHOW ME WHAT YOU WANT ME TO DO.

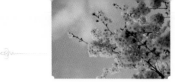

I cannot ask Thee to restore / The years of canker and of blight, / For Thou hast called me o'er and o'er, / And sought me thro' the long, dark night; / I cannot ask it, Lord, but see— / I bring a broken heart to Thee!

—MARY ARTEMISIA LATHBURY

BRING YOUR HEART

"The years of canker and of blight." It's old language but the words deeply resonate if we have spent many years living far from God, spending our lives in what will not last, seeking for a joy we could never find. Indeed, being far from him is like living in a "long, dark night."

We may look back across years where we lived our own way and wish we could get them back. If only we had sought God sooner. If only we had heard that voice calling us "o'er and o'er." Then we could have saved ourselves much pain and heartache.

God will not turn back time, but he readily accepts broken hearts. He specializes in taking hearts beaten and bruised by life and healing them.

Come to him with your broken heart, your fragmented soul, your worn baggage. He will make you whole.

Read Psalm 51:17.

LORD, I COME TO YOU AS I AM. MAKE ME YOURS.

If we look for the happy ending in this world and according to the standards of this world, we'll never find it.

—MADELEINE L'ENGLE

HAPPILY EVER AFTER

We love the happy endings in fairy tales. The prince rescues the fair maiden and rides off into the sunset. Good triumphs over evil. Everything works out right.

The world's definition of a happy ending can often be found on the nearest bumper sticker: "Visualize world peace." "He who dies with the most toys wins." If we're looking for a happy ending that matches a bumper sticker slogan, rest assured we will never find it.

God's version of the ultimate happy ending, however, was born through the Savior's agony on the cross. Jesus suffered and died to provide a happy ending for the sins of all people. That happy ending is coming. A place where the curse of sin is gone. A place where we will see our Savior face to face. A perfect forever.

How's that for a happily ever after?

Read Revelation 22:4–5.

JESUS, YOU ARE MY PRINCE AND ONE DAY WE
WILL HAVE A HAPPILY EVER AFTER.

It takes faith to come to God simply to be with Him. It proves, first of all, that we believe He exists. And that He is our greatest gift.

—Stormie Omartian

THE GREATEST GIFT

Sometimes we get to the end of a long day and flop exhausted into the nearest chair, only to find ourselves asking, "What did I really accomplish today?" Maybe our accomplishments were many, but we found no joy in them. Or perhaps of all the tasks we did, nothing seemed very valuable or worthwhile in the grand scheme of things.

Stormie Omartian suggests an action that will put every other thing we do into its proper perspective: Come to God simply to be with him.

In the fast pace of today's world with its focus on achievement and financial success, we may lose sight of our greatest treasure—our relationship with our loving God. The best way to grow more deeply in love with him is to carve out time every day to be with him.

Simply bask in his goodness. He is your greatest gift.

Read Psalm 31:19.

IT'S AMAZING—YOU WANT TO SPEND TIME WITH
ME. SO HERE I AM TO WORSHIP YOU.

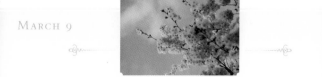

It is one thing to stand in truth, to believe it, and to embrace it, yet, there's more than this in girding our loins with truth; we are to walk in truth.

—KAY ARTHUR

WALK IN TRUTH

We long for truth. We appreciate the people in our lives who tell us the truth. Truth means we can count on it. Even if it's a difficult observation or statement, we at least have a foundation to work from to make a change.

As believers, we count on God's Word as truth. We stand on it, we believe it, we embrace it. But we must do one more thing—we must *walk* in it. What we do, what we say, how we live, the example we set, the attitudes we show—all of these must line up with the truth to which we have committed our lives.

It isn't always easy, but it's vital. We have found the truth that changes the world, changes lives, changes hearts. Let that truth affect every step you take today and every day.

Read Psalm 86:11.

LORD, LET MY ACTIONS REVEAL MY
FAITH IN YOUR WORD AS TRUTH.

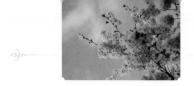

Giving unlocks our own hearts to God's comfort and His new plans for our lives after tragedy and grief have done their worst.

—EUGENIA PRICE

STRENGTH TO GO ON

She used to volunteer regularly at her church's food pantry, but after the sudden death of her newborn son eight months earlier, she retreated as she and her family mourned.

"I wondered if I would ever feel anything but sadness again in my life," she said. "But I felt a glimmer of joy when I returned to volunteer at the food pantry and placed some groceries in the arms of an elderly man. He smiled at me. I smiled back at him. It had been a long time since I'd smiled."

If tragedy and grief have done their worst, Eugenia Price would advise, then after your time of mourning, find ways to serve others. You may not feel like you have much to offer, but giving unlocks your heart to receive God's comfort. He will provide the strength to go on.

Read Psalm 119:50.

PLEASE STRENGTHEN ME TO SERVE ANOTHER
TODAY, O GOD OF ALL COMFORT.

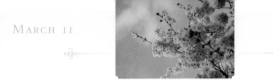

He sat for a long time and thought to himself that he wished he knew how to pray, yet he knew, untaught, how by abandonment of himself to let the quietness take hold of him.

—ELIZABETH GOUDGE

BE STILL

How can we let the quietness "take hold" of us? Our lives are so very busy. Finding time to be still, to be quiet, seems like an unattainable luxury.

But we must try. Days will pass and, if we wait until we have the time or the attitude or the setting to pray, we may never get around to it. We will wonder why we feel so harried and why God seems so far away. At that time we must remember what we already know—that we must abandon ourselves and let the quiet take hold.

"Be still, and know that I am God," wrote the psalmist (Psalm 46:10). God invites us to, at least for a few moments, cease our physical and mental activity and simply bask in who he is. We don't need to *do* or *say* anything; we simply need to *be* with God.

Read Psalm 46:10.

HERE I AM, GRACIOUS FATHER. I JUST WANT TO SIT HERE QUIETLY WITH YOU.

Your friendships are vital to your relationship with God. Your friends are either pulling you down (away from God) or pulling you along and/or up (toward God).

—ELIZABETH GEORGE

TRUE FRIENDS

Ever think of your friendships as a vital part of your relationship with God? Those hearts knitted together with you and God are gifts from on high. Such friends pull us up toward God, always encouraging us to seek him. We learn from one another's experiences. We're encouraged to break out of mediocrity and stretch into the persons we were created to be.

Some friends influence our dreams. Some mentor us. Some connect us to other important relationships. And our dearest friends would tear off the roof to set us before Jesus!

Friends can also pull us away from God if we let them. Some friendships can send us in wrong directions. We need to discern these and set them aside.

Thank God for good friends. Keep them close. Pray for them, care for them, love them. They are God's gift to you, for now and for eternity.

Read Mark 2:2–4.

JESUS, THANK YOU FOR YOUR FRIENDSHIP. HELP ME BE A TRUE FRIEND TO OTHERS.

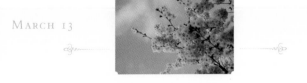

We are not only striving towards victory but fighting from the position of victory.

—CORRIE TEN BOOM

WE WIN!

If a soldier knew that no matter how hard he fought, his army was going to lose the war, he would probably drop his ammunition and desert. On the other hand, if word came down that victory was absolutely assured, he would fight on with renewed strength.

We are in a battle, make no mistake about it. Simply by being followers of Christ we are archenemies of Satan. We are targets—and many of us face his attacks every day.

But guess what? Jesus already told us the outcome of the war. We win!

Victory is assured in the war, but many battles are to be fought in the meantime. As Corrie says, we are not just striving for victory, we are fighting from the position of victory. Every battle we win pushes back the darkness a little further. Every soul saved is another life rescued for God's kingdom.

Fight on.

Read 1 John 5:4.

I AM READY FOR BATTLE TODAY, LORD.
THANK YOU THAT WE WIN!

Oh! for the mighty, convicting, convincing power of the Holy Ghost! Oh! for faith to remove mountains, to expect them to be removed! Pray for us, for the mountains are very tangible, and our faith is very weak.

—AMY CARMICHAEL

FAITH TO MOVE MOUNTAINS

As Amy Carmichael penned these words, she was on her way to Japan to serve as a missionary. Even she, now looked upon as a model for world missions, admitted that she struggled with trusting God. The mountains that stood in the way of sharing Christ were tangible and seemingly impassable. Her faith seemed too weak to move them. So she prayed for the Holy Spirit to fill her with the faith she needed.

Take comfort in that, dear sister. You don't need to have "perfect faith" in order for God to use you. You only need to be willing. When you feel weak, you can go to the Source who promises to give you the faith you need.

What mountains are on your horizon, threatening to block God's work? What challenge seems more than you can handle? Cry out to God. He will give you faith to move mountains.

Read Matthew 21:21–22.

LORD, I DO BELIEVE. HELP ME OVERCOME MY UNBELIEF.

God lays down certain physical laws. Yet we seem to be continually expecting that He will work a miracle—i.e. break His own laws expressly to relieve us of responsibility.

—FLORENCE NIGHTINGALE

YOUR HANDS, YOUR FEET

You sit bedside with an ailing friend. You hug a neighbor receiving tragic news. You agonize over a child living with sin's consequences. *They don't deserve this*, you think. *Why can't God relieve the torturous pain?* As Florence Nightingale reminds us, God lays down certain physical laws. In some cases, he will break through with a miracle. At other times, he does not. Our desire to see a miracle must not be in order to relieve us of responsibility.

What is that responsibility? Perhaps it is to pray fervently. Perhaps it is to maintain an unwavering faith that witnesses to others. Perhaps it is to seek God's approval as reward enough. Nobody knows the bigger picture or the thoughts of God. Whatever he chooses to do, he needs you, for you are his hands and feet in the world.

Your touch, your words, your prayers bring him into your hurting world.

Read James 2:15–17.

TAKE MY WORDS, MY HANDS, MY FEET INTO YOUR WORLD TODAY, LORD.

Satan isn't called the Father of Lies for nothing. He opened his cozy chat with [Eve] using a deliberate lie—misquoting God, even putting words in the Lord's mouth.

—LIZ CURTIS HIGGS

KNOWING TRUTH

We don't like to be lied to, but sometimes we fall for lies in spite of ourselves. It all depends on what we're looking for. If we're desperate to look younger, we'll believe anything about the special cream sold on TV. If we want quick wealth, we'll fall for the online ad with all its impossible promises.

You see, Satan plays on our weaknesses. Just as he sensed that Eve wanted to know more about God and so built his cozy chat with her around that very information, so he observes where we are most vulnerable. He's looking for ways to get us off track spiritually—even sometimes quoting God's Word—because he wants nothing more than to come between us and God. If we listen, we lose.

Our best defense is intimate knowledge of the truth found in God's Word. Read it. Study it. Talk about it. Understand it.

How will you know the truth? Open God's Word. He'll gladly reveal it.

Read Psalm 119:30.

HELP ME, FATHER, TO STUDY YOUR
WORD SO I KNOW THE TRUTH.

I love neither the world, nor the things of the world; nor do I believe that anything that does not come from Thee can give me pleasure; everything else seems to me a heavy cross.

—TERESA OF AVILA

WORLD-WEARY

World-weariness isn't a twentieth-century phenomenon. Teresa of Avila faced it as she wrote these words in the sixteenth century. She was tired of chasing things that disappointed and seeking satisfaction in that which ultimately fell flat. She describes these pursuits as a "heavy cross." Only that which came from the hand of God could give her true pleasure.

All around us messages promising pleasure fill our senses. We are told to buy this, taste that, watch this, and we will be happy. Only when we learn to no longer love the world or the things of the world, only when we understand that seeking pleasure in these worldly pursuits is merely a heavy cross—only then will we begin to understand where true pleasure lies.

Your greatest joy, dear sister, is found in seeking after God and enjoying what he gives. Anything else will disappoint.

Read Isaiah 55:2–3.

FATHER, MY GREATEST JOY IS FOUND
IN SEEKING AND FINDING YOU.

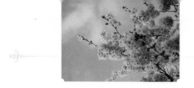

We must believe that God permits failure—that a loving God permits hard things; because the hard things bring the greatest victories, the deepest lessons, the most lasting changes.

—CAROLE MAYHALL

BEAUTY FROM ASHES

The thought of it causes our faces to turn red and our heads to drop in despair. FAILURE. We don't always understand why it is a part of life. We try to avoid it. Yet, in spite of our best efforts it happens. Shame, disappointment, and humiliation hit us like a tidal wave. People distance themselves from us. Ministry crumbles before our eyes.

From the ashes of devastation, God can bring beauty. God permits hard things—yes, even failures—because he knows that through the failures come great victories, deep lessons, lasting changes.

God can bring beauty from the ashes of our failure, too, if we let him, if we choose to believe he is still at work, if we trust him enough.

Are you facing hard things today? Trust God for the victory, the lessons, the changes. He loves you. He wants to bring beauty from the ashes.

Read Isaiah 61:3.

> GOD, I TRUST YOU WITH MY HARD THINGS TODAY. I KNOW YOU CAN BRING BEAUTY FROM ASHES.

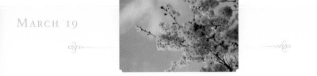

If we are willing to be molded by His hands, the Lord will shower us, our men, and our relationships with abundance. That is the way He works.

—SHAUNTI FELDHAHN

OUR SACRED SCULPTOR

When a potter picks up his clay, it's usually a stiff, cold, shapeless block. It takes patience and strong hands to soften the clay before it can be molded. During this time, the artist gets to delight in the process of creation and dream about his finished product.

Picture our heavenly Father, with his strong hands, desiring to shape you for his glory, for your benefit, and for others' blessing. How much patience will he need to make you pliable? How resistant are you to changing shape? Are you willing to take on the shape he has in mind for you, or are you set on a shape of your own? As Shaunti Feldhahn reminds us, God wants to mold us. When we are willing to let him shape our lives, he showers us with his abundance.

God is molding and shaping you. Will you let him be your Sacred Sculptor?

Read Romans 9:20–21.

SACRED SCULPTOR, MOLD ME. MAY I BE PLIABLE IN YOUR HANDS.

Worshiping needs to come before asking. In our prayers, there needs to be more praise than petition.

—JOYCE MEYER

PRAYER AND PRAISE

Some people only call when they want something. Their short greeting is quickly followed by a request. We know the minute we hear a certain voice on the line that we need to put up the boundaries and be ready with a reason for our yes or no. After awhile, we don't like to hear from those people at all.

When we approach God, are we guilty of being like those difficult friends? "Hi God," we say, followed by, "Here's what I need from you." Joyce Meyer explains that the privilege of even approaching God with our requests is granted to us at great cost to our Savior. The least we can do is open our prayers with worship and praise to our great God.

Adore him. Thank him. Praise him. Let your mind focus on his greatness. Then bring your requests humbly to him. He will be honored and glorified by you.

Read Psalm 150.

LORD, I PRAISE YOU FOR YOUR GREATNESS AND POWER. THANK YOU FOR HEARING ME.

[I resolve] . . . to search for the Face of God not only in prayer but in having no other intention in my work, words or sufferings.

—MOTHER VERONICA NAMOYO

SEEING HIS FACE

Picture the homeless traveler. His clothes are dirty and he wears no shoes. Is it possible to see God in him? Yes. Jesus looked that way at times.

Visualize a frowning boss, holding out unreasonable demands. Is it possible to see God in this situation? Yes. Jesus faced accusers who pointed and demanded. He forgave them.

Remember the sickness or the aches and pains you have struggled to overcome. Is it possible to see God in these? Yes. Jesus suffers with us.

Mother Veronica was born into a Communist family and raised by parents who denigrated faith and denied God. Yet she started to believe at a young age and, through her example, they too became followers of Jesus. She went on to set up monasteries in North Africa.

Mother Veronica resolved to find Jesus everywhere. To those who are paying prayerful attention, God shows himself. Where will you see him today?

Read James 2:8–9.

HOLY SPIRIT, GUIDE ME. HELP ME SEE JESUS
IN THE PEOPLE I MEET TODAY.

When difficult circumstances come into my life, I hear God's voice saying, ". . . let me be the blessed controller. Surrender. Accept my timing. Accept my ways. Accept my outcome. Let your trust be in me alone."

—LINDA DILLOW

SWEET SURRENDER

One word in Linda's quote can be easily overlooked—the word *when*. Not *if*, but *when* difficult circumstances come into our lives, we are called to listen for God's voice. Maybe you're going through a peaceful season right now and your load is light. What better time to start practicing? Wake up each morning and say, "Lord, I'm giving you full control of this day and all that concerns me."

And if today is full of difficult circumstances, God calls you to let him take control. Surrender it all to him. Accept the timing of his answers, the ways he will answer, and the outcome he has planned.

Let go, dear sister. During the good times and the bad, God lovingly calls you to trust him alone. Begin the obedient act of falling back into his waiting arms. Trust him. He'll catch you every time.

Read Isaiah 55:8–9.

PRECIOUS LORD, I SURRENDER TODAY TO YOUR
TIMING, YOUR WAYS, YOUR OUTCOME.

I was able to look at my weaknesses calmly, honestly and with hope because I knew I was standing in the presence of a Father who loved me. Looking at him made it easier to look at me.

—ANN SPANGLER

MIRROR, MIRROR

We've all had a bad hair day. No matter what we do, we just can't get the hair to lay right, curl right, act right. We've all had our "bad hair days" spiritually as well. We look in the mirror and see only weaknesses and failures glaring back at us. It's hard enough to go out in public on a bad hair day—but when we think that even our weaknesses are exposed, hopelessness begins to set in.

Ann Spangler suggests that we stop staring at our flaws and instead look calmly, honestly, and with hope. God made us in his image. He is good and gracious, forgiving and faithful, humble and holy, loving and loyal.

Looking at him will make it easier to look at yourself. When you're standing in the presence of the Father who loves you, you see the beauty he sees—the beauty you are.

Read Psalm 45:11.

GRACIOUS FATHER, THANK YOU FOR SEEING ME AS BEAUTIFUL.

I am his child; but in his great wisdom, he let me realize that nowhere else in the whole wide world, nowhere in all creation, can I go from his presence. He wouldn't let me go.

—JAN DRAVECKY

HE WILL NOT LET YOU GO

The six year old, angry that mom won't give him ice cream for lunch, packs up his belongings in a plastic bag and declares that he is running away. Mom keeps an eye out, watches him head to the neighbor's home, and makes a quick phone call. Then she watches and waits. Her son will soon return. In short order he discovers that he needs his mom, that no other place offers the comforts of home, and that mom loves him and wants the very best for him—which doesn't include ice cream for lunch!

At times we are frustrated at God, angry at his refusal to give us what we want. We figuratively pack our bags to run away—only to discover that we cannot get away from his presence. He is watching, waiting, loving.

He loves you too much to let you go. So unpack your bags. You're home.

Read Psalm 139:7-10.

FATHER, THANK YOU FOR YOUR LOVING PURSUIT
OF ME IN MY WILLFUL WANDERING.

*If I had been told what I was to learn through these lengthy
sufferings, I am afraid I would have shrunk back in terror, and
so have lost all the sweet lessons God proposed to teach me.*

—ELIZABETH PRENTISS

SWEET LESSONS

What if we could know what the future holds? It seems
like a good idea. If we could know what's going to
happen to us, we'd be better prepared, right?

But what if the future holds suffering? What if we discover that
the coming years will bring pain, difficulty, or sorrow? To know
would cause us, as Elizabeth Prentiss says, to shrink back in
terror—not wanting to take another step toward the pain.

It is much better for us not to know too much, but instead to
live life fully every day. Then, when suffering comes, we trust
in God's promises of his grace to endure. And beyond that, we
watch for the sweet lessons he proposes to teach us in the midst
of our suffering—lessons we could not learn any other way.

In your suffering, dear sister, God has sweet lessons for you. Let
him teach you.

Read Psalm 119:124.

TEACH ME THE SWEET LESSONS YOU HAVE
FOR ME, LORD. I AM YOUR STUDENT.

To be holy is to be wholly satisfied with Christ. Above all, it is to reflect the beauty and the splendor of our holy Lord in this dark world. . . . You will fulfill and experience all that God had in mind when He created you.

—NANCY LEIGH DEMOSS

WHOLLY SATISFIED

The flame of a lit candle is inconsequential during the day. But take a candle into a deep cave, and its light will make the difference between safety or stumbling, between finding your way or being lost, even between life or death.

Shine the candle into your life. What do you see? In a dark world, secret and habitual sins can be hidden. But seek holiness, and your candle will show where Christ needs to cleanse your life of sin, clear away the baggage of the past, and help you become more like him. Like a candle in a cave, the holiness Christ gives will keep you safe, help you find your way, and reflect the beauty and splendor of Jesus into a dark world.

To walk in holiness is to experience all that God had in mind when he created you. You will find that you want nothing more.

Read Leviticus 11:44.

FATHER, MAY I DESIRE HOLINESS MORE THAN ANYTHING ELSE.

To be candid without ostentation or design—to take the good of every body's character and make it still better, and say nothing of the bad—belongs to you alone.

—JANE AUSTEN

KIND WORDS

What fills our conversation about others? Are we full of praise about others' goodness? Or are we eager to gossip about their faults?

The words of Jane Austen remind us that, while we have our opinions, we would do well to choose to speak of the good in people's character and say nothing of the bad. When talking to friends, co-workers, neighbors, or church members, the choice belongs to us alone to see the strengths in others and remain silent about their weaknesses. Usually a person's weakness is glaring anyway and our help is not needed in bringing attention to it. Would we want other people talking about our glaring weaknesses—the weaknesses of which we are painfully aware?

Christ knows our every shortcoming and, thankfully, he wants us, welcomes us, and loves us. Let your words about others be uplifting and kind, reflecting Jesus' love for you.

Read Proverbs 16:28.

TODAY, LORD, LET MY WORDS ABOUT OTHERS BE POSITIVE, HELPFUL, AND ENCOURAGING.

I sprang to my feet, shouting "hallelujah," and then for the first time I realized that I had been trying to hold the world in one hand and the Lord in the other.

—FANNY CROSBY

TWO HANDS

Our lives are full, without a doubt. We literally and figuratively "have our hands full" as we seek to juggle family, friends, job, community responsibilities, and trying to take care of ourselves in the process. Too often, however, we find ourselves dropping the balls and watching them bounce all over our lives.

What's the problem? Perhaps we're trying to juggle life with one hand, at the same time holding the Lord in the other. Fanny Crosby discovered that doing so didn't work. Why keep the Lord separate from all aspects of our busy lives as if he doesn't apply? Why not put the two together?

God should be imbued into *every* arena and detail of our lives—every shopping trip, every assist with homework, every service project, every relationship. Juggling with both hands is so much easier.

Hallelujah!

Read Psalm 16:8.

I WANT YOU TO BE INVOLVED IN EVERYTHING I DO TODAY, MY LORD.

I am a little pencil in the hand of a writing God who is sending a love letter to the world.

—MOTHER TERESA

GOD'S LOVE LETTERS

There's something about a handwritten note that means so much more than even the kindest e-mail or text message. A thank you, an "I love you," a note that says "I'm thinking of you" when written by hand above your signature sends a special message to the receiver: "You are worth it."

You are like the precious pencil in God's hand. God is sending a love letter to the world—and you are that personalized note. He sends you when someone needs love, tenderness, companionship, encouragement, courage, or kindness. Your small stroke of a smile or your willingness to erase others' mistakes sends an unmistakable message of God's love. A pencil? Seems small and unimportant and certainly not high-tech, but it is oh so powerful.

Like Mother Teresa, you are a little pencil in God's hand, writing a love letter to the world. What message is he sending through you today?

Read 1 John 3:11.

GOD, USE ME TO WRITE YOUR LOVE ON
THE HEARTS OF OTHERS TODAY.

Imagine how different our days would be if we had our cups filled by Christ first thing in the morning.

—BETH MOORE

A CUP IN THE MORNING

The alarm rings. As our minds wake from the fuzziness of slumber, thoughts of the day come rushing in. Our day may have some unpleasant tasks ahead, or perhaps our to-do list is so long it makes us tired before we even begin. In any case, some mornings we'd rather stay in bed so we don't have to face the day at all.

But as Beth Moore states, imagine how different our days would be if we had our cups filled by Christ first thing in the morning!

When Christ fills our cups, he gives us his love, his joy, his peace and patience. We're able to be kind, good, faithful, gentle. And hey, a little bit of self-control might come in handy at an opportune moment as well!

Christ wants to fill your cup to the brim. He knows just what you need for the day ahead.

Read Psalm 5:3.

FILL MY CUP, LORD. YOU KNOW JUST WHAT I NEED FOR TODAY.

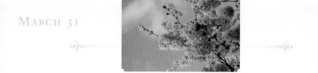

Often we do not know our own gifts. That's why it's a great help to self-knowledge if we have family and friends who can tell us honestly, "This is what you do well."

—INGRID TROBISCH

UNWRAP YOUR GIFTS

Can you remember a moment during your childhood when a trusted adult noticed that you had an aptitude for something? Perhaps your sixth grade teacher encouraged your interest in science. Or a piano teacher cheered on your musical talent. Perhaps a grandparent affirmed your communication skills. Until that person noticed, you may not have been fully aware that something special was happening in your life.

We all want to serve God well, and we want to use the gifts he has given us. But what, exactly, are those gifts? And how will we know?

We will know when we hear it from those who know us best. When they truly compliment something we do well, something we already love to do, we'll know we have discovered a gift from God.

Then the next question is, "Where, God, do you want me to use my gifts for you?"

Read 1 Corinthians 12:4–7.

SHOW ME MY GIFTS, LORD, AND SHOW ME WHERE TO USE THEM.

APRIL

Today I believe in miracles. Out of brokenness can come good: Character can be deepened, relationships can be restored, emotions can be steadied, and a mind can be healed. Now, isn't that miraculous?

—PATSY CLAIRMONT

OUT OF BROKENNESS

When things in our lives are broken, confused, and hopeless, we want nothing short of a miracle. We know that, in order to solve the problem, it will take something out of the ordinary, something beyond the realm of possibility.

Then, sure enough, hope shines through. Out of brokenness comes good. Relationships thought long lost are restored. Emotions considered too overwhelming are steadied. Even minds are healed. Through it all, we find a depth to our character we didn't know existed.

That too is a miracle.

God wants us. He wants our full selves, and sometimes it takes brokenness for us to turn to him. He doesn't want to be our "fair-weather friend"; he wants to show himself miraculous in our lives through the storms and valleys we face.

Miracles? They happen every day when God is involved. Look around. You'll see them everywhere.

Read Psalm 77:14.

HELP ME, FATHER, TO TRUST YOU TO WORK YOUR MIRACLES IN ME.

O when once the heart is gained, how easily is all moral evil corrected! It is, therefore, that God, above all things, requires the heart.

—MADAME GUYON

A NEW HEART

Her life had not turned out as she planned. In fact, difficult situations had sent her spiraling into a lifestyle she hated. Her parents would not be proud of her. Her "friends" only drove her desperation. She sought happiness but, when it seemed she found it, it was short-lived. She sought love, but that didn't last long either.

Then one day she met Jesus. His words touched and healed her broken heart. His forgiveness was complete, for he had taken the punishment. His love was the purest she had ever experienced. He showed her that a life following him would give her all the happiness she craved and all the love she sought. Her desperate search was over. In exchange for her heart, Jesus gave her life. His forgiveness set her free to live her best life possible—for him.

Jesus wants your heart. He'll cleanse it and make it new.

Read Ezekiel 36:26.

JESUS, TAKE MY HEART. IT'S YOURS. MAKE IT NEW.

The more we know God, the more deeply we love God.

—JANE RUBIETTA

COME CLOSER

Something's missing. You accepted Christ as your Lord and Savior and you love him. You attend church on Sunday mornings and pray both morning and night. But still . . . something's missing. There's an emptiness that hasn't been filled. Sure, the love of your family and friends warms you, worship and Bible reading sustain you—but that empty feeling remains.

Suddenly within your heart you hear sweet, soft words, "Come closer."

God wants you to come closer, to come and know him better, to feel the warmth of his presence. He wants you in a relationship with himself. And as you come to know him more deeply, you experience the immense love he has for you.

The more we know God, the more deeply we love God.

It is then, in that closeness with your God, that your emptiness will be filled.

Read Ephesians 1:17.

GOD, I LONG TO KNOW YOU BETTER SO THAT
MY EMPTINESS MAY BE FILLED.

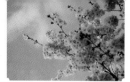

This whole business of guidance, obviously, is a highly personal thing. . . . All I can do is recommend to anyone who is troubled or uncertain or confused that they ask for it—and see what happens.

—RUTH STAFFORD PEALE

TAKE HIS HAND

During his short years here on earth, Jesus frequently asked for God's help. He went to God on the mountain for guidance about the choice of twelve disciples. He wept with a broken heart in the Garden of Gethsemane as he faced the future. Jesus modeled how to recognize human limits and ask for divine direction.

When we are troubled, uncertain, or confused, we are invited to ask our loving, wise Father for guidance. He will pour it out onto us. Freely. Abundantly. We don't have to beg him or force him—he *wants* to guide us. He knows the future and specifically what we need. He will replace our ambiguity with decisiveness, our bewilderment with good sense, our troubled hearts with peace.

He desires to take you—his precious child—by the hand and lead you today. This guidance from God? It's personal; it's yours. Just ask.

Read Psalm 48:14.

I PLACE MY HAND IN YOURS, DEAR LORD. LEAD ME. GUIDE ME.

Often God delays purposely, and the delay is just as much an answer to your prayer as is the fulfillment when it comes.

—EMILIE BARNES

GOD'S DELAYS

From Instant Messaging to microwave dinners, we are accustomed to receiving what we want or getting our tasks done right now—or at least within seconds. When answers to our prayers don't come according to our desired timeline, we become as frustrated as small children who want dessert before dinner.

No wonder we get so impatient with God. We pray. He delays. We get flustered and frustrated. We want the answer *now*.

Just as a loving parent knows we need nourishment before treats, God knows the perfect order and timing of the answers we desire. He also knows that waiting on him will bring us even greater satisfaction when he finally sends his answer.

The delay is as much an answer as the answer itself. As your patience grows, so will your faith. God is waiting too—waiting to know that you want *him* more than you want answers.

Read Psalm 27:14.

FORGIVE ME FOR BEING DEMANDING AND IMPATIENT.
TEACH ME TO WILLINGLY WAIT ON YOU.

It is not enough to pray for answers if we are too stubborn to listen to what the Lord is telling us.

—ALLISON BOTTKE

FIRST, LISTEN

As a milestone event approaches, we shop for a new dress. We know exactly what we want or else we search until we find *the* perfect one. No sales clerk can change our minds. We *know* what we want.

How often do we petition God with the same determination? We know our needs and we know exactly how we want them to be met. We know *what* he should provide for us, *when* he should provide it, or *how* he should deal with that person who hurt us. We aren't ready to hear another alternative. We may not recognize when God sends a friend or a Scripture to soften our hearts in order to hear him. If we're too stubborn to listen to what God is saying, we miss his perfect answers.

Listen with an open heart. God's answers may surprise you.

Read John 10:27.

LORD, HELP ME LISTEN SO THAT I HEAR YOUR
BEST ANSWERS TO MY REQUESTS.

Enable me to fulfil all my duties perfectly. . . . To You, my Beloved, I offer myself so that You may fulfil in me Your holy Will.

—THERESE OF LISIEUX

THY WILL BE DONE

The media says, "Demand what is yours." To be a *servant* is equated with masochism. Few want to serve if it means giving up something they want.

Therese of Lisieux was a nun who died in 1897, at age 24. As a child she dreamed of being a missionary, imagining she would do big things for God. But her body was too frail for such a life.

Instead she prayed, "Thy will be done," and God showed her that she could make each day a gift. She became a servant to anyone in need. She shared music, laughter, and prayer with those around her. She showed great courage even when she was suffering. She offered herself to her Beloved Lord to do his will in her life.

To do the will of God is a beautiful act. It enables you to fulfill all your duties perfectly.

Read Mark 14:35–36.

LORD, NOT MY WILL, BUT THY WILL BE DONE. LET MY LIFE GLORIFY YOU.

Love of Jesus, wider far / Than the widest heavens are: /
Deeper than my sin can be, / Who shall separate from Thee? /
Safe from self and safe from sin, / Love of Jesus, shut me in!

—MARY ARTEMISIA LATHBURY

SAFE IN HIS LOVE

The love of Jesus is wider than the widest heavens, deeper than the deepest darkness. Nothing can separate us from that love.

When Jesus enfolds us in his arms, we are safe. Safe from ourselves—from our uncanny ability to make the wrong choices, to turn from God when we most need him, to think we can find our way alone. And we're safe from sin—the sin nature within us that plagues, the sin around us that tempts, the sin-darkness that wants to take away our joy.

Only Jesus provides that safety. Only his love is wide enough and deep enough and high enough and long enough to shut us in safely and to protect us from the storms.

No love is greater, wider, deeper, truer, or more constant than the love of God. He calls you his beloved. He promises to never let you go.

Read Romans 8:35–39.

JESUS, WRAP ME IN YOUR LOVING ARMS. NEVER LET ME GO.

Every single time I confess my self-reliance and submit my life to God's will in a particular area, I am worshiping God.

—Barbara Hughes

WHAT WORSHIP LOOKS LIKE

We long to please God, but in the heat of the moment we often do the opposite of what God would have us do. When someone hurts us, we retaliate. When someone betrays us, we get angry. If our rights are denied, we're ready for a fight.

But what if we decided to submit to God's will in every situation?

What if, instead of doing what comes naturally, we obeyed God? This is what that might look like: We'd show love to our enemies and pray for those who persecute us. We'd submit to our husbands, even when we disagree. We'd honor our parents, even when they're difficult. We'd pray instead of worry. We'd forgive instead of holding a grudge. We'd confess our self-reliance. We'd submit to God's will.

You prove God's worth to you every time you choose to obey him. And that is true worship.

Read Romans 12:2.

LORD, I SUBMIT TO YOUR WORD AND WILL. I LONG TO WORSHIP YOU IN ALL I DO.

I stumbled upon a mystery without a solution, a mystery so immense that I gave up trying to find an explanation because the whole mystery defied belief.

—ANNE RICE

THE GREAT MYSTERY

A well-written mystery keeps us glued to the pages of the book. The characters engage us, the plot twists surprise us, and we can't wait to discover the resolution. We'd be very angry if we got to the end and the mystery was still unsolved: "They never knew who did it. The End."

The author Anne Rice stumbled across a mystery without a solution in her journey to becoming a Christian. The mystery of God's love, of a God who would die in our place, of salvation bought and paid for, of a Savior who would take up residence in us to help us live for him, of a God who prepares heaven for us—it all makes no sense. It's a mystery so immense that we can't wrap our minds around it. The mystery defies belief yet draws us to believe.

Fortunately we don't need to have all the answers. We only need to trust the One who does.

Read Colossians 1:26–27.

THE MYSTERY IS BEYOND MY UNDERSTANDING,
LORD. BUT I TRUST YOU.

I feel that it is better to continue to try to teach or live equality and love than it would be to have hatred or prejudice.

—ROSA PARKS

LEVEL GROUND

God is an amazing Creator. He could have made all people look exactly alike, but he chose to build variety into humanity. Whether our differences are eye and hair color, or whether our skin is a different shade, God says we are all his children.

Rosa Parks is famous for standing up for equality. She built her convictions based on her Bible, which taught her that all people are equal in God's sight. We are called to live knowing we're all God's children. He wants his people to teach and live equality and peace, not prejudice and hatred. We reach across racial barriers with the love of Jesus. He breaks down the divisions.

No matter what the color of our skin, we are all saved the same way—by the red blood of Jesus. The ground is level at the foot of his cross.

Read Revelation 14:16.

THANKS FOR LOVING US EQUALLY. HELP ME TO
MODEL THAT TYPE OF LOVE, LORD.

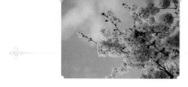

Evil is real—and powerful. It has to be fought, not explained away, not fled. And God is against evil all the way. So each of us has to decide where we stand, how we're going to live our lives.

—CATHERINE MARSHALL

STANDING ON GOD'S SIDE

The attacks can come out of nowhere, blindsiding us. They rip into our hearts and lives—the sin that besets us, the temptations that assail us, the fear that overtakes us. Satan has many weapons in his arsenal and he's ready and eager to use them all to battle against Christ's followers.

We cannot explain away the battles or pretend they don't exist. There's truly nowhere to run. Instead, we have to decide where we stand. Are we willing to serve as soldiers of Christ? Are we willing to do battle against the darkness?

We aren't left to our own devices. We depend on God's power and wear the armor he provides. Then we go out to fight the battles. Every inch of ground we take back from Satan brings light and hope to our embattled world.

Dress in your armor. You are needed on the battlefield.

Read Ephesians 6:11–17.

FATHER, I CHOOSE TO SERVE YOU ON THE BATTLEFIELD TODAY.

Beloved, whenever you are in doubt as to which way to turn, submit your judgment absolutely to the Spirit of God, asking Him to shut every door but the right one.

—L. B. COWMAN

CHOOSING WITH CONFIDENCE

Life is filled with choices. Simple ones like the choice between chocolate or vanilla, and more complicated ones like whether to accept a new job or to take on that responsibility at church or to buy a car. Some choices are easy because we see clearly that one is better than the other, or even that one is right and one is wrong. But sometimes we're choosing among several good options and we just don't know what to do.

Like that old TV game show *Let's Make a Deal*, selecting "door number one" instead of "door number two" seems daunting. But unlike a game show host, God isn't trying to confuse or deceive you. He *wants* to show you the best choice for you. Submit your judgment absolutely to his Spirit, asking that he close every door but the right one.

Then the choice is easy.

Read Acts 16:6–10.

LORD, I WANT TO CHOOSE YOUR BEST FOR ME. SHOW ME THE RIGHT WAY.

The Bible teaches that God is the sole source of the entire created order. No other gods compete with Him; no natural forces exist on their own; nothing receives its nature or existence from another source.

—NANCY PEARCEY

THE SOLE SOURCE

The Bible tells us that God is the sole source of creation—absolutely nothing exists without his having created it. No other gods compete with him; nothing exists on its own; creation did not just "happen."

So what do we learn about God by looking around at what he has created? We conclude that he is a God of beauty, of order, of creativity—and we might even conclude that he has a sense of humor as well.

You, as a part of creation, find your source in God as well. You exist because he created *you*. That longing in your heart, that desire for love and relationship, that search for meaning in your life—all can be found when you go to your Source. Look no further than God. As your Creator, he knows the plan for you. All you need to do is ask.

Read Psalm 19:1–6.

FATHER, THANK YOU FOR YOUR MAGNIFICENT CREATION. THANK YOU FOR CREATING ME.

When we focus primarily on knowing about God, we add to our to-do list. Yet as we concentrate on enjoying God—being with Him, in His presence—we begin to relax and appreciate Him.

—JOAN C. WEBB

BEST FRIENDS

What if our faith were just about facts? What if we had to do nothing more than memorize a list of the attributes of God, know the books of the Bible in order, and recite a few verses? What if we just had to go to church to learn *about* God, but there was nothing more?

Now think about what our faith *is*—a relationship with the God of the universe. We walk every day with God our Friend. We cry on the shoulder of God our Comforter. We converse with God our Guide. We lean on the arm of God our Strength. We seek advice from God our Father.

Our relationship with our Lord is not a dutiful act to be checked off a daily list; instead, being with him is joy and refreshment.

Today, *enjoy* being with God, your best Friend. After all, he enjoys being with you!

Read Psalm 28:7.

I ENJOY BEING WITH YOU, LORD. YOU ARE MY BEST FRIEND.

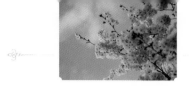

Nearer, my God, to Thee, nearer to Thee! / E'en though it be a cross that raiseth me, / Still all my song shall be, nearer, my God, to Thee. / Nearer, my God, to Thee, / Nearer to Thee!

—SARAH ADAMS

EVEN NEARER

We long for nearness to God. What does it feel like? What happens when we are *near* God?

First we must ask *how* we can be near God. The answer is in the beloved hymn itself: *E'en though it be a cross that raiseth me.* We come near to God because of what Jesus did for us on the cross. His death allows us—sinful human beings—to approach the holy God.

And oh what joy that nearness brings. When we draw near to God, he is beside us, within us, before us, behind us. His very closeness brings us protection, peace, and safety. Like a young child reaching for her mother's hand, nearness to God means his hand reaches down to grasp ours.

Such nearness is a gift from Jesus to you. Such nearness offers you joy and peace beyond imagining. Let your song always be, "Nearer, my God, to Thee."

Read Hebrews 7:19.

LORD, I LONG TO BE CLOSE. DRAW ME NEARER TO YOU.

God never comes to take sides. He comes to take over.

—BETH MOORE

GOD IN CHARGE

Have you ever prayed specifically about a certain situation, perhaps for several years, but then the opposite happened? It can be devastating, especially if the request was right and good. At those times we might cry, "God, how could you let this happen? I thought you were on my side!"

But we can be sure he has not left us. We may feel like he switched teams, but the reality is, he doesn't come in and take sides.

As Beth Moore describes it, he comes in to take over. As our faith is challenged, we learn to acknowledge that God's plans are always better than ours. As we watch situations unfold, we learn to trust that God has the bigger picture.

It's not easy, this issue of trust. But with God, it's the only way. Trust him enough to let him take over.

Read Psalm 9:10.

LORD GOD, I TRUST YOU TODAY TO TAKE CHARGE OF MY LIFE.

All prayers were not answered immediately. Otherwise there would be no need to pray without ceasing, as Scripture said to do.

—KAREN KINGSBURY

UNCEASING FELLOWSHIP

Pray without ceasing. It seems like an almost impossible task. Even when you need an answer soon, how do you pray in the midst of working, playing, concentrating on business, and interacting with others? Talk about multitasking! But Jesus knows your thoughts and hears them regardless of what you're doing, who you're with, or where you are. Speaking your prayers silently as you go about your day opens the door to continual prayer.

Think about it. Constant fellowship with the Lord! Yes, you're engaged at your job, concentrating on balancing the checkbook, or disciplining your child, but if somewhere in the background of your mind you're aware of his presence and inviting him in, that's prayer.

He may not always answer quickly. He wants the joy of your constant communication. When you pray without ceasing, your words strengthen the bond you have with your first love.

He hears you. And he smiles.

Read 1 Thessalonians 5:17.

LORD, TEACH ME TO PRAY WITHOUT CEASING,
INVITING YOU INTO EVERY ASPECT OF MY LIFE.

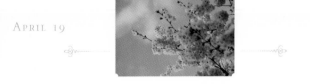

There's wealth enough; I need no more. / Farewell, my pelf; farewell, my store. / The world no longer let me love; / My hope and Treasure lies above.

—ANNE BRADSTREET

HOPE AND TREASURE

What if everything you owned was suddenly taken from you? Anne Bradstreet wrote these words after her home burned, destroying all her family's belongings and leaving her, her husband, and their eight children homeless. She understood that even though everything she owned was gone, her hope and treasure were safe in heaven.

We have no guarantees in this life. No written contract with God states that we will have earthly riches if we work hard. Nothing anywhere says we are assured a house, a car, and good health. In fact, God doesn't even promise we will live to see tomorrow.

However, there is one guarantee in which we can trust: Jesus will be with us and never let us go. No matter what life holds for us, he will be there to celebrate or to comfort.

Love not the world. If your hope and treasure lie above, you have all you will ever need.

Read Matthew 6:19–21.

> LET ME NOT LOVE THE WORLD, LORD. MY HOPE AND TREASURE LIE WITH YOU.

The name of Jesus wasn't just some way to sign off on my prayer, a spiritual "Over and out.". . .The name of Jesus was the authority I had stamped on my life, enabling me to come boldly to God.

—NETA JACKSON

IN JESUS' NAME

In Jesus' name, Amen." We often end our prayers this way, sliding across the closing words. But what do those words mean? It's not a spiritual "over and out," as Neta Jackson explains. The name of Jesus—and only the name of Jesus—allowed us access to God in the first place. That Jesus gives us the authority of his name when we come to the Father in prayer is a privilege we must not pass over lightly. We are saying, in effect, "God, your Son Jesus introduced me to you, and he told me I could talk to you at any time and even call you my Father. I have his authority."

With that authority stamped on your life, you can come boldly into God's presence. Jesus said so; he made the introduction.

Come on in. Talk to God. Jesus' name makes it okay.

Read Hebrews 4:14–16.

> I COME TO YOU IN JESUS' NAME, KNOWING I'VE BEEN INVITED. THANK YOU, JESUS.

I found it harder to forgive the treachery of the smiling friend who betrayed me to the stake than to forgive the men who lit the fire.

—ELIZABETH GOUDGE

AT HIS FEET

Betrayal is painful. A friend turns on you. A husband strays. A trusted mentor fails. Such hurt squeezes our heart like an iron fist and refuses to let go. Like Elizabeth Goudge, we would prefer to know of a person's hatred and deal with it than to have someone we trust turn on us.

As Jesus shared the Passover meal with his disciples, he was aware of the betrayal that was ready to explode in the heart of his friend Judas. Yet Jesus washed his disciples' feet—including those of Judas. From this position of humility and service, Jesus looked into the eyes of his friend as he washed and dried his betrayer's feet.

As always, Jesus is our example. He fully understands your hurt, for he has been there. Bring your pain to him and ask him to show you today how to honor him through this painful time.

Read John 13:21–30.

IN THE FACE OF GREAT PAIN, JESUS, I TRUST YOU TO GUIDE ME.

If only we could see that every single sin is a big deal, that every sin is an act of rebellion and cosmic treason, that every time we choose our way instead of God's way, we are revolting against the God and King of the universe.

—NANCY LEIGH DEMOSS

YOUR CHOICE

Sin. Do we take it as seriously as we should?

Our world glosses over all kinds of behavior. But Nancy Leigh DeMoss would have us pull our heads out of the gray mist and realize that every single sin *is* a big deal. It is an act of treason against the King of the universe.

Sound a bit too dramatic? Then think for a moment that this very King sent his Son to die so that we could draw close to God and know his will for us. In the face of that, when we choose our way instead of his, we are disobeying the One who gave his life for us. Instead, we should so desire to be close to God that we only want to choose his way.

The One who died for you wants what is good for you. The choice, moment by moment, is yours.

Read 1 Peter 2:24.

FATHER, I WANT TO CHOOSE YOUR WAY AND
ONLY YOUR WAY—TODAY AND EVERY DAY.

In order to expand your borders beyond where they are, God wants to move you beyond where you are.

—DARLENE WILKINSON

CATCH THE VISION

Too many people just "settle" because they don't feel like they have the time or ability or strength to do anything for God. They figure he has set them aside, so why not put up their fences and stay in where it's safe?

God doesn't want his people to settle. He doesn't want us fenced in. He wants to expand our borders. He wants us to dream bigger.

You don't need to change your address or find a new job— although that's not out of the question. More important, God wants you to catch a new vision of what he can do in and through you right at your current address and phone number.

Perhaps it's time to step out of your place of comfort and explore, looking for God's new possibilities.

Catch the vision. God has great plans and wants you to join him!

Read 1 Chronicles 4:10.

LORD, GIVE ME COURAGE TO DREAM BIG AND
SEE WHAT YOU'VE GOT WAITING.

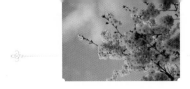

There is hope! The home you've always wanted, the home you continue to long for with all your heart, is the home God is preparing for you!

—ANNE GRAHAM LOTZ

MAGNIFICENT CONSTRUCTION

Life can be overwhelming, and on some days, so can our homes. Unfinished work and repair projects fill our to-do list and pile up around us. Strife moves in and peace moves out as we face challenges in our relationships. Exhaustion fills the rooms during a long battle with sickness or disease. Emptiness and loneliness close in on us, even in a beautifully decorated house or among people we love.

When your heart aches for something better, remember what's under construction for you. The place you dream of and long for, God is at this moment building. Imagine—a place where everything works the way it's supposed to, where there is no more darkness, and where there is no more sickness or death or crying.

That place is *your* place! As you live in a less-than-perfect home today, let the hope of your eternal home give you peace and joy.

Read Revelation 21:4.

THANK YOU, GOD, FOR THE HOPE OF A HOME WITHOUT BLEMISH.

I'm not afraid of the storms, for I'm learning how to sail my ship.

—Louisa May Alcott

LIFE'S STORMS

As we sail our ship through life, we face times of calm when the sea is like glass beneath us. Other times, the perfect storm comes, splashing waves across our bows, spraying mist in our faces, tossing our ship about, threatening to sink us. It takes an expert captain to navigate a ship through a storm.

Louisa Mae Alcott decided not to fear the sudden squalls in life, but to take the helm, grab the wheel, and learn how to sail the ship. Only the most trying times make the expert captains. Experience in rough water is the best teacher.

Are you sailing choppy seas? Is your ship taking on water? Now is the time to learn how to sail the ship. God promises to teach you how to make it through life's squalls.

Do not fear the storms. The Captain is at the helm with you.

Read Luke 8:22–25.

THANK YOU, LORD, FOR TEACHING ME HOW TO
NAVIGATE THROUGH LIFE'S STORMS.

Love is creative. It does not flow along the easy paths, spending itself on the attractive. It cuts new channels, goes where it is needed.

—EVELYN UNDERHILL

CHANNELS OF LOVE

It's like love has a mind of its own. When we think about the fact that God *is* love, then, maybe it does. God knows where people are hurting. He knows who needs love.

Jesus saw the woman with uncontrollable bleeding, the untouchable leper, the lonely little man in a tree, and he showed love. He saw the young woman tormented by demons, the blind man who begged for attention, the promiscuous woman who sought true love, and he showed love.

When we let God's creative love guide us, he sends us to unexpected people and places. When we love as Jesus loved, he sends us to those who are in extra need of a loving touch.

When you need love, God is there. When others need love, he commissions you to cut new channels and take love where it is most needed.

Read John 15:12.

THANK YOU FOR LOVING ME. HELP ME TO LOVE AS YOU LOVE.

As we walked through the destitute place, our souls cried out to God for help.

—MARY MCLEOD BETHUNE

CRY OUT TO GOD

The destitute place. It looks different for each of us, but we've all been there.

It's a place where nothing makes sense. It's a place where what we thought we understood is turned upside-down, where what we thought we had is taken away. It may be the loss of a job or a home, a wandering child, an unexpected attack, the loss of a friendship, a divorce, a death. It's a place where darkness descends, envelops, overwhelms. Where do you go? Who do you turn to? Who can possibly bring sense back to a world of confusion?

Mary Bethune knew. In that destitute place, our souls cry out to God for help.

Only he can turn your world right-side-up again. Only he can give you the wisdom to move forward from the destitute place and back into life.

He's there. Just call out to him.

Read Psalm 40:1.

FATHER, IN THESE TIMES OF HARDSHIP AND TROUBLE, MY SOUL CRIES OUT TO YOU.

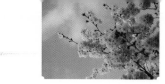

*God can do everything, that's true, but if nothing bad happened
in our lives, we might get the idea that we didn't need him. . . .
He lets life happen, and sometimes what we think is a burden
is really a blessing.*

—LORI COPELAND

FROM OUT OF NOWHERE

We don't plan for trouble. It comes on its own, out of
nowhere. A company downsizes and renders us jobless.
An accident limits our activities. Grief or sorrow overwhelms us.

So often our first response to trouble is to ask, "Why, God?"
We explain to God all the reasons why this specific trouble
isn't fair. We want God to make life easier. But if life were easy,
perfect, with no problems, we would not be driven to our
knees, bringing to him our dilemmas that only he can solve.
He says, "My child, I am with you, aware of your trouble. I
care about you. This trouble may have seemed to come from
nowhere, but I've got it all under control."

Never forget how much you need him. Only he can turn what
you think is a burden into a blessing.

Read Hebrews 10:22–23.

> DEAR GOD, I KNOW THIS TROUBLE DOES NOT
> SURPRISE YOU. I NEED YOUR HELP TODAY.

The older I get, the greater power I seem to have to help the world; I am like a snowball—the further I am rolled the more I gain.

—SUSAN B. ANTHONY

GROWING IN GOODNESS

We women resist growing older. Wrinkles and age spots and gray hair can cause us no end of frustration. We try creams and gels and hair color to stave off the inevitable.

While it's healthy to care about our appearance, the outside of our bodies doesn't define the beautiful "us" inside.

Oh, if we would just have Susan B. Anthony's perspective. As we age, we can be like rolling snowballs, gathering experience, skills, connections, friends, wisdom, and spiritual maturity and insight. The more we live, the more we gain, and, hopefully, the more we realize we have the resources to share wisdom, offering depth of insight and help for those in need.

Have a few wrinkles and gray hairs? Thank God for allowing you to grow older. Embrace these days. Accept your age—and all that comes with it—as a gift to give others.

Read Proverbs 20:29.

PRECIOUS LORD, HELP ME TO MATURE WITH
MY YEARS SO I CAN HELP OTHERS.

What happens if the functions or circumstances in which a woman places her identity changes? . . . We need to place our identity in what will not change.

—VONETTE BRIGHT

UNCHANGING IDENTITY

Where do we place our identity? If we put our identity in what we *do*—in our job description or our service record or our child-raising skills—we may find ourselves disappointed, for all those circumstances can change. We can lose our job; we could face a sudden illness that affects our ability to serve; our children will grow up and leave us with empty nests.

What happens to our identity then?

Vonette Bright has a better idea. We need to place our identity in what will not change. And the only thing we can totally depend upon to never change is our Lord Jesus himself. He is the same yesterday, and today, and forever. With our identity in him, we know we always have a place in his kingdom to serve.

You are his forever, dear sister, no matter what changes are happening in your world today. Place your identity in him.

Read Hebrews 13:8.

JESUS, THANK YOU THAT I CAN PUT MY IDENTITY IN YOU.

God wants us to stand out as women who know we have something valuable to offer the world. . . . The people around us can have full confidence in us because we have full confidence in God and we live accordingly.

—DONNA PARTOW

IN HIS IMAGE

Every woman has a "bad hair day" or pulls on her "fat jeans" once in a while. On those days, we just don't feel very good about ourselves, and it shows as we interact with others. Our focus is inward and it's hard to get things done.

The next time you have a crisis of self-confidence, take another look in the mirror and see what God is looking at: his empowered creation. He doesn't notice extra flab or blemished skin or unmanageable hair; he sees the potential of your gorgeous, bold spirit. And if you go about your day with that image in mind, you can accomplish everything God sets before you. People react and respond with trust to those who exude unmistakable confidence.

Exchange your insecurity and lack of self-confidence with God-confidence. You have something valuable to offer the world. Your confidence will be electrifying.

Read 2 Corinthians 3:10–12.

MAKE ME BOLD TODAY FOR YOU, LORD. WE HAVE WORK TO DO!

To believe in God is the beginning. To hear Him call your name is the start. To dance in His arms is real life.

—ANGELA THOMAS

DANCE WITH THE DIVINE

To dance in His arms is real life." As women who love God, we may find it easy to believe in him and to hear him call our name. We're willing to be his servants and carry out the work he puts before us.

But what does it mean to *dance* with him?

God doesn't only want us to know who he is and to work for him, he wants a joyful, exhilarating relationship with us! Dancing with someone requires intimacy. It requires confidence. It requires trust. When we dance with our God, we offer him ourselves.

Do you believe he finds you so interesting and intriguing that he wants to dance with you through this life? Do you understand that God accepts you for who you are—his own beautiful creation?

Look up. He's standing there, hand outstretched, ready to lead you to the dance floor.

Read Jeremiah 31:13.

LORD, YOU TAKE THE LEAD;
I'LL BE YOUR DANCE PARTNER FOR LIFE!

Help me, Lord, to remember that religion (Christianity) is not to be confined to the church . . . nor exercised only in prayer and meditation, but . . . everywhere I am in Thy Presence.

—SUSANNA WESLEY

ALWAYS IN HIS PRESENCE

Our faith does not have walls. We gather in churches or storefronts or homes to worship together, but those are not the only places we can worship our Lord.

And our faith does not have limits—it is exercised not just by prayer and mediation, but also by our work, acts of service, and fulfilled responsibilities. We worship our Lord as we care for our children, work at our jobs, take a meal to a sick friend, or hug a grieving neighbor.

Christ-followers cannot be silenced. We cannot be hemmed in or separated by walls. We are not confined to buildings. We are not limited to prayer and meditation. Wherever we go, whatever we do, we are in our Lord's presence and we are living out our faith.

Everywhere you go, you are in your Lord's presence. May your tasks today be imbued with worship.

Read 1 Corinthians 10:31.

EVERYWHERE I GO TODAY, LORD, I AM IN YOUR PRESENCE, LIVING FOR YOU.

Don't let the circumstances fool you. . . . God's love is so powerful it can touch any heart, even the heart that seems impossibly far from him.

—CAROL CYMBALA

UNFAILING PURSUIT

When a loved one is far from the Lord, our hearts ache. The pain cuts like a knife. We toss and turn through many sleepless nights. Our tears could fill a bathtub. We know we shouldn't do it, but we blame ourselves. If only we had said this, or not said that. If only we had done something a little differently.

Then we wipe our tears and look to heaven. Where is God? Why isn't he doing something? Surely this is a prayer within God's will. Doesn't he want everyone to be saved?

Don't fret, dear one. God's unfailing love is pursuing your loved one. His grace doesn't stop—he died to save sinners, so sin doesn't stand in his way. His love knows no boundaries.

Keep on praying. Keep on living as you know God would have you live. Trust that your loved one is being chased by the God who will not give up.

Read Psalm 77:1–12.

LORD, HELP ME TO REMEMBER THAT YOU LOVE MY LOST LOVED ONE EVEN MORE THAN I DO.

*O Beloved, what is yours because you are His? Pursue it per-
sistently. Ask, seek, knock. Jesus is the One who tells you to do
this. It is both a command and a loving invitation.*

—KAY ARTHUR

KEEP ON ASKING

Sometimes we get to the place where our prayers seem
pointless. Maybe we've prayed for the same person, the
same request, the same need for five years, a decade, or even
longer. And the questions abound: If God hasn't answered yet,
will he ever? Does God's silence mean the answer is no? Does
it mean our request isn't in his will? Should we just give up?

Jesus' answer to all our questions is clear—keep on asking, keep
on seeking, keep on knocking. In other words—we must not
give up! We must pursue persistently.

As Kay Arthur says, persistence in prayer is both a command
and a loving invitation. Jesus loves to see you come. He loves to
hear your voice. He delights in your dependence on him.

You are his. He is yours. He will answer, at just the right time,
in just the right way.

Read Luke 11:9.

LORD GOD, IT'S ME . . . AGAIN.

Do not ask "what can I do?" but "what can He not do?"

—CORRIE TEN BOOM

NOTHING IS IMPOSSIBLE

We try, we really do—cleverly designing the solution, pushing and sweating to make it work, pulling an all-nighter to finish the project. Hard work leads to success—that's what we've learned, it's in our DNA. But when we hit the impossible, the unthinkable, the immovable, we don't understand. What then?

How about, instead of focusing on "What can I do?" we ask, "What can God not do?" Nothing is impossible with God. And nothing is impossible with you, when you depend on him. Here's the most amazing thing—God is pleased to work in and through us whenever we ask him to do so.

Do your best, but realize that it's not all about you and what you can do. It's about you being available to be used by God. That's a whole different perspective. Through you, what can he not do?

Read Jeremiah 32:17.

> LORD, WHAT CAN YOU NOT DO TODAY?
> NOTHING. REMIND ME OF THAT.

Jesus is my Husband, my Savior, my Beloved. I am not alone.

—ROBIN LEE HATCHE

NEVER ALONE

Loneliness. Married or single, young or old, rich or poor, we all sometimes feel alone—like no one is there for us, no one cares. But those of us who love Jesus have his constant presence, even in the times when we don't feel him close. Whether we are joyful and fully content or struggling with grief or discouragement, Jesus is with us. We are never alone when we have him.

He is better than the most perfect husband—he knows your needs and gently cares for you. He is your Savior—he willingly gave his life so that you could be set free from sin and have this always-and-forever relationship with him. He is your beloved—loving you with an everlasting love. The One who runs the whole universe is your Husband, your Savior, your Beloved. He has you always on his heart.

You are never, ever alone.

Read Hebrews 13:5–6.

*BELOVED JESUS, THANK YOU SO MUCH FOR
YOUR CONSTANT PRESENCE WITH ME.*

In a culture that says, "Don't go there," those of us who call ourselves followers of Christ really must go there—go to the cross, go to the grave, go to others and say, "Come and see for yourself."

—LIZ CURTIS HIGGS

GO THERE!

Each of us has things we feel passionate about . . . our hometown team, a great hair stylist, or an amazing new cereal that causes teeth to gleam and weight to drop off. We can't wait to invite our friends to give it a try and become fans too.

Sadly, sometimes we rein in our enthusiasm for Jesus. We think it might be inappropriate, make someone uncomfortable, or even offend, so we steer clear of conversations that involve prayer, supernatural peace, consequences of sin, or salvation. These topics are at the very core of what sustains every believer, yet we avoid them for fear of . . . *of what?*

Causing someone a moment of discomfort, or even having them reject us altogether, is such a small risk. You *must* go there—eternal souls are at stake.

Invite them to come and see for themselves.

Read Romans 1:16–17.

LET ME NEVER BE ASHAMED OF MY FAITH SO
THAT YOU MAY NOT BE ASHAMED OF ME.

I wonder how many times I've received from the Lord what I had asked for but just didn't recognize it.

—PATSY CLAIRMONT

RECOGNIZE ANYTHING?

She wants to make a difference for God. As a believer in Christ, she knows it is her mission in this world. Her heart aches for those who don't know the Savior. She passionately inquires of the Lord where she should go, which nation will be first.

Morning greets her with a phone call. Her plans for the Lord will have to be put on hold—her elderly aunt is ill and needs her help. She'd really like to do bigger things today than sit with this woman she barely knows. But she goes, she serves, she shows her love.

Weeks later she receives a call from her mom. "Your aunt passed away this morning but not before she accepted Jesus, thanks to the love of Christ that she saw in you."

God sent her not to a nation, but to an elderly woman who needed him.

Where will he send you today?

Read Mark 11:24.

LORD, HELP ME TO RECOGNIZE ALL THE ANSWERS
TO PRAYER THAT YOU HAVE GIVEN ME.

May we yield to His pruning and know the hand that holds the knife is a wounded one—wounded for you and me.

—JILL BRISCOE

YIELD TO HIS PRUNING

Gardeners understand that pruning is part of the process of growth. They know that they must cut away certain stems and leaves to allow a plant to bloom to its full potential. The plant may look a little worse for the wear for a short time, but when the blooms come, they will be full and healthy.

So it is in our lives. The Master Gardener knows us better than we know ourselves. Because he wants the very best for us, he prunes away anything that would stunt our growth or choke our potential.

Perhaps you are feeling the clippers cutting away at you right now. It hurts. You wonder why certain parts of your life are being so drastically changed. Be reminded, dear one, that each cut is done with precision and care. Only the Gardener knows how you will look in full bloom.

Read John 15:1–2.

LOSS AND CHANGE ARE PAINFUL, LORD. SHARE YOUR VISION OF WHEN I RECOVER AND THRIVE AGAIN.

Faith and prayer are the vitamins of the soul; man cannot live in health without them.

—MAHALIA JACKSON

VITAMINS OF THE SOUL

We want to stay healthy, so we take our vitamins. We eat our vegetables and fruit; we watch our sugars and carbohydrates. We have this one body and, in order to serve God well, we need to keep it as strong as we can.

The Bible provides advice about a different type of health—that of the spirit. God is the Great Physician who is invested in our spiritual health. He prescribes faith and prayer—the "vitamins of the soul"—to keep us living vibrant spiritual lives. A daily intake of faith helps us see beyond our current circumstances to God's promises. It allows us to hope for that which we do not see. Prayer strengthens and supports our vital connection with the Great Physician who watches over our souls.

Open your Bible. Take your vitamins. Your spiritual health depends on it.

Read Romans 12:11–12.

MY GREAT PHYSICIAN, MAY FAITH AND PRAYER BE MY DAILY VITAMINS SO I CAN SERVE YOU.

When one really cares, the self is forgotten, and the sacrifice becomes only a part of the activity.

—DOROTHY SAYERS

OVERFLOWING FOR GOD

Sometimes we care—and want to help—but it's too inconvenient. We'd take that meal, but the family lives too far away. We'd contribute to the offering, but our finances are tight. We'd volunteer, but our schedule is filled to capacity.

Dorothy Sayers explains that, when we really care, we don't focus on ourselves and the sacrifice we must make. The sacrifice becomes only a part of the activity; the rest is wrapped up in love for God, love for others, and desire to serve.

We just need to learn to forget about ourselves. Not easy, but possible.

Today, tune your heart to the Holy Spirit's gentle voice. Is he asking you to really care? Don't do something because you feel manipulated, pressured, or guilty. Do it out of willing obedience to him.

When you forget about yourself, your acts of service overflow with joy and love. And God in heaven smiles.

Read Romans 12:1.

EVEN THROUGH SACRIFICE, JESUS, HELP ME
FORGET MYSELF AND DO AS YOU ASK.

Until the will and the affections are brought under the authority of Christ, we have not begun to understand, let alone to accept, His Lordship.

—Elisabeth Elliot

HIS LORDSHIP

As a group, women are adverse to the thought of anyone lording over us. We've been trained to believe that no one should stand in the way of our goals and dreams—that we have the right to do anything we want.

But as believers, we have a different view, for we must willingly submit ourselves to the lordship of Christ. We put him in charge. We turn our lives over to him. We ask him to guide us; we follow. It doesn't mean we don't make plans or pursue our passions; it just means we hold the plans and passions loosely, always seeking God's will.

As Elisabeth Elliot says, we must bring both our will (what we want) and our affections (those passions that send us following our hearts) under Christ's lordship.

Until he is Lord of all, he is not really Lord at all.

Read James 4:7.

I WANT YOU TO BE LORD OF ALL MY LIFE.

The secret of God is upon our tabernacle; / into His mystery I dare not pry. Only this I know: / With Him is strength, with Him is wisdom, / and His wisdom hath set darkness in our paths.

—HELEN KELLER

DIVINE SECRETS

Helen Keller, blind and deaf, knew about darkness. She understood, probably more than any of us, what it meant to be lonely, alone, left in the darkness and the silence. Did she ever question God: "Why did you choose to take those two senses from me? Why did you leave me dependent on others for the rest of my life?" In spite of that understandable frustration, this is what she writes: It is in God's wisdom that we don't understand. God knows what's best for us. Sometimes what is best for us is to *not* have all the answers.

Are we content to learn what God wants to teach us, or are we constantly trying to pry into mysteries that he has chosen to keep hidden? Be content, sister, to let your Father teach you his lessons in his time.

His strength and his wisdom are enough.

Read 1 Corinthians 13:12.

LORD, I DON'T NEED TO HAVE ALL THE ANSWERS
BECAUSE I KNOW YOU'RE IN CONTROL.

Praise is not a response to our circumstances, which constantly fluctuate. Praise is a response to the goodness and love of a God who never changes.

—NANCY LEIGH DEMOSS

KITE FLYING

Flying a kite in an open field or on the ocean shores is pure joy when the weather conditions are right. The kite whips through the air, dipping and dancing in the sky . . . until the wind stops. Then it falls helplessly to the ground.

When our praises are tied to changing circumstances, they are just like that kite. Soaring one minute, grounded the next. When our praises are tied instead to an unchanging God, we can respond to God's goodness and love regardless of what's going on in our lives.

No matter what you're feeling today and no matter what the circumstances look like around you, God hasn't changed. He is the same yesterday, today, and tomorrow. He never changes. And that alone is a fact worth praising!

It's always perfect kite-flying weather with God. Let your kite fly! Let your praises soar.

Read Psalm 44:8.

HELP ME TO PRAISE YOU, LORD, REGARDLESS OF THE WEATHER.

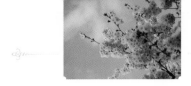

Blessed assurance, Jesus is mine! / O what a foretaste of glory divine. / Heir of salvation, purchase of God, / born of His Spirit, washed in His blood.

—FANNY CROSBY

BLESSED ASSURANCE

Ever been absolutely sure of something—so sure you would bet your life on it? We can pretty much count on the sun rising in the morning and that summer will follow spring, but beyond that, few things in life are certain. People and situations change. Promises are broken.

As believers, however, we do have absolute assurance in one thing: Jesus is ours—in our lives, in our hearts. Having him gives us a foretaste of what is to come, the glory he promises us in heaven with his Father. We are guaranteed salvation because we have been purchased by God with the blood of his Son. That blood has washed away our sin and made us clean. And we have been reborn by his Holy Spirit. We are brand new from the inside out.

You can be certain of this—Jesus is yours. And his promises are yours as well.

Read 2 Corinthians 1:21–22.

THANK YOU FOR GIVING ME BLESSED ASSURANCE IN YOU.

How I need to order my life around one incredible thought: God is to be honored in all I do. My heart's desire is to be so overwhelmed with . . . God that my life cannot help but bring Him glory.

—CYNTHIA HEALD

SUNRISE

I n those early-morning moments when your eyes first open, what goes through your mind? What gets you up and out of bed?

Perhaps a fussy infant gets you moving, or a long list of responsibilities. Maybe it's the smell of fresh-brewed coffee, or the song of sparrows. But have you ever considered that you and the sun share the same reason for rising?

God created you and the sun to display his glory. The sun displays the glory of his sustaining and creative power. You display the glory of the risen Christ who lives in you!

Imagine that. As the sun warms the earth, you radiate the warmth of God's love. That's why you're here. And every single thing you do falls into the category of showcasing God's glory and goodness. Order your life around the incredible thought—God is to be honored in all you do.

Read 2 Corinthians 4:6.

LORD, I WANT TO HONOR YOU TODAY IN EVERYTHING I DO.

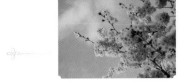

It is to you I owe everything, O my Deliverer, and I have infinite pleasure in owing it to you.

—MADAME GUYON

IN DEBT

Being in debt is usually not a good thing. We can become bogged down in what we owe—money to credit companies, time to organizations, work that has passed deadlines. We are easily overwhelmed as we try to keep track of what we owe and to whom.

However, there is one debt that we can never repay. When Jesus paid for our sins by dying on the cross, he offered eternal life in exchange for . . . nothing. His ultimate sacrifice cost him his life, yet he offers it to us at no cost. It's absolutely free. We couldn't pay him back even if we tried!

To him we owe our lives, our salvation, our fulfillment, our futures, our hopes. What a pleasure to owe it all to him. With staggering gratitude we return to him our love, our praise and worship, our service.

Read Romans 5:8.

THANK YOU, JESUS, FOR MAKING THE ULTIMATE SACRIFICE
FOR ME. IT IS A DEBT I CAN NEVER REPAY.

For wisdom is more than just seeing our problems through God's eyes—it's also trusting Him even when the pieces don't seem to fit.

—JONI EARECKSON

FITTING THE PIECES TOGETHER

When we scatter the pieces of a puzzle across a table, nothing makes sense. We start with the edge pieces and then work from the photo to help guide us. But what if we have to put together the pieces without knowing what the picture is?

Our lives are exactly like that. Pieces of problems are scattered across life's table and nothing makes sense. Nothing fits. And we don't even know what the final picture is supposed to look like.

That's when we trust. If the puzzle manufacturers can deliver exactly the right pieces that will all fit in the end, then all the more, our Creator God knows how to form our puzzle-problems together into a beautiful picture.

When the scattered pieces don't make sense, know that the puzzle of your life has already been solved by God. Look through his eyes and trust him.

Read Ecclesiastes 3:11.

> THOUGH MY PUZZLE PIECES DON'T SEEM
> TO FIT, LORD, I WILL TRUST YOU.

Oh! if only once for an hour, all we could bear to know of what Calvary meant to the Father, Son, and Holy Ghost, could be flashed upon our hearts, burned deep into them.

—AMY CARMICHAEL

COMFORT IN OUR SORROW

Separation from loved ones makes our hearts ache. Whether children are off to college or moved to another state or deployed to war, we can't help but long to wrap our arms around them and protect them. They need us close—or maybe it's the other way around.

Now imagine how it must have felt for the Father, Son, and Holy Spirit, who are One from time immemorial, to be separated, torn from each other's presence as the direct result of *our* sin. Jesus took upon himself the penalty of human sin, died, and was separated from the Father for the sole purpose of providing our freedom. Amy Carmichael suggests that if only once in our lifetimes—for just an hour—we would feel the pain of that separation, we would be different people. We would be overwhelmed with the immensity of what Jesus did for us.

For you.

Read Isaiah 53:4–6.

FATHER, SON, HOLY SPIRIT—THANK YOU FOR
EXPERIENCING SEPARATION SO I COULD JOIN YOU.

For this little pain that we suffer here, we shall have a high endless knowing in God . . . and the harder our pains have been with him in his cross, the more shall our worship be with him in his kingdom.

—JULIAN OF NORWICH

WORTH THE COST

This is hard teaching. Pain, suffering, hardship . . . that's not what we signed up for. We responded to the message of peace that surpasses all understanding, of grace greater than we could ever imagine, of an unfailing love. No one said anything about pain.

But what, really, did we expect? That becoming believers would make our bills go away, our relationships suddenly perfect, and accidents no longer happen? In this world we have trouble. That's just the way it is. We would encounter some difficulties with or without Christ. The difference is, the more we respond in faith and act with integrity when we suffer, the more Christ is honored.

Facing pain is never easy. Is it worth it? Be assured of the answer. The answer is yes! Not maybe, not kind of, not probably, but absolutely, undeniably *yes!*

His kingdom is coming, and it will be perfect.

Read James 1:12.

LORD, HELP ME TO SAY "YES! FOR YOUR
GLORY"; IT'S WORTH THE COST.

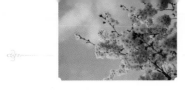

*Letting go of our grip on predictable results and trusting God
with our heart offering is one of the most challenging choices
we make.*

—CAROL KENT

INVITING UNCERTAINTY

Our days can become routine if we let them. The alarm
clock squawks loudly, we make coffee, get dressed, and
go through the motions . . . again and again. Maybe it's boring
but at least it's safe. We like the predictability of our mundane
days.

But God just might have something better. What if we let go of
our grip, set aside our desire for control over every portion of
our lives, and let God take the wheel? Can we trust him with
our heart offering—that which is nearest and dearest? Are we
willing to open ourselves up to God's unexpected blessings?

By stepping out of our worn path and trying something new,
we risk stumbling and falling flat. But as we ask the Lord where
he'd have us go—stretching out an open hand to let him lead us
into new territory—we will find his surprises.

It's a challenging choice. Can you trust God that much? Will
you?

Read Psalm 61:2.

---

*HELP ME STEP OUT OF MY COMFORTABLE
ROUTINE INTO BLESSINGS UNSEEN.*

That's always my prayer—that I can be totally present with the person I'm talking to, not thinking about the next thing I'm going to ask—not filling up the awkward spaces with words.

—CATHLEEN FALSANI

ESTEEM OTHERS

It's difficult to not think about ourselves. Our minds keep us consumed with how *we* look, how *we* feel, what *we* want. . . . Even during conversations we are often thinking about ourselves. We want to keep the conversation going so we don't look awkward. We're so busy thinking about the next question we don't hear the answer to the one we just asked!

Cathleen Falsani advises that we pray for the ability to be totally present with others and to trust God with our needs as we shift our attention outward. We don't have to fill up every space with words. We need to allow for conversation, back and forth, and even the silence of reflection. This shows that we are engaged and that we care.

Let God guide your conversations today. Be totally present for those with whom you converse. After all, that's just how God listens to you.

Read Philippians 2:3–4.

LORD, I AM SELF-FOCUSED IN MANY AREAS. I NEED YOUR GRACE TO LET GO OF ME AND HEAR OTHERS.

Sometimes we become so mired in the small pieces and petty frustrations of our days that we forget the bigger picture. . . . We have a present promise and a future certainty.

—SHEILA WALSH

LIFE'S MURAL

Every thread of a tapestry is important to the whole piece. Up close, the tiny threads don't make a lot of sense, but when we step back, we see how all of those tiny fibers combine to make a detailed mural.

Our lives can sometimes feel like endless loose threads. We try to follow God's plan, but still feel mired in meetings, soccer practices, and a thousand other things during our days. We can't see how the threads of our lives make any sense at all.

Then one day, God will tell us to step back and take a look. Those tiny filaments, those small pieces and petty frustrations, have come together in a beautiful mural no one else could create.

God sees the big picture, and he cares about the details. He is at his loom weaving the threads of your life into something amazing.

And that's a promise.

Read Matthew 10:29–31.

*MAKE ME FAITHFUL IN MY SMALL "THREADS," LORD,
SO THE MURAL COMES OUT PERFECT!*

[W]e hear, "I can't be a Christian because I can't believe in the virgin birth," as though faith were something which lay within the realm of verification. If it can be verified, we don't need faith.

—MADELEINE L'ENGLE

TRUE FAITH

Faith means believing without seeing. If we can see it, verify it, explain it, and make perfect sense of it, we don't need faith. Faith, by its very definition, requires us to trust in something we don't understand.

Much of Scripture requires us to take that step. Virgin birth? Unbelievable. Calming the sea? Can't be done. Raising people from the dead? Impossible. And so some turn away and decide that they can't be Christians when, in reality, those questions *are* that first step. Knowing that something is unbelievable or impossible means that a higher power has to be involved. That knowledge leads to a choice. Are we willing to believe the unbelievable? Are we willing to have faith?

You may never understand the reason for some events of life on this side of heaven. But God is pleased when you have faith in him even when you can't understand.

Read John 20:29.

LORD, MAY I SEE THROUGH THE EYES OF FAITH.

Whatever burden or care we take to Jesus, if we would get the peace promised, we must leave with Him as entirely as the little child leaves his school troubles with his mother. . . . We must say, Christ has taken that.

—HARRIET BEECHER STOWE

LETTING GO

Jimmy has had a very bad day at school. First, he forgot his homework. Second, he fell and ripped the knee of his jeans. Third, he found out one of his friends is moving. He trudges home with the weight of the world on his shoulders. As he tells his mom, Jimmy sobs a little (he can do that in front of her). And then, he feels a little better. Mom is sharing the burden with him. She gives him a hug. Things will be all right.

We carry so many worries and cares. We go to Jesus to give them to him, and then we take them right back as if we don't quite trust him. If we really want the peace he promises, then we have to let go. Really, how hard is that?

Give it all to Jesus and then say with confidence, "Christ has taken that."

Read Psalm 68:19.

LORD, I GIVE YOU MY BURDENS TODAY. HELP
ME NOT TO TAKE THEM BACK.

The first characteristic of true love is humility: the pouring of oneself down lower and lower in self-effacement and self-denial The message of running water always is, "Go lower. Find the lowest place. That is the only way to true fulfillment."

—Hannah Hurnard

GOING LOWER

Humility doesn't come naturally. We want people to notice us, admire and respect us, and to not take advantage of us. We want to be treated fairly and shown consideration. After all we do, how kind we are, how generous—it's only fair, right?

Beloved, we're called to something greater. We're called to love those around us and to find our worth not in ourselves but in Jesus. The more we strive for others' approval, the more frustrated we become. According to Hannah Hurnard, the only way to true fulfillment is to "go lower."

What does that mean for us? It means self-denial. It means putting the interests of others before our own. It means exalting Jesus because of our love for him, and always seeking to put him first.

You show your love by pouring yourself out. That is true fulfillment.

Read John 3:30.

THANK YOU THAT YOUR LOVE NEVER FAILS. HELP ME TO LOVE OTHERS IN HUMILITY.

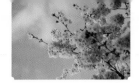

That rippling water is a subtle reminder that little things often lead to bigger things in the divine plan of our heavenly Father.

—RONDA RICH

THE RIPPLE EFFECT

One kind word. But to the cashier at the grocery store, it means the world. She picks herself up from her doldrums, and she greets the next person in line warmly and with genuine concern. It's the ripple effect.

One small act of kindness. It had been a long time since someone noticed him, there behind his desk. But today, a thank you note appeared, expressing appreciation for his good work. It restores his hope in the human race. It makes him feel *part* of the human race again. He passes the thanks on to someone else in his world. Ripple.

One young life surrendered to Christ. But to a whole next generation, this has eternal significance. Ripple.

One little act. One heartfelt prayer. The ripple is started and it spreads across the world.

Toss a pebble today. Start a ripple.

Read Ephesians 3:20–21.

THANK YOU, LORD, THAT WHAT MAY SEEM SMALL
TO ME CAN HAVE GREAT EFFECT.

Obedience is easy when you know you are being guided by a God who never makes mistakes.

—CORRIE TEN BOOM

A TRUSTWORTHY GOD

A young child jumps when her father is there to catch her. A well-trained dog comes to his master's whistle in spite of any obstacles. And a Christian . . . well, too often the Christian hesitates at God's call to obedience. We wonder if we really want to obey. Maybe it is going to be difficult, or it won't make us feel good, or it goes against what everyone else is doing.

What if we just obeyed simply because God told us to—without questioning, without dithering, without worrying? What if, since we know God never makes mistakes, we simply trusted that his call to obedience is not a mistake either?

Your God never makes mistakes. When you see obedience from the perspective of his perfection and his love, you can trust that when you jump into his waiting arms, he will catch you.

Read 1 John 5:3.

GOD, HELP ME TO OBEY YOU, TRUSTING
THAT YOU NEVER MAKE MISTAKES.

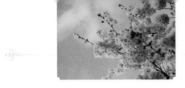

The more you comprehend the greatness of God's forgiveness of you, the more you will love.

—KAY ARTHUR

EXQUISITE FORGIVENESS

It's perfect. Beautifully stitched. Signature details. The more you study this magnificent work, the more you love it. The more you want to share it with others.

It's called forgiveness.

It's just what we need when life gets hard. Our guilt consumes us and wears us down. We lose peace, contentment, joy. But just when we feel that all hope is lost, the comforting cover of God's forgiveness soothes the pain. Wrapped in it, we begin to have the faintest understanding of the greatness of what he offers.

Wrap yourself in the garment of God's forgiveness. Drape the luxurious material over your shoulders. Lose yourself in the rich folds of God's mercy and grace. Remember Christ, who wore a crown of thorns on a wooden cross as he died for our sins. His example of forgiveness becomes the garment we not only wear, but one we wrap around others as well.

Read Psalm 51:7–12.

THANK YOU FOR YOUR FORGIVENESS THAT
WRAPS ME UP AND COMFORTS ME.

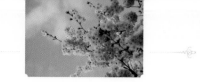

It was no accident . . . that the seasons came round and round year after year. It was the Lord speaking to us all and showing us over and over again the birth, life, death, and resurrection of his only begotten Son.

—FRANCINE RIVER

THE MASTER TEACHER

Spring, summer, autumn, and winter—it's predictable. Every year brings the same rotation of seasons. Each season continuously reveals the glory of our awesome God.

Think of it. We never have to worry that winter might come between spring and summer this year. And what is God showing us over and over again? His constant love and desire to have relationship with us. He is a predictable and purposeful teacher, sending Jesus Christ as his audio-visual. Just as the seasons cycle through the calendar, reminding us that some things never change, Jesus was born, lived, died, and rose again to prompt us that God never changes.

As you look out your window today, thank God for his reminder over and over again of his love for you. He created this world and its seasons for you to enjoy. You are his precious child; live out and enjoy his love for you.

Read Daniel 2:21.

THANK YOU FOR THE BEAUTY OF THE SEASONS AND THEIR REMINDER OF YOUR LOVE FOR ME.

JUNE

Do some small things with great love. Help somebody. Maybe just smile . . . and you will find Him.

—MOTHER TERESA

SMALL THINGS

Although Mother Teresa did "big things" by founding worldwide centers for the poor and devoting her life to serving the sick, she encouraged others to do small, everyday actions with great love. It is the *love* that counts, not the scope of our work.

God may call some of us to great acts of service in the public eye, as he did Mother Teresa. Most of us, however, won't gain national attention for what we do. That doesn't make our service any less valuable. The meal you deliver to a sick neighbor provides for her family. Your friendly smile to the cashier brightens a tough day at work. The grouchy family member who comes home to the smell of cookies baking remembers that you love him.

The small things add up. They matter to the people who receive them.

When you pour out love, you find Jesus. And others find him too.

Read 2 John 5–6.

FATHER, HELP ME TO BE WILLING TO DO THE
SMALL THINGS FOR OTHERS WITH LOVE.

I will not force you to do anything. I have given you a free will to walk with me or walk away from me.

—SHERI ROSE SHEPHERD

YOUR CHOICE

Every day, every moment, we have a choice. Will we choose to walk with God and follow his example and commands? Or will we choose to walk in the other direction?

When temptation to sin presents itself, we have a choice. Walk with God, or head into the sin. When a frustrating situation arises, we have a choice. Walk with God and act with love and patience, or walk our own way—losing our temper. When we have an opportunity to do good, we have a choice. Walk with God and eagerly serve, or decide we're too busy to get involved.

God doesn't force us to do the right thing, he gives us the choice. We have the free will to walk with him or to walk away.

In every moment of this day, God graciously gives you the choice to walk with him.

Read Proverbs 8:10.

DEAR GOD, TODAY I CHOOSE TO WALK WITH YOU.

Here's the secret to serving with the right attitude: take your eyes off the physical people you are serving, and place your eyes solely on the One whom you must ultimately serve.

—PRISCILLA SHIRE

WHOM DO YOU SERVE?

It's workday at your church, and you're assigned the lowliest, most unpleasant job on the list—deep-clean the bathrooms.

Not very glamorous.

The chemical smell is only a little worse than, well, the typical bathroom smells. Dirt is ground in. You can't imagine how any place could get so dirty. In the middle of wiping around the third toilet, you realize that this is just going to get dirty again (quickly) and no one is going to notice or recognize your hard work.

And then, by the fourth toilet, Jesus has let you know that it's not about you, it's not about toilets, and it's not about the rest of the church members. It's about serving. And it's about him.

God is pleased when we consider our service for others as a service to him. Even when it includes cleaning bathrooms.

In the end, serving him is what matters most.

Read Ephesians 6:7.

> O GOD, TEACH ME TO ENJOY SERVING OTHERS
> AS A WAY OF SERVING YOU.

I thought I had lost my way. Actually I did lose my way—in order to follow God's way.

—JAN DRAVECKY

FIND YOUR WAY

Picture yourself in a rowboat in the middle of a large lake. The sun is setting. You see your destination on the shore, so you grab your oars and paddle toward it. Suddenly fog feathers around you, getting denser as dusk settles. You can no longer see the shore. You paddle in what you think is the right direction. You should have reached the shore by now! Panic rises in your throat.

Then you hear a voice calling from a distance behind you. The shore is the other way! You turn and paddle toward the voice, the only way home.

Sometimes we have to lose our way in order to find God's way. Sometimes we need him to call us from the fog and turn us around.

God has a plan for you, a place for you, and a journey for you.

Listen. Can you hear him calling?

Read Luke 19:10.

*SHOW ME THE WAY, LORD. I'M LOOKING
FORWARD TO GOING WHERE YOU LEAD!*

As you come to "dark places" in your life, just reach out for the Hand of the Shepherd.

—HELEN STEINER RICE

VALLEY OF SHADOW

She held him tightly, mourning his numbered days as cancer devoured the body of her loving husband. During those dark days, very little light or laughter crept into her world.

Life has its dark, scary places. Nobody welcomes emotional or physical pain, disappointment, or death. At one time or another we all walk through a valley of shadow.

The bright spot is assurance that we can reach out to a gentle Shepherd to guide us through. We can rest in his goodness even in the badness of a situation. During the days—or weeks or months—when you cannot see the light or know what to do or say, simply reach out for his hand. He's there. He promised to never leave you, even when you walk through the valley of shadow. He's there to comfort, sustain, empower, and provide for you.

He may not lighten your dark places, but he will lighten your load.

Read Psalm 23.

> *I'M REACHING OUT FOR YOU, GENTLE SHEPHERD.*
> *TAKE MY HAND THROUGH THIS DARK VALLEY.*

God has designed a life plan for each one of us. It was custom-fitted to our talents and personality, and it usually involves a step of faith. But that step, the first one, is always up to us.

—MARTHA BOLTON

THAT FIRST STEP

God has a job for you to do that no one else can do. No one else is so perfectly suited by way of talents, personality, background, or life experiences. You are unique, created by God for a purpose. As you walk with him through life, he will show you exactly what he created you to do.

But that first step? That step of faith that tries something you've never tried before, that takes you out of your comfort zone, that asks something beyond what you think you can do—*that step is all up to you.*

Will you take that first step? Like a toddler who gingerly lets go of the edge of the couch, settles shaky legs, and then ventures out across the room one wobbly step at a time, so you need to let go and take the first step into God's plan.

It's up to you.

Read Jeremiah 10:23.

ONE STEP AT A TIME, LORD. GUIDE ME ONE STEP AT A TIME.

Do not build towers without a foundation, for our Lord does not care so much for the importance of our works as for the love with which they are done.

—TERESA OF AVILA

LOVING SERVICE

We want to do great and important things for God. Nothing wrong with that; it's certainly a noble desire. Yet even if we are given the opportunity to do great things— to give large amounts of money, build churches, speak to thousands, bring salvation to many—the Lord is looking more closely at our attitude than at the works themselves. He is looking at the foundation on which our tower of works is built; he is looking for an attitude of love.

Those great things we do for God—are they done for attention, accolades, a name on a building, an award? Or are they done simply out of gratitude to God and love for our fellow human beings?

Your works—whether as small as reading to your child or checking in on your elderly neighbor—when done in love, are of great value to your Lord.

Read Mark 9:41.

LORD, HELP ME TO SERVE OTHERS FROM THE SOLID FOUNDATION OF YOUR LOVE.

I have always, essentially, been waiting. Waiting to become something else, waiting to be that person I always thought I was on the verge of becoming, waiting for that life I thought I would have.

—SHAUNA NIEQUIST

CONTENT WITH NOW

Some people spend their entire lives waiting. Days pass, people come and go, relationships wither, opportunities disappear—all because they had their eyes focused on the horizon, waiting for something better. If we wait for the life that we thought we would have, we miss the life right in front of us. That would be a sad legacy indeed.

It is hard to just be happy in the now, especially if *now* doesn't look like you had hoped or planned. When planted, the seeds of discontent will grow into full-fledged bitterness and despair. How much better to look around at the now, be content with all that God has given, and thank him for the blessings he has provided.

Let God take what you thought life would be and give you a new focus. Contentment will get you there.

Read 1 Timothy 6:6.

FATHER, I WANT TO BE CONTENT WITH ALL
THAT YOU HAVE GIVEN. THANK YOU.

By our worrying and fretting, we are really saying, "I don't believe in any God who can help me, and I do not trust Him."
...We need to develop a sense of dependence on the Fatherliness of God.

—CATHERINE MARSHALL

FEAR NOT

The role of father is to be protector and provider. Our heavenly Father does this for us. We have nothing to fear when we truly believe in him. We know we can trust him to both protect and provide.

Why, then, all this anxiety? Why do we spend so much time afraid—wondering if we will be provided for, cared for, protected? Do we not understand that when we worry and fret we are basically telling God that we don't trust him to handle our problems?

If we trust we don't need to worry ... do we?

When anxiety creeps in, as it does for all of us, we can use it as a wake-up call. Worry time is the perfect time to surrender. We need our Father. He has not left us. Our Father knows our needs.

Are you worrying and fretting today? Depend on your heavenly Father. He will protect. He will provide.

Read Luke 12:22–26.

HEAVENLY FATHER, I PLACE MY
TRUST IN YOU. I DEPEND ON YOU.

know that disobedience can lock and bolt the door against God's still, small voice.

—JOYCE HUGGETT

OPEN THE DOOR

We can feel justified in doing our own thing—and few people can tell us we're wrong if we've already made up our minds. We don't want advice, so we avoid anyone who offers it. We close our Bibles. We excuse ourselves from worship and sermons at church, counting on God's grace to make up for our losses; hoping against hope that, even in our disobedience, he'll cut us some slack because he knows what we're up against.

All the while we ignore the possibility that our disobedience is causing our hearts to grow hard against God and his still, small voice. We choose to go our own way. We shut ourselves inside our disobedience, locking and bolting the door.

Oh, we can stay in there as long as we like. Eventually, however, we'll find ourselves miserable, missing God. Then we hear a quiet, gentle knock.

It's him!

Read Revelation 3:20.

> LORD, MAY I ALWAYS BE ABLE TO HEAR YOUR
> GENTLE VOICE AND YOUR QUIET KNOCK.

Right is right, even if no one else does it.

—JULIETTE LOW

STAND UP

Children are famous for saying, "*Everybody's* doing it!" when they want permission to have their way. But moms are just as famous for their retort. In fact, you can almost hear mothers across the continent speaking in unison, "If everybody jumped off a cliff, would you jump too?"

Going against the flow is uncomfortable. It's hard to buck the system, and even harder to stand up for what is right when no one else stands with you. These days it seems that fewer and fewer people stand for what is right. In your situation, you may indeed be the only one!

Be assured that you are not alone. When you take a stand for what is right, Jesus is beside you, providing strength and fortitude to stay strong. And you never know the influence you have on others. Your decision to do what is right may inspire others to do the same!

Read Matthew 7:13–14.

LORD, GUIDE ME TO DO WHAT IS RIGHT,
EVEN IF I HAVE TO DO IT ALONE.

The special people God gives us along the way make us stronger to face the trials of an ugly world.

—GRACIA BURNHAM

LEAN ON ME

We are never alone. Even when it might feel that way, God puts people in our lives at strategic moments to comfort us, to give us encouragement, and to help us find strength to face the next trial. The Bible has many examples: Adam had Eve, Moses had Aaron, David had Jonathan, Mary had Elizabeth, Paul had Timothy.

When times are tough, God will be there. He'll send messengers at the moments when we need them most. They may be strangers, trusted friends, or unexpected acquaintances. They may not be what we expect.

Be open, dear sister, to the words and touch of those around you. In this sometimes ugly world, they may just be exactly who—and what—you need.

And be open to how God may use you. *You* may be that special person in someone else's life, providing them strength to make it through their day.

Read Galatians 6:2.

MAKE ME RECEPTIVE, FATHER, TO THE
PEOPLE YOU SEND INTO MY LIFE.

God is offering Himself to you daily, and the rate of exchange is fixed: your sins for His forgiveness, your hurt for His balm of healing, your sorrow for His joy.

—BARBARA JOHNSON

DAILY BLESSINGS

God offers himself to you daily. Think of it! Who else does that? Who else comes running whenever you have a need? Your mother? Your father? A dear sister? A friend? And even if you have many loved ones who are faithful to assist you, how much can they really do? Their efforts are limited by their humanity.

But, think of it. God, the Creator of the universe, the Ruler of heaven and earth, watches over you every moment of every day. And nothing is impossible for him. He stands ready to exchange your sins for his forgiveness, your pain for his healing, and your sorrow for his abundant joy. God is able to walk you through your problems and meet your needs according to his wisdom and his timing. He chose you, bought you, calls you by name, and enjoys taking care of you.

Take him up on it.

Read Psalm 86:1–4.

I PRAISE YOU, LORD GOD MY FATHER, FOR WATCHING OVER ME. I WORSHIP YOU.

Forgive me for accusing you of making a mistake when you made me. From now on, I accept with joy your decision to make me average. I surrender myself to you.

—KAY WARREN

PRICELESS

We've all played the comparison game. *She* has longer eyelashes than I do; *she's* more organized; *she's* in better shape; *she's* a gifted speaker. Why do we insist on playing a game that we always lose?

When we play comparisons, we're also accusing God of messing up when he made us. That, by extension, says he's not perfect—and at that point we're on very thin ice indeed.

Instead, let's decide to accept *exactly* how God made us. We may feel that our flaws make us merely average, but as any collector knows, the imperfections are often what make a work most valuable.

God loves you—flaws and all. When you surrender to him and stop comparing yourself to others, he is free to use the gifts and abilities he implanted in you for his glory.

Thank him today for how he made you, flaws included. You are priceless.

Read Isaiah 64:8.

> HELP ME SURRENDER MY SELF-CRITICAL SPIRIT
> AND APPRECIATE HOW YOU CREATED ME.

God is more interested in teaching me through a situation than in using me in a situation.

—CAROLE MAYHALL

LET HIM WORK IN YOU

We desperately want to be out working, serving, and doing for God, but at times we feel sidetracked. Wrapped up in raising children, housebound with an illness, separated from projects and people that we care about—we feel that we are not doing anything at all for God's kingdom. If he's not working through us, then, well, nothing good can be happening. We want to be anywhere but where God has us.

Instead, God says, "Wait, my child. Sit quietly. Let me work *in* you." As our hearts catch up to that understanding, the dissatisfaction and disappointment dissipate. Restlessness and grumbling are replaced with praise and thanksgiving to God. Our minds and spirits open to hear God's instruction. Our hearts soften to soak up God's love.

With God working in you, you're never sidelined, never useless He will teach you wherever he has you.

Read Psalm 37:7.

> I PUT MY DESIRES BEFORE YOU, GOD, READY
> TO RECEIVE YOUR INSTRUCTION.

[God] is absolute good. . . . The more we contemplate Him, the more we enjoy of His good.

—JULIA WARD HOWE

ENJOY HIS GOODNESS

Absolute good. What does it look like? Such perfection is unfathomable in our imperfect world where even simple goodness seems to be in short supply.

Yet absolute good does indeed exist in the person of God Almighty. And he invites us to enjoy that goodness by enjoying him, by drawing close to him. As we contemplate his goodness, we let it sink into our lives. God's goodness is so overwhelming, so rich, so immense, that our very contemplation immerses us in that goodness.

God has given us many ways to know him and see facets of who he is: creation, his Word, stories from fellow Christians of his faithfulness, goodness, and care. Now add contemplation of his goodness to the list.

In these moments, contemplate God's goodness to you. You will be filled to overflowing. Take that goodness and spread it around your world today.

Read 1 Peter 2:9.

> YOU ARE ABSOLUTE GOODNESS, DEAR
> LORD. I IMMERSE MYSELF IN YOU.

How wonderful that we serve a God who formed us and there-fore understands our frailty and susceptibility yet has grace-fille[] plans for us.

—Patsy Clairmon[]

IN HIS SIGHT

How often do we go around disqualifying ourselves from God's plans for our lives? We say to ourselves, "Now I messed up. No way God can use me now," or, "I've sinned so badly, God is not going to want anything more to do with me[] We can accept that he'll forgive us, but we cannot imagine tha[] he can still use us for his purposes and glory.

That's a lie, dear sister. Not only does he forgive—he knows our weaknesses and *still* has glorious, God-sized plans for our lives.

For *your* life.

Don't let your past, not even your yesterday, dictate your futur[] Instead, let his past—his perfect atonement for your sins on th[] cross—decide who you are and what you will do. He died to deal with sin—every sin.

He can and will use you for his purposes. You just need to let him.

Read Acts 9:13–15.

YOU KNOW ME AND MY FAULTS. THANK YOU
THAT YOU CAN STILL USE ME.

The true test of walking in the Spirit will not be the way we act, but the way we react to the daily frustrations of life.

—BEVERLY LAHAYE

CHASING OUT THE PESTS

When we can anticipate problems, plan for events, and manage our time, it's easy to be on our best behavior. But oh, those other times. Those pesky irritations and annoyances that pop up when we're least prepared for them. A traffic jam, a ringing telephone, a too-long line at the checkout, a misplaced purse, or something that doesn't go our way. If we'd been able to prepare, we might have known how to act. Instead, we react to these situations with complaints, muttering, impatience, and anger.

Actions *and* reactions tell the story of our walk with God. What is God revealing to you today about your walk with him? Is there something he wants you to repent of, change, learn, or make right? What a comfort it is that the Holy Spirit helps as we pick ourselves up, dust ourselves off, and try again to deal with the daily frustrations of life!

Read Galatians 5:16.

GOD, HELP ME TO WALK CONSCIOUS OF
YOU TODAY AS I REACT TO LIFE.

The principle make no decision without prayer keeps me from rushing in and committing myself before I consult God. It guards me against people-pleasing.

—ELIZABETH GEORGE

ASK GOD FIRST

How many times have you been asked to do something—a perfectly God-honoring, mission-fulfilling task—and you said "yes" only because you knew that's what the person asking wanted to hear? And how many times have you regretted that "yes" as soon as you hung up the phone? Consider this: That task may have been a burden you were not meant to bear.

Suppose you do as Elizabeth George suggests: make no decision without prayer. Imagine not feeling the pressure to say "yes" when everything in you is shouting "no." Imagine the joy of conferring with God in the decision-making process. Imagine the relief when he says, "No, this is not something I want you to do," or the excitement when he says, "Yes, I will enable you to do this task. It's perfect for you."

No more people-pleasing. Your job is to be God-pleasing. That's what matters most.

Read Philippians 4:6–7.

LORD, REMIND ME TO MAKE NO DECISION
WITHOUT TALKING TO YOU FIRST.

There is no pit so deep that He is not deeper still.

—CORRIE TEN BOOM

THE VIEW FROM THE PIT

In the pit, we are enveloped by darkness. It's cold. Dank. And very lonely. Our cries go unheard and eventually all we can do is whimper into the darkness, hoping against hope that someone will hear, someone will call down to us from above, someone will find a way to rescue us. But as our tears fall to the ground, we know that we may be here for a long time.

Where is God?

The truth is, dear sister, he is here. In the pit. He knows the trial that has sent you into this pit of darkness. Abandonment, uselessness, grief, fear, depression. He desires to help you out of the pit. To raise you back to the sunshine and fresh air. To refresh you to serve again.

Corrie ten Boom lived it. "There is no pit so deep that He is not deeper still." Grab onto God and don't let go.

Read Psalm 40:2.

THIS PIT IS DARK, LORD, BUT I AM HOLDING ON TO YOU.

Savior, like a shepherd lead us, / much we need Thy tender care; / In Thy pleasant pastures feed us, / for our use Thy folds prepare. . . . Blessed Jesus, blessed Jesus! / Thou hast bought us, Thine we are.

—DOROTHY THRUPP

LEAD US

Savior, like a shepherd lead us. Call us each morning to you. Gather us together. As you set off into the day, we simply follow.

We watch you as you move ahead of us. We trust you. You will take us to pastures of green grass so we can eat. You will be careful to bring us to still waters, for you know that we can easily be swept away by swiftly flowing streams. You will not take us on paths too rocky for our hooves to handle or too steep for us to climb. You will tenderly care for us should we get caught in the briars or stumble on the path. And, when the sun sets, you will return us safely to the fold.

You bought us. You know us. We are yours.

Your Shepherd calls you today to follow. You can trust him wherever he leads.

Read Isaiah 40:11

I TRUST YOU, GOOD SHEPHERD, TO LEAD ME TODAY.

True surrender is not a single action but a posture in life, yielding ourselves—our whole selves—to God.

—MARGARET FEINBERG

DAILY SURRENDER

Surrender. The word brings to mind wounded and bloodied, battle-weary soldiers trudging back to camp, shoulders hunched and faces downcast. Surrender can mean humiliation and failure.

But surrender can also be a positive word. Surrendering our lives to God is not the result of losing a battle. God does not intend humiliation and failure for us, but rather life in his abundance. When we surrender—we win! This new picture of surrender is not of heads hanging in failure but of hands raised in victory.

And as Margaret Feinberg suggests, this surrender is not a single action. We must surrender daily. Each morning before our feet hit the floor, we surrender to God, asking him to take over, to walk us through the battles, to bring his victory into our lives.

Wave the white flag. Surrender daily.

In the end, you win.

Read Psalm 25:4–5.

> LORD, I TRADE MY POSTURE OF DEFEAT FOR ONE
> OF VICTORY BY SURRENDERING TO YOU.

This life of faith, then, about which I am writing, consists in just this,—being a child in the Father's house. And when this is said, enough is said to transform every weary, burdened life into one of blessedness and rest.

—Hannah Whitall Smith

BE A CHILD AGAIN

Security—that's the feeling a child has in a home with caring parents. She knows that her needs will be met to the best of her parents' ability because she is loved and cherished. A tender plant such as she can blossom in this environment.

Those who are privileged to belong to the household of the heavenly Father can have this expectation as well. The life of faith is a childhood of sorts, where we grow under the Father's tutelage. While this is not a license to cling to childish behavior, it is a reminder that we have the time and the room to grow in a nurturing environment. We also have a standing invitation to bring our concerns to the all-powerful God. The knowledge of God's love provides this assurance.

What a comfort to know this "blessedness and rest" is ours.

Read John 1:12–13.

FATHER GOD, I'M THANKFUL THAT I BELONG TO YOUR FAMILY.

Let us never say, "God has given me nothing to do." He has. It lies on our doorstep. Do it, and He will show you something else.

—ELISABETH ELLIOT

THE WORK ON OUR DOORSTEP

There's nothing to do," the child whines, only to have mom answer, "Well, I can *find* you something to do . . ." Moms have a great way of finding chores for a bored child; there is *always* something that needs to be done.

It's the same with our Christian lives. We look around, bored, thinking that God has given us nothing to do. However, as Elisabeth Elliot says, the next job we can do for him is right on our doorstep. The job may not seem very spiritual. It may not even be noticeable. But if God has placed it in front of you, chances are he wants you to get it done for him.

It just boils down to paying attention, listening, and keeping an eye out at the front door. You never know what God's going to bring your way.

In God's kingdom, there is always something to do.

Read Ecclesiastes 9:10.

GOD, HELP ME TO SEE AND DO THE WORK BEFORE ME.

Old homes, new homes, tiny cottages, magnificent palaces, little huts, big tents, a sleeping bag on a wanderer's back, or a trailer—whatever the home of the believer, the astonishing and breathtaking promise is that God will live with us.

—EDITH SCHAEFFER

HOME

When he came to dwell among us, God chose to be born in a stable—a place most of us wouldn't even consider sleeping! Yet another sign, dear sister, of the astonishing lengths God has gone to . . . to be with us!

By choosing a stable, God also sent another message: he cares about our hearts; not how clean our houses are. We don't need to meet a certain standard of living. He doesn't care if our house is not as nice as the one next door. He'll even join us in the tent! You see, he simply wants to *be* with us. He wants to experience life as it is *with us*, to live with us and spend time with us wherever we live. That fact takes our breath away!

Beloved, is Jesus knocking at your door? You can let him in— no need to vacuum first.

Read John 14:16–17.

FATHER, I AM ASTONISHED THAT YOU WANT TO
SPEND TIME WITH ME. THANK YOU.

I felt invincible. My strength was that of a giant. God was certainly standing by me.

—CARRIE NATION

INVINCIBLE

As women we sometimes feel it isn't ladylike to be assertive or bold. We may think it's not our place to speak out. Scripture, however, reveals many examples where a woman's boldness was right, necessary, and appropriate. Deborah led an army; Ruth followed Naomi to a new land; Esther put her life on the line; Mary offered her finest perfume to wash Jesus' feet. God blessed those who obeyed his prompting and acted on their convictions.

Just as Carrie Nation felt invincible, you, too, can do mighty—perhaps historic—acts through him. When God calls you, he will give you the strength of a giant. He will stand beside you. He will empower you to do his will. Your faith in God will result in the boldness and confidence you need to do what may seem to be impossible.

With God beside you, you are invincible.

Read 2 Samuel 22:30.

LORD, GRANT ME STRENGTH TODAY TO
SAY AND DO WHAT IS RIGHT.

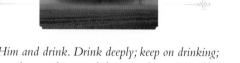

Come to Him and drink. Drink deeply; keep on drinking; let Him quench your thirst; and then, watch as rivers of living water flow out through you to quench the thirst of those around you.

—NANCY LEIGH DEMOSS

DRINK DEEPLY

The ice is clinking in the pitcher of freshly squeezed lemonade. You're invited! The door is open. The welcome mat is out. The table is set.

Come, join him at the table. Stay awhile. Savor his Word, rest in his presence, and listen for his voice. Let God quench the thirst of your soul like water hydrates after an intense workout, like a deep breath in the mountain air clears your lungs, like a swim in a beautiful, cool spring rejuvenates your tired limbs.

Are you thirsty today? Thirsty for meaning in life? Thirsty for love that will not fail? Thirsty for peace or joy or contentment? Come to him and drink. The well is deep; the supply endless. And then, when you've drunk your fill, that living water flows out through you to the thirsty souls around you.

Who will you refresh today?

Read John 7:37–38.

QUENCH MY THIRST TODAY, GOD. THEN LET
ME REFRESH SOMEONE ELSE.

sit on my favorite rock, looking over the brook, to take time
away from busy-ness, time to be . . . it's something we all need
for our spiritual health, and often we don't take enough of it.

—MADELEINE L'ENGLE

TIME TO BE STILL

So many people try to cram fifty hours of activity into twenty-four-hour days. That seems to be the expectation of the world. Yet our souls cry out, "Stop! Be quiet. Seek silence. Just *be*." When we take a break from the constant running, a door opens into heaven.

Attend to the mysteries of your soul by quieting your mind before the Lord. Nothing is more valuable than this time with God. No schedules, no chores, no plans are more important than the need to sit in the presence of his glory.

Create a space for quiet. Create a place for prayer. Maybe it's that favorite rock by the brook, or a favorite chair in your bedroom. Wherever it is, that is your place for taking time to *be* and to renew your spiritual health.

The paradoxical truth is that you're too busy *not* to take time for God.

Read Mark 1:35.

I JUST WANT TO SIT HERE AND BE WITH YOU,
LORD. THANK YOU FOR THIS QUIET TIME.

Descartes said, "Because I think, I am." Because I am, I pray.
. . . We do this not . . . to curry favor for some hoped for life be-
yond this one. We do this because we've got to talk to somebody.

—MARJORIE HOLMES

SOMEONE WHO LISTENS

The urge to talk to the Creator is a part of who we are—an urge created in us by the One who made us. Because we are, because we are alive and breathing, we pray. As Marjorie Holmes explains, we pray not to get favor; we pray because we have to talk to someone.

Sometimes the pain goes so deep, we just don't want to share it with others. At times, in the still quiet of a sleepless night, we need to take our worries and fears—the ones that don't seem quite so troubling in the daylight—and bring them to someone who cares and understands. Then there are the days when our hearts are so full of joy they are about to burst, and we've got to share it with the One we know is responsible.

Do you need to talk to someone? Pray. God is listening.

Read Lamentations 3:55–58.

LORD, I BRING YOU MY TROUBLES. I TRUST IN YOUR HELP.

The greatest honor we can give Almighty God is to live gladly because of the knowledge of his love.

—JULIAN OF NORWICH

KNOWING HIS LOVE

There's nothing quite like being in love. When we're in love and know that love is returned, the whole world is rosy. Love is a gift that causes even the most mundane aspects of life to seem wondrous. We even smile at others more.

The gospel is a love story—the story of God's love for a wayward people, poignantly displayed through the death of his Son on the cross for our sins. The knowledge of this precious love lifts the soul and imbues even mundane aspects of our lives with a patina of richness.

A love like that deserves a response. We can best acknowledge this love by honoring the Lover. We can offer him praise. We can serve others in the overflow of that love.

You are loved. Bask in the thought. Then honor the One who loves you by living in the knowledge of his amazing love.

Read 1 John 4:7–12.

LORD, IN GRATITUDE FOR YOUR LOVE, I WISH
TO HONOR YOU WITH MY LIFE.

JULY

God lovingly came to me in my heap of despair and disaster and seemed to kiss the elbows and knees I had scraped in the fall.

—BETH MOORE

HE COMES TO YOU

In a world filled with violence and disasters, illness and disappointments, there is no shortage of hurt, pain, and tears. They're all around, driving you deeper into hopelessness. Blinded by your troubles you stumble into the pits of despair. Lying there bleeding and wounded, you wonder: *Where is my hope?*

But God shines down a light of hope in his Son, Jesus Christ.

Jesus' outstretched hand reaches to you; gratefully, you place your hand in his. Lovingly, Jesus lifts you out of the pit and stands you up. He cleanses your wounds and kisses them. In Jesus, your hope is renewed.

God doesn't want to leave his beloved children in disaster or despair. He came to give them fullness of joy. So, he lovingly comes to you, no matter what difficult situation you're in. That's where he does his best work.

Read Psalm 18:28.

LORD, SHINE THE LIGHT OF CHRIST UPON ME THAT
MY DARKNESS AND DESPAIR MAY BE GONE.

The Lord already knows the best itinerary for our lives. When he shines a light on the path by his Spirit and hands us a map in his Word, let's stop hesitating and start walking!

—LIZ CURTIS HIGGS

OUR TRAVEL GUIDE

You've just arrived in a foreign country for the first time. You don't speak the language, are all alone, and have to get to a meeting across town. You're exhausted from the flight and feeling out of sorts. You have a map you've printed from the Internet with basic directions, but emerging out of the airport in the twilight hours, you struggle to get your orientation.

Don't you wish, in such circumstances, for a friend you can trust who knows the way? For someone you trust to take the lead and show you the way to go?

God has given us his Word to guide us, to lead us in the way everlasting, and to direct us even to the end. Trust the words you read, dear sister. They are words of truth and of life. God knows our itinerary, and he delights in leading us home.

Stop hesitating. Start walking!

Read Psalm 119:133.

I WANT TO KNOW HOW TO LIVE, FATHER. SHOW ME YOUR PATH THROUGH YOUR WORD.

The latch on the door is on the inside.

—CATHERINE MARSHALL

UNLATCHED

It's an undeniable truth—the doors of our heart can only be opened by us. Our friends can't open them. Our pastor cannot. And Jesus chooses not to force them open, either. Instead, he waits patiently—and knocks. We may have opened the salvation door to Christ, but what about the door that holds back our fears? Or the door that closes off our deepest hurts? Catherine Marshall compels us to open those doors too. She assures us that Jesus is a trusted houseguest.

If you want peace—unlatch the door.

If you want joy—unlatch the door.

If you want blessings—unlatch the door.

If you want fulfillment in your life beyond what you can imagine—unlatch the door.

Jesus wants to come in and be a part of your whole life. But only you can unlatch the door.

Read Psalm 36:5–9.

HEAVENLY HOUSEGUEST, YOU ARE WELCOME
IN ALL THE ROOMS OF MY HEART.

Joy is God in the marrow of our bones. And His joy never changes.

—EUGENIA PRICE

THE PURSUIT OF JOY

I just want to be happy," we say, as if saying it will help us understand exactly what that means, or keep happiness from escaping us when the winds of life change. The Declaration of Independence proclaims that we have the right to "the pursuit of happiness," but what a difficult pursuit it is.

The Bible tells us that God promises us something quite different than the external, fleeting emotion of happiness. He promises us joy so much a part of us that it is in the marrow of our bones. It is an internal state of contentment that is the result of communion with him. God alone is our source of joy and, because of that, it never changes. It runs deep, unaffected by circumstances on the surface.

It's just what we've been searching for.

Read Psalm 90:14.

LORD, IN YOUR PRESENCE ALONE WILL I DISCOVER
JOY IN THE MARROW OF MY BONES.

The Bible describes our relationship with Jesus as being similar to the relationship between the Eastern shepherd and his sheep—a relationship based on His voice. . . . His voice is God's Word, the Holy Bible.

—ANNE GRAHAM LOTZ

KNOWING HIS VOICE

Sheep are easily frightened and have almost no natural defense. They also have to be led everywhere—to pasture, to water. So, when we learn that sheep are used as a metaphor for followers of Jesus, we hope there's a compliment in there somewhere.

Sheep may need a lot of guidance and they may be prone to wander (also sounds very much like us humans), but they do have a well-tuned sense of hearing. They *know* the voice of their shepherd as distinguished from every other voice. When they're called out of the pen by their shepherd, they follow his voice. They know who is taking care of them.

As Jesus' sheep, we should be so tuned in to our Shepherd's voice that we always hear it. He speaks to us through his Word. His voice rings loud and clear through the pages of Scripture.

Are you listening?

Read John 10:3–4.

HELP ME TO RECOGNIZE YOUR VOICE, DEAR SHEPHERD.

In the order of creation, rest-ful night came before the work-ing day, assuring us that rest is part of the natural rhythm and restoration of our fragmented lives.

—JANE RUBIETTA

TAKE A BREAK

Soft pillow, comfortable blankets, tired body relaxed into the mattress—the ingredients for a restful night. Mind at ease—no fretting over jobs incomplete today or tasks to do tomorrow, no tossing and turning with worry. When we get a restful night of sleep, we know it in the morning. We awaken refreshed and renewed. Face it, life always looks a little better after a good night's sleep.

We need it. God, who created our bodies, gave us rest as part of the natural rhythm and restoration of what Jane Rubietta calls "our fragmented lives." We may be able to multitask like the best superwoman, but it does take a toll on us. We must give our bodies the rest they need and deserve.

Do you want to enjoy everything God created for you? God created rest. Take a break. You deserve it.

Read Proverbs 3:24.

LORD, HELP ME NOT FEEL GUILTY FOR TAKING
A BREAK. I WANT TO REST IN YOU.

The mystery is that God is not so much an object of our knowl edge as the cause of our wonder.

—JOYCE HUGGET

DESPERATE FOR HIM

When we first met God, we wanted to know all about him. At the time of our salvation, we learned about his deeds and his faithfulness through many generations. We continued to absorb all we could from the Bible. We will continue to gain more knowledge about God throughout our lives and on into eternity. All that we learn should show us that we will never know all there is to know.

And that, in turn should be a cause for wonder. The very mystery of a God who would give his creation choice, and then send his only Son to die to correct the wrong choice, is beyond our comprehension. The very wonder of a God who seeks to be with us and in us, who loves us so much that every hair on our heads is numbered—well, we cannot imagine.

We can only be thankful.

Read 1 Chronicles 16:8–12.

GOD, I THANK YOU THAT I KNOW I BELONG TO YOU. IT'S ALL I REALLY NEED TO KNOW.

A holy life is not to be confused with a "holier than thou" life. A holy life is a life that pleases God. It is a life of humble, quick obedience and generous, glad service.

—JILL BRISCOE

A HOLY LIFE

Perfection. Piety. Pretense. Too often "holiness" is construed as one of these three attitudes. To be holy means to be perfect. To be holy means to live a life of piety. Or a person's holiness may look good but be skin-deep, nothing more than pretense.

But, as Jill Briscoe makes clear, holiness does not mean "holier than thou." In other words, holiness is not something to slap others with; to use as a comparison to make yourself feel better; to say, "I am so much better than *that* person."

Instead, a holy life is one that pleases God. What kind of life pleases God? "A life of humble, quick obedience." When God shows us what to do, we do it—without delay. And, it is a life of "generous, glad service." When God shows us where to serve, we do it—with delight.

Read Micah 6:8.

HELP ME TO LIVE TODAY, GOD, IN A WAY THAT PLEASES YOU.

Today I know that Jesus is the destination. And because he is also the Way, I know that the goal and the journey are one. With hindsight I can reconstruct the route by which we've come.

—ELIZABETH SHERRILL

LOOKING BACK

For believers, Jesus is our goal, our destination. Yet Jesus also describes himself as "the Way." Elizabeth Sherrill explains that Jesus is both the goal and the journey.

As the Way, he has been journeying with us along every unexpected turn, every high mountain, every deep valley, every rocky road. With a little hindsight, we look back and realize that our Companion had been there all along, whether we knew it or not. The spiritual signposts are now clearer too. What we thought were coincidences were really carefully laid guides that helped us stay nearer to God's designed path. Studying a mental map, we are more assured of our future direction. With 20/20 hindsight, our forward thinking to eternity becomes more focused.

When you reconstruct the journey of your life, see Jesus. He's been there all along. And one day you will reach your destination and see him face to face.

Read John 14:6–7.

THANK YOU, JESUS, FOR BEING MY TRAVELING COMPANION.

*He knows the journey is difficult. He knows life is rarely fair.
. . . Jesus invites us to cast our doubts, our fears and anxiety
upon him, to discover how much he really does care.*

—JOANNA WEAVER

THE CARING SAVIOR

So when does "happily ever after" really start?

Life has moments of joy and laughter, times of beauty and pleasure. But those happy moments have a way of being cut short by the sadnesses of loss, or pain, or sin, or death.

It's true: Life is rarely fair. The journey is difficult.

All this reminds us of what we really should know already—that this world isn't our home. While we travel here, however, we have a traveling companion. When the hurt of life creeps in, Jesus invites us to cast everything on him. When the burden is too heavy or the pain runs too deep, when sorrow overwhelms, we can ask him to help us carry the load. When we do, we find how much he really does care.

The "happily ever after" part? That's coming. We have his word on it.

And that is enough.

Read 1 Peter 5:6–7.

*JESUS, THANK YOU FOR TRAVELING WITH ME,
AND FOR HELPING WITH THE LUGGAGE.*

Those who abandon ship the first time it enters a storm miss the calm beyond. And the rougher the storms weathered together, the deeper and stronger real love grows.

—RUTH BELL GRAHAM

HOLD ON FOR THE CALM

Storms hit our lives out of nowhere. Gale-force winds knock our sails; waves splash over the bow and across the deck. When life hits choppy waters, our first response may be to go below, to give up and abandon the ship to the waves.

To do that, however, is to believe that the storm will never pass, to abandon hope that life will ever get better. But after the storm comes the calm. And that calm will seem so much greater after having faced the storm.

If you give up hope and abandon the ship in choppy seas, you miss "the calm beyond." When you've weathered the storms with those you love, the bonds created will draw you that much closer.

In your choppy seas, hold on tight. The storm will pass, the sea will grow calm, the love you share will be stronger.

Read Proverbs 10:25.

LORD GOD, YOU ARE MY ONLY HOPE. I TRUST YOU THROUGH THE STORM.

Have you noticed when you run out of places to turn, He's always there?

—PATSY CLAIRMONT

A PLACE TO TURN

A check left in our mailbox. A box of clothes dropped on our doorstep. A casserole dish thrust into our arms. Just when we think we've run out of resources, God's love shows up in the hands and feet of people around us.

And just when we think our tears will never stop flowing, God gives us his merciful presence. Peace that envelops us like a cozy quilt. Balm that soothes and heals our wounds. Calm that washes over us like a gentle spring rain or a cool, bubbling brook on a hot summer day.

When a brick wall leaves us nowhere to turn, God hasn't disappeared. He is there. When we run out of options, he is there. When we think hope is gone, he is there.

Take your impossible situation to God. When you have nowhere else to turn, turn to him.

He is there.

Read Psalm 18:3–6.

LORD, HELP ME TO REMEMBER TODAY THAT YOU ARE HERE.

Every day something else failed to make sense, something else grew too heavy. "Will You carry this too, Lord Jesus?"

—CORRIE TEN BOO

BURDEN-BEARER

Some days the weight on our shoulders feels like too much to bear already, and then—something else happens; something else doesn't make sense, and yet another weight is placed on our stooping back. This time it *is* too heavy. We can't possibly carry this one.

Corrie ten Boom watched her world spin out of control from behind the fence of a Nazi prison camp. Nothing made any sense. Every day a new burden was added to her overloaded psyche and it was too much to bear. Where was Jesus?

He was right there with her. She took the encumbering confusion and handed it to Jesus. He willingly carried the load for her.

Are you struggling under a burden? Jesus never intends to give you too much. He offers to shift the weight of your burdens onto himself.

"Will You carry this too, Lord Jesus?" you ask. He smiles. Yes. He will.

Read Matthew 11:28–30.

WILL YOU CARRY THIS BURDEN, LORD JESUS?
IT'S TOO HEAVY FOR ME TO BEAR.

Love is not a feeling. It is an overmastering passion to help and bless and deliver and comfort and strengthen and give joy to others just as the Lord Jesus always did.

—HANNAH HURNARD

JUST LIKE JESUS

When Hannah Hurnard went to Israel in 1932 as a missionary, she didn't go as a high-profile worker or evangelist. She went as a hospital housekeeper. She cleaned rooms, did laundry, and eradicated bugs on a daily basis—far from any glamorous roles or dreams. She did this out of love. Did she *feel* like washing those soiled sheets or cleaning out the bedpans? More than likely not, but she served out of a desire to be like Jesus.

She understood what many of us do not. Love is not a feeling. If we wait until we *feel* like it to do good or care for others or share Christ, it may never happen. Instead, we love God and love the people around us by blessing, comforting, strengthening, and giving joy . . . no matter our feelings at the moment.

Just like Jesus. It's really not more complicated than that.

Read 1 Corinthians 11:1.

> LORD, I WANT TO LOVE PEOPLE, TO HELP, BLESS,
> AND COMFORT THEM AS YOU DO.

The Lord doesn't disappear when you turn away from Him, He remains.

—ANNE RIC

WHY, GOD?

What would cause us to turn away from God? Perhaps a deep, heartfelt plea we brought to him was refused. O maybe we have talked to God about a request for so long that we tire of bringing it anymore. We shake our fists at heaven. We stand dazed and confused, crying out, "Why, God?" We fee angry and disappointed. And, finally, we decide it's easier just to turn away than to face the constant silence from heaven.

You may turn away, but God stays by your side, seeing your pain and knowing your hurt. He never leaves, never turns his back. He constantly walks beside you whether you sense his presence or not.

A day will come when the light will break through. You'll look back and see God's fingerprints everywhere. You'll look around and there he is.

He's been waiting for you.

Read Luke 15:20.

*FATHER, I LAY DOWN WHAT I DON'T UNDERSTAND.
I CHOOSE TO TRUST IN YOU.*

The more I am spiritually exercised, the more strength I have to cope with the sudden stresses brought about by adverse circumstances or attacks from the enemy.

—EVELYN CHRISTENSON

DAILY REGIMEN

You didn't see it coming. The enemy thinks a blindside attack will knock you down. A wave of exhaustion consumes you. You retreat to bed and pull the covers over your head so no one can hear you whimper. The enemy thinks you're defeated.

Though you are reeling, your mind becomes strong with deposits of God's Word. Under the covers, his light shines. After a little rest, God reminds you of his love, grace, and mercy. He is your fortress and your strong tower. He's the One who lifts your head off the pillow.

Because you followed your internal regimen of prayer and quiet time with him, you are ready for battle. You have regularly spent time with God, and that spiritual exercise gives you the strength to endure no matter what happens.

Get your daily spiritual workout. Open the Bible. Read. Talk to God. Simple, but so very powerful.

Read 1 Timothy 4:8.

JESUS, I SPEND TIME WITH YOU TODAY, EXERCISING
SPIRITUALLY SO I'M ALWAYS PREPARED.

Men say there are no atheists in foxholes. Women can testify that there are no atheists in delivery rooms . . . never is she so a the behest of forces beyond herself.

—MARJORIE HOLMES

SOMETHING BIGGER

People look to something bigger when they face forces beyond themselves. In the foxholes of wartime, most men want to know that a God watches over them, and that, should they die, their sacrifice will matter and their life will go on in a better place. In the delivery room, where women push life into being, they too know that something bigger than themselves is happening and they have no control over it. They know that a higher power and a higher purpose is involved.

What foxholes are in you right now? What part of your life is spinning out of control? That's the time to look to the One who alone knows the reason and the outcome. When forces beyond you press in and threaten to undo you, look to God, your Creator and Sustainer.

He's got it all in his hands. Nothing is too big for him. Even the winds and the waves obey him.

Read Matthew 8:24–27.

WHEN LIFE GETS TOO BIG FOR ME, LORD, PLEASE CALM THE WINDS AND THE WAVES.

It's not half so sensible to leave legacies when one dies as it is to use the money wisely while alive, and enjoy making one's fellow creatures happy with it.

—LOUISA MAY ALCOTT

LEGACY

What legacy will you leave? What will those left behind say of you after you are gone?

"She really worked hard to get to the top."

"Her house was spotless."

"She always dressed so nice."

"She left behind a lot of money."

Sounds a little empty, doesn't it? Especially when life is in front of us to be lived and enjoyed! The resources you have should be used to make your "fellow creatures happy," as Louisa May Alcott said. So what if your home is not spotless? All of the neighborhood kids enjoy gathering there. So what if your clothes are a little ragged? You choose to put your money toward something more lasting.

What better legacy to leave than memories of the joy we gave to others? What if we lived knowing that all that makes us unique—our talents, love, passions, and resources—are to bless others? The possibilities are thrilling!

Read 2 Timothy 4:6–8.

LORD, HELP ME BRING JOY TO THOSE IN MY WORLD TODAY!

Prayer might not change things, but it will change my perspective of things. Prayer might not change the past, but inevitably, it changes my present.

—MARGARET FEINBERG

PERSPECTIVE-CHANGING PRAYER

In Scripture, prayers are likened to incense. Every time we petition the Lord, our requests curl upward as a pleasing aroma to him. We can imagine him inhaling our sweet gratitude, our humble confessions, and our desperate pleas. He lovingly savors and considers what we—his special children—are concerned about.

God's responses, however, are so far beyond our understanding that they may not make sense. We may even misinterpret that our prayers are unanswered. His *yes* might mean "Yes, but . . ." His *no* might mean "Not quite yet, my child." Our prayers are heard, but God may be more interested in changing our perspective than our circumstances.

The fragrant offering of your prayers opens your tender heart for change, in God's way, in his time. The past cannot be changed. The present? Well, God can do anything when we are open to his answers to our prayers.

Read Revelation 8:3–4.

LORD, I LIFT UP MY PRAYERS TO YOU.
LET ME SEE WITH YOUR EYES.

*When emotions are unchecked by the Holy Spirit, one negative
emotion can easily feed another, joining together as links in a
chain of bondage.*

—BETH MOORE

BROKEN CHAINS AND QUENCHED FLAMES

It begins with a tiny flutter deep down. Something—or
someone—ignites a spark of anger. Or rebellion. Or lust,
guilt, jealousy, greed. There it sits, smoldering in our hearts
until something else fans the flame. The heat intensifies; a link
is forged. Then another, then another. The links join together
in a chain that wraps itself around us, trapping us in negative
thoughts and emotions.

When unchecked by the Holy Spirit, our emotions can send
us into bondage. With the Holy Spirit, however, we have the
ability to keep our emotions in check, to look realistically
at a situation and not fly off the handle, to turn away from
temptation, to turn the other cheek. We can keep the chain of
bondage from being forged in the first place.

Jesus came to release us. He can unlock chains. He can extin-
guish the flames within.

Read 2 Corinthians 3:17.

GOD, SATURATE ME WITH YOUR SPIRIT AND
QUENCH THE EMBERS OF SIN.

In everything God has told us in His Word, He makes one thing very clear: He loves us. Not merely as a faceless world population, but one by one . . . individually and by name.

—JAN KARON

AMAZING!

We long to be known. Our friends know our name and perhaps parts of our history. They smile when they see us coming. They remember our special days. If they run into us unexpectedly in a crowd, they stop to chat. And in each instance, we are reminded that someone knows us, someone cares.

Every single person in every location on the planet—from the deepest jungle to the most populated city—is that well known by God. He knows each name. He knows each person's history, each person's joys and fears, each person's thoughts.

And that is how he knows you. In the eyes of your heavenly Father, you are not an anonymous face in the crowd. He knows every detail about you and cares about every single facet of your life more than you can comprehend.

You're on a first-name basis with the Creator of the universe, who knows you and loves you more than you can imagine.

Read Psalm 139:13–18.

> *FATHER, THANK YOU FOR YOUR AMAZING CARE IN EVERY DETAIL OF MY LIFE.*

Waiting silently is the hardest thing of all.

—ELISABETH ELLIOT

WORTH THE WAIT

It seems all we ever do is wait—in lines, on the phone, for people who are late. There are even rooms dedicated to the inaction of waiting.

Sitting in a long line of cars, stuck in traffic, we feel the urge to honk our horn. It's not going to help us move one inch further, yet we honk the horn anyway. We're busy women, and waiting is just a pure waste of time. Frustration bubbles up and sometimes we sound off.

But that's not God's way. God tells us to wait on him. What's more, he tells us to be still and wait patiently. In our hurry-up lives, God is aware of the benefits that come from slowing down and waiting. He is right beside us, urging us to be still long enough to think of him, to spend time with him.

Your Lord is always worth the wait.

Read Psalm 38:15.

*IN MY HURRY-UP LIFE, HELP ME, LORD,
TO BE STILL AND WAIT ON YOU.*

Just like a plant with its roots hidden underground, you and I—out of public view and alone with God—are to draw from Him all that we need to live the abundant life He has promised His children.

—ELIZABETH GEORGE

BLOSSOM

Growth happens very slowly. We plant our gardens in the spring and wait patiently for the tiny green sprouts to appear. We nurture them, care for them, but the real work is going on below the surface. The roots spread, holding ground, soaking in water from the rain above, gaining nutrients from the soil. All of this hidden activity allows the plant above the soil to stretch tall toward the sun, to sprout leaves, and to blossom.

You are a delicate flower, reaching toward the Son. To have spiritual strength and vitality, your roots need to be strong. That growth happens in the quiet places, alone with God. As you draw the abundant life from him, you are prepared for life's changing seasons: hibernation, vibrant spring, lazy summer days When strong winds blow, through drought and rain, you stay strong.

God's handiwork unfolds as you grow and blossom.

Read John 15:5–6.

LORD, HELP MY ROOTS GROW DOWN DEEP AND STRONG IN YOU.

"Remember, girls . . . purity at all costs," Mamma had said. "May be old-fashioned, but it's God's way . . . and the best way."

—BEVERLY LEWIS

THE BEST WAY

We all have a common need—pure drinking water. Water-bottling companies make millions selling what's advertised as a pure product—no toxins, pollutants, or microbes to be found. But even minus the marketing, our sense of taste is sensitized to naturally help us avoid salty or putrid water.

What about purity in life? The word has lost all meaning unless you're describing drinking water. Few people talk about the value of young men and women remaining pure sexually, following God's plan. Our sex-saturated culture scorns purity and advocates casual sexual encounters. Yet each time a woman has sex outside of marriage, she gives away a little piece of herself. God wants better for his daughters. He intends for that physical act to connect a man and a woman only when they're joined in marriage.

As Mamma said, it may be old-fashioned, but it's God's way. It's the best way.

Read Psalm 119:9–11.

LORD, GUIDE ME TO FOLLOW YOUR WAY OF
PURITY IN EVERY PART OF MY LIFE.

Our spirits need the balance that comes from taking in the "whole counsel of God," not limiting ourselves to those passages that seem particularly appetizing

—NANCY LEIGH DEMOS

A BOUNTIFUL BANQUET

Some Scripture passages call out to us again and again. We feast on what lies before us, devouring each word as if it were a delectable morsel of our favorite food. Others, like certain vegetables, bring a lump to our throat as we stare at them. They simply don't look appetizing. We know they will be difficult to swallow because of the texture, shape, and what we think they will taste like.

Eat your vegetables! It is the refrain parents, doctors, nutritionists, and dieticians delight to sing, telling us what we already know deep in our hearts. Our bodies need nutritious food and a balanced diet to keep us healthy. So do our spirits. God has prepared a bountiful banquet for us in *all* the words of the Bible. A feast full of color, flavor, and, yes, the nutrients we need.

Open God's Word and feast on the banquet he has generously provided.

Read Ezekiel 3:1–3.

HELP ME, GOD, TO FEAST ON ALL THAT YOU
HAVE FOR ME IN YOUR WORD.

Consider your own limitations not as obstacles but as opportunities for God to show his limitless power and unlimited love.

—CAROL CYMBALA

LIMITATIONS LIMITED

We all have limitations. Maybe we just can't cook to save our lives, or we have difficulty staying organized, or we can't seem to make any set of numbers add up the same way twice. Face it, not one of us is good at everything.

Where we have limitations, someone else excels. Where we're gifted, someone else needs our help. And through it all God puts the pieces together, showing his limitless power and unlimited love.

Consider your limitation as an opportunity. Can't cook? Check in with your elderly neighbor and spend some time learning a few of her special recipes. Need to be better organized? Call upon that friend who in turn is feeling bad about herself for not being able to add—and let her shine as she organizes your life.

See how it works? God can use even your limitations for his glory.

Read Ephesians 4:11–13.

HELP ME TO LOOK AT MY LIMITATIONS AS YOUR
LIMITLESS OPPORTUNITIES, LORD.

Sharing the gospel isn't so much what you know as who you know. If you know the Savior and are surrounded by friends and family who haven't met him yet, then who better to handle the introductions than you?

—LIZ CURTIS HIGG

RIPPLES

When Jesus *kerplunked* into the pool of your life—the still, ordinary-ness of your world—the waves he created began with you at the center. He took up residence in your heart, began to work through your hands, mouth, and feet, and started a ripple effect through the sea of relationships you have.

The people within your sphere of influence may just be bobbing along life's waters when the ripple of your Jesus-relationship becomes noticeable. They see the wave coming, feel it lifting them up when it reaches them, and are left changed in its wake. You've touched them in some special way with the gospel.

The Lord wants all to know him. And since you do, he wants you to have a ripple effect on others for him. Let those in your life get caught in the current. And help them become part of the heavenly tide.

Read John 4:39–42.

JESUS, USE ME TO MAKE A DIFFERENCE IN THE LIVES OF OTHERS. LET'S MAKE RIPPLES.

Here by faith in Him to dwell! / For I know, whate'er befall me, / Jesus doeth all things well.

—FANNY CROSBY

CONFIDENCE IN HIM

Unpredictable. Part of life's delight—or dread—is never knowing what will occur, who we'll meet, or what new doors will open or close. Many people fear the unknown because it takes the control out of their hands.

Fanny Crosby was wrongly blinded as an infant. Her tragedy could have made her bitter. Instead, she grew up to write thousands of hymns praising her Savior who "doeth all things well." She had a confident loyalty to Jesus. She knew that all things work for the best when he is in charge.

Rest in your Savior's loving arms. Whatever happens, be assured that Jesus will weave it together to fit into his design and purpose for your life or for others. Faith is maintaining confidence in his character, not in your circumstances.

Whatever befalls you, Jesus doeth all things well.

Read Romans 8:28.

JESUS, I DON'T KNOW ABOUT TOMORROW BUT I TRUST YOU WILL WORK EVERYTHING TOGETHER FOR GOOD.

We exhausted, futile travelers, losing the way, falling in the dark, struggling on again, will ultimately get there. . . . It is an immense hope and is the gift of faith.

—ELIZABETH GOUDGE

YOU'LL GET THERE

We find ourselves sidetracked and turned around many times: choosing things of the world over God; filled up with pride over achievements; waiting until we are desperately in need and only then turning to him. As Elizabeth Goudge puts it, we fall and fall again.

Our reassurance is from Jesus, who came for sinners such as us. When we repent and set out again on the journey home, he will give us strength. He shines a light in the darkness.

The spiritual journey requires a habitual effort to put God first in our lives. When we do this, the world loses its appeal. God's love is so great, so awe-inspiring, and so graciously given to sinners, that all else pales in comparison.

Persevere in virtue. Then when you fall, Jesus stretches forth his hand to pick you up and set you on the path again.

You'll get there. He promises.

Read Hebrews 12:1–3.

LORD JESUS, I'M TIRED AND OFTEN SIDETRACKED.
HOLD MY HAND. GUIDE ME.

believe that this life is not all; neither the beginning nor the end. I believe while I tremble; I trust while I weep.

—CHARLOTTE BRONTE

THE GIFT OF LIFE

We mostly grab quick snatches of ourselves in the mirror while we're in a hurry, but every once in a while we steal a moment to take a good, long look at the women we have become. We notice more gray hair that stubbornly reemerges despite the valiant efforts of our hairdressers. Lines and wrinkles have made their appearances around our eyes and mouths.

We can't help but think back to the days when we were young. And we might feel a bit melancholy. But dear sister, look again. Youth is gone, replaced by the gray hair of wisdom and the wrinkles of a life lived with concern, care, and laughter.

Time is fleeting and precious. God has entrusted each of us with this precious gift called life to fulfill a unique and divine purpose.

With eternity in view, it's time to live, work, and love—passionately, joyfully, purposefully, reverently.

Read Proverbs 16:31.

I WANT TO LIVE MY LIFE WITH PASSION, JOY, PURPOSE, AND REVERENCE. THANK YOU, LORD.

God can make you anything you want to be, but you have to put everything in his hands.

—MAHALIA JACKSON

THE TRUST EXERCISE

A trust exercise is where you fall backward into someone's arms. The trust part, of course, is in being willing to believe that the person behind you is going to catch you. It isn't easy. You look back to make sure the person is actually there, ready. And even then, you have to turn around, close your eyes and fall.

God desires that his people make the trust exercise a lifelong discipline. He wants us to throw everything into his hands and trust that he'll do what's best. Sometimes we glance back in fear, wondering if he'll catch us. But instead of giving God a doubtful glance, we can remind ourselves of the ways that he has proven himself trustworthy.

God can do anything with you . . . amazing things that you cannot today imagine. You just need to trust him enough to put everything in his hands.

Read Proverbs 3:5–6.

FATHER, I WANT TO PUT EVERYTHING
IN YOUR HANDS. I TRUST YOU.

AUGUST

A Christian has no business being satisfied with mediocrity. He's supposed to reach for the stars. Why not? He's not on his own any more. He has God's help now.

—CATHERINE MARSHALL

REACHING FOR THE STARS

Look up," Scripture tells us. Look to the stars and remember who made them. Look to the mountains and worship their Creator.

Much of the activity of our lives requires daily, repetitive tasks that keep us focused on earth. We can easily get sucked in to mediocrity. But God has a higher calling. He wants us to do everything with our best effort—even beyond that, to reach for the stars. That means as we work and serve our Lord, we refuse to be satisfied with the mediocre. We refuse to just get by, to do just enough. We are so passionate about serving our Lord that we want to always do our best work.

Don't worry, sister. This is not a new standard for you to attempt to reach. You have God's help now. That's what enables you to reach the stars in the first place!

Read Psalm 121:1–2.

FATHER, IN ALL I DO, LET ME REACH FOR THE STARS!

Always be faithful in little things, for in them our strength lies.

—MOTHER TERESA

THE LITTLE THINGS

Little things matter. Too often we focus on the big things of our faith and miss the little things. But as Mother Teresa explains, we need to first be faithful in the little things. That gives us the strength for the "big" things.

It's subtle, but we can find ourselves rationalizing some sins— "I deserve a break . . . No one will know . . . I'm not hurting anyone." But those very choices eat away at our character, undermining the strength we need to handle the powerful temptations, the weighty responsibilities. If we can't handle the small things, it follows that we cannot handle the big things either.

So focus on the small stuff. Quiet honesty. Hidden acts of kindness. Willingly turning away from temptation even when no one else will know.

Only faithfulness there lays the foundation for faithfulness in the big areas of life.

The little things really do add up.

Read Song of Songs 2:15.

LORD, HELP ME TO BE FAITHFUL IN THE LITTLE THINGS.

Progress has a price; and becoming a person who never gives up will cost you.

—JOYCE MEYE

PRICELESS

What might it cost us to walk closer with Jesus, to move forward and deeper in our relationship with him? Might we have to lose a friend who is holding us back? Might we have to set aside some habits that we know are detrimental to our spiritual growth? Lose a few extra minutes of sleep in order to have a daily quiet time? Risk annoying a family member who thinks we've jumped overboard?

Moving forward always has a price. Risks are involved. Often we enter into uncharted territory. Dangers may come our way. Like Pilgrim in the classic book *Pilgrim's Progress,* our journeys to the Celestial City take us through all manner of sloughs and valleys.

But the only way to get where we're going is to never give up. To walk closer with Jesus is priceless. The cost isn't worth counting.

Read Matthew 16:24–28.

JESUS, I WANT TO NEVER GIVE UP AS I DRAW CLOSER TO YOU.

Lord, teach me to worship You with my whole heart the way You want me to. Make me a true worshiper. May praise and worship of You be my first response to every circumstance.

—STORMIE OMARTIAN

GIVE IT YOUR ALL

It would do us good to consider our first responses to every situation we encounter in a given day. First response to no milk left in the fridge for breakfast. First response to a traffic jam. First response to plans changed due to a child's sudden cough. First response to a perceived slight. First response to the long line at the store to buy the needed milk.

What if our first response to *every circumstance* was praise and worship? Is that even possible?

It is when you ask God to help you. He can show you what worship with all your heart in every circumstance looks like and feels like.

When you worship God with your whole heart in grateful contemplation of his majesty and love, there's little room for self-pity or anger—those typical first responses. Instead, God gets in and infuses even the frustrating situations with renewed grace.

Read Psalm 71:14.

TEACH ME TO PRAISE YOU TODAY IN EVERY CIRCUMSTANCE.

Forgiveness may be excruciating for a moment. Anger and bitterness are excruciating for a lifetime.

—BETH MOORE

AGE OF BITTERNESS

Everyone avoids her angry eyes. She enters a room and looks at no one. She sits alone in the back. She glares straight ahead. One might have guessed the hurtful incident happened weeks or a few months ago.

"My, she's aged since I last saw her."

"I'd like to talk with her, but the look on her face is never welcoming."

"It's been twenty-four years . . . ."

The pain she felt had become rock-hard anger and bitterness, sucking away her life. The person who hurt her had moved on—for right or wrong—but she was stuck in her emotional pit, hurting no one but herself.

How much better if she had been willing to forgive twenty-four years ago. So much life missed in the meantime.

Forgiveness helps *you* move on.

Read Hebrews 12:14–15.

JESUS, SHOW ME WHEN I NEED TO FORGIVE.

Greatness is never achieved nor dreams realized apart from great discipline.

—KAY ARTHUR

GREAT DISCIPLINE

Behind the few seconds of a gymnast's vault stand hours, weeks, and years of training. For many hours a day, she practiced running and vaulting. She landed hard a few times, developed some bruises, and went back to try again. Run, vault. Run, vault. Run, vault. She practiced all those years so that her five seconds of running and vaulting might bring home an Olympic medal.

She will be the first to tell you that greatness and dreams cannot be realized without discipline.

We do not all have Olympic dreams or Olympic abilities, but we have God-given gifts. We are responsible to discipline ourselves to develop those gifts for his glory. The greatness we achieve and the dreams we realize may not put our pictures on a cereal box, but we will accomplish what God had in mind when he created us.

And that is enough.

Read Romans 12:6–8.

LORD, GUIDE ME TO HAVE THE DISCIPLINE TO
DEVELOP THE GIFTS YOU GAVE ME.

Sometimes it is the simple act of grazing that gets a sheep into trouble. Nibble a little here, a little there, a little more over in another area, and pretty soon, they are far from the shepherd. And then a lion comes.

—FRANCINE RIVERS

CLOSE TO THE SHEPHERD

The grazing sheep has its eyes focused on the ground, the next blade of grass, a little more over there, just a few more steps to the next tasty patch. Before long, the sheep looks up and has wandered far from the shepherd.

We are so much like sheep! We have our eyes focused only a few inches in front of our nose. We like this, we want this, we need this. We just keep moving along to what comes next. Finally, we look up and realize that we have strayed far from our Shepherd.

How can we avoid this? We take our steps with our eyes always on the Shepherd. We make sure that no new "patch of grass" is distancing us too far from him.

The grass might look greener out there, beyond the Shepherd's eye. But think again—because out there is where the lions wait

Read Psalm 79:13.

SHEPHERD, KEEP ME EVER CLOSE TO YOU;
BRING ME BACK WHEN I TRY TO ROAM.

"Come, come," He saith, "O soul oppressed and weary, /
Come to the shadows of My desert rest, / Come walk with Me
far from life's babbling discords, / And peace shall breathe like
music in thy breast."

—HARRIET BEECHER STOWE

COME AWAY

C ome away with me," Jesus invites. "Let's spend some time
together and talk. Your soul will find peace." And he set
us an example of doing just that, for he himself got away from
the hubbub and the hustle and bustle of the crowds, away even
from his friends, in order to find a quiet place to talk with his
Father.

Do you have a quiet place, a safe place where you can go and
meet with God, undistracted by the noise of the world? Dear
sister, if Jesus needed to get away, how much more do we
need to escape to truly hear our Savior's voice! It may be early
morning, late at night, in a room in our home, at the library, or
in the park.

Your Savior will meet you wherever you are, so come away to
a place where you can listen.

Read Matthew 14:23.

JESUS, IN THIS QUIET PLACE I WANT
TO SPEND SOME TIME WITH YOU.

"I am love," said the King . . . and the very first characteristic of true love . . . is the willingness to accept all other human beings just as they are.

—HANNAH HURNARD

AFFECTIONATE ACCEPTANCE

Acceptance is such a basic human need. Babies crave it. Adolescents seek it. And puppies wag their tails at it. But for some, acceptance from others comes at a very high cost. Or it doesn't come at all.

In God's eyes, however, we are all worthy. We are all loved. And we are all the same. This is what Hannah Hurnard was trying to illustrate: no matter how much another person hurts us, mistreats us, irritates us, or ignores us, his or her soul has the same eternal value as ours. God sees that person's eternal worth the same as ours. So since there are no half-priced humans in the kingdom of God, we are to love (and accept) them—even if their offensive ways stay the same.

Challenging? Yes, but well worth the effort to please the One who is love itself.

Read Luke 6:27–31.

PRECIOUS KING, HELP ME TO LOVE OTHERS AS YOU DO.

Patience withholds: It withholds vengeance, revenge, and retaliation, and endures instead. It endures ill treatment, it refuses to be angry, and it desires the offender's good.

—ELIZABETH GEORGE

FOLLOWING GOD'S EXAMPLE

When a friend hurts you more deeply than an enemy ever could, when harsh words cut like daggers, when co-workers accuse—what should you do? Elizabeth George suggests withholding vengeance, revenge, and retaliation. She says we should patiently endure ill treatment, refuse to be angry, and desire the offender's good.

But how can we do that when the wound still bleeds and the anger still burns? The healing begins when we realize what God has done for us. He sent his only Son to pay the penalty for our sins. When we trusted in Jesus, God wiped our slate clean. He hurled our iniquities into the depths of the sea. He remembers our sins no more.

The more fully we understand what God has done on our behalf, the better we'll be able to treat others with patience.

After all, how many times has God been patient with you?

Read Romans 2:1–4.

LORD, HELP ME TO FORGIVE OTHERS JUST AS YOU HAVE FORGIVEN ME.

God comes looking for us and brings us home, away from the danger we got ourselves into. He loves us so much that He doesn't want to lose even one of us.

—TRACIE PETERSON

STAY CLOSE

When a shepherd discovers a sheep is missing, he can stand and shake his head over that stupid animal, or call out the sheep's name but simply give up on it if it doesn't come. But a shepherd who cares about his sheep goes out in search of the creature who has gone astray. He knows the sheep may be lost, stuck, or in danger from a predator. He will keep looking until he finds it.

Jesus, our Great Shepherd, doesn't give up when he calls and we don't answer. He doesn't leave us to make our own way home. He doesn't stand and scold when he finds us stuck in thorns after we've wandered away. He tenderly pulls us out of the thornbush and offers medicine for our wounds.

Oh that we would learn that the best place is to stay close by the Shepherd's side.

Read John 10:11–15.

MY SHEPHERD, THANK YOU FOR CARING FOR ME
ENOUGH TO LOOK FOR ME WHEN I WANDER.

Incredible, isn't it? To imagine God's love reaching across the boundaries of time, encircling us in his ceaseless embrace. Do you yearn to feel his heavenly arms around you? Holding you, comforting you, cherishing you?

—LIZ CURTIS HIGGS

IMMEASURABLE LOVE

It is truly beyond our comprehension. A God who loves us. A God not of stone or marble but a living being. A God who existed before time itself.

This God reaches across time and space to encircle us in a ceaseless embrace. This love is beyond our imagination, so he shows it in thousands of ways he knows we can process. Sense his beaming face when you help a neighbor. Feel his comfort in a friend's kind words. His love is conveyed through the hug of a child, the smile of a stranger, the hand-squeeze of an elderly acquaintance. His love warms us with the sunshine and refreshes us with the rain.

When you need a reminder of God's incomprehensible love, you need only look around to witness the many wonderful ways he lavishes it on you.

Feel his comforting, cherishing embrace. His love will not let you go.

Read Psalm 108:4–5.

EVEN THOUGH I CAN'T UNDERSTAND YOUR INFINITE LOVE, I SEE IT ALL AROUND. THANK YOU.

Knowing where you are going takes the uncertainty out of getting there.

—ANNE GRAHAM LOTZ

A SURE THING

Distress. Disappointment. Disease. Death. Struggles in life can make our hands tremble, our hearts pound, and our knees buckle.

Until we reflect on our final destination.

When we know we're going to heaven, certainty fills our heart as we look forward to the joy, beauty, and welcome that we know will meet us there. As we fix our eyes on our ultimate destination, we have the courage and the hope to handle whatever comes our way.

The road you're on today may be littered with fear, anxiety, or worry. The future may not look or feel like a sure thing.

Look up! Heaven is a sure thing. God can be counted on. Keep going, regardless of the twists, turns, and unexpected detours on your journey. Keep going, certain of the One who saved you. Keep going, letting the picture and promise of heaven fill your steps with confidence and hope.

Read John 14:1–3.

THANK YOU, GOD, FOR REMINDING ME WHERE I'M
GOING SO I CAN CONFIDENTLY FACE TODAY.

Suffering opens our eyes to the centrality of the cross in the Christian life, enables us to lift up the crucified Savior to the rest of the world.

—ELISABETH ELLIOT

GLORY OF THE CROSS

Few of us would voluntarily ask for a cup of suffering. Most of us get one anyway.

We are not alone. The cup of suffering has been drunk by generations of saints before us. Suffering is the very cup Jesus willingly accepted in life and in death. When we drink from the cup, we can allow the bitter aftertaste of suffering to overwhelm us, or we can have faith that God can use that suffering to transform us.

Take the cup of suffering you hold in your hands today and bring it to God. Sit at the foot of the cross. Think of your Savior there, willingly dying so that you could be saved.

Through your pain and the faith you show in the midst of it, you are lifting up your crucified Savior to the rest of the world. Others see in you the glory of Christ's cross.

Read Isaiah 53:10–12.

HELP ME, GOD, TO SHOW CHRIST
TO THE WORLD IN MY SUFFERING.

You may have no idea when or how God will answer your prayers, but don't stop praying.

—NANCY LEIGH DeMOSS

PRESSING ON

When it feels like our prayers are being met with silence we experience great discouragement. When we've talked to God for a long time and haven't seen any impact from our prayers, it's easy to become weary or to decide that God just isn't going to get involved with this situation at all.

Waiting days, weeks, years for God to answer tempts us to give up. It's quite different from "waiting" in our culture of instant gratification, where problems are solved within a sixty-minute TV show.

The truth is, we don't know when or how any of our prayers will be answered. What we *do* know is that God promises to answer. So we keep praying, for in those deep conversations with God we are forging deep trust and developing strong faith.

No matter how silent God seems, dear sister, don't stop praying.

Read Psalm 13.

GOD, GIVE ME THE ENDURANCE TO KEEP PRAYING,
FOR I KNOW YOU WILL ANSWER.

"Wherever you are, God is there," Mama always said. "He'll meet you wherever you are."

—RONDA RICH

MAMA ALWAYS SAID . . .

What did your mama always say? Or your grandmother? Or that teacher who inspired you? If you're lucky, someone along your journey took the time to impart his or her wisdom to you.

Ronda Rich's mom wanted her to remember that wherever she went, God was there. It sounds almost mundane until we think about it.

In the days of joy and thankfulness, God is there. In the time of sorrow and grief, God is there. When worry assails us, God is there. When temptation entices us, God is there. When uncertainty tears us apart, God is there.

The Great I AM is rejoicing, sorrowing, comforting, guiding, strengthening. He is walking with you. He is willing to carry the burden when it gets too heavy.

Do you need him today, but feel you need to "get in a better place" first? No matter what your circumstances, he'll meet you wherever you are.

Read Psalm 37:23–24.

THANK YOU THAT WHEREVER I AM, LORD, YOU ARE THERE.

The faith that gets us through unthinkable circumstances begins with being flat-out needy and allowing God's love to wrap us up, hold us close, and dry our tears.

—CAROL KEN

TREMBLING FAITH

Has it happened to you yet? Have you experienced something so painful that you never would have believed you could survive? If not, surely you've marveled at someone who has endured unthinkable circumstances, faith intact.

Faith borne of desperation is a strong faith—a faith that can get us through. When the pain is too immense or the trial insurmountable, we know we can't do it alone. At that point, we come to a crossroads. We can choose to give up, continue flailing and fighting on our own strength, or surrender to the One who is *able* to carry us through. We come to him with our trembling faith and our complete neediness.

And that's okay with him.

When it's all just too much to bear, allow God's love to wrap you up, hold you close, and dry your tears.

Read Psalm 6:6–9.

I AM SO GRATEFUL FOR YOUR LOVE, LORD. PLEASE HOLD ME CLOSE AND DRY MY TEARS.

Make an investment that lasts longer than a lifetime.

—BRENDA NIXON

WISE INVESTMENTS

Financial counselors warn that those who hoard their money fail to build a strong nest egg. So, they advise diversifying one's investments to secure strong future returns.

You may not have worldly wealth and your nest egg may be cracked; still, you can use your personal reserves to make a difference in someone's life.

"What reserves?" you may ask.

Your prayers for a hurting soul. Your kind words of friendship. Sharing the love of Christ. Encouragement. A smile. All are diversified resources to invest in others. And an investment in others pays the highest dividends. Your life will be enriched in return.

The life of the Christ-follower is a paradox: when you give away, you receive. As Jesus generously invested in you, do so to others. Your godly reputation will last beyond your earthly years.

Use his gift of today to give to others, and your legacy will be valued for generations.

Read Luke 6:38.

LORD, THANK YOU FOR TODAY'S OPPORTUNITY TO MAKE
INVESTMENTS THAT WILL OUTLAST MY LIFETIME.

Beginning with sin instead of creation is like trying to read a book by opening it in the middle: You don't know the characters and can't make sense of the plot.

—NANCY PEARCEY

STARTING ON PAGE ONE

In the beginning God . . ." Everything in life has God as its reference point. The story begins on page one. And what is this story about? It's about us. Where did we come from? Who are we? What is the meaning of life—and of our lives? What caused all this bad stuff that goes on in the world? What will make it all better?

The answer to every question is all there, right in the pages of his Word.

The world has big questions. These questions require big answers. Sometimes we worry that we don't have the answers, we don't understand how it all goes together.

So start at the beginning, page one. It is ultimately the story of God's love and care for the human race he made. Read all the way to the end.

The grandest story of all begins and ends with God.

Read Genesis 1:1.

FATHER, THANK YOU FOR THE GRAND
STORY OF YOUR LOVE FOR US.

True, genuine religion . . . is the anchor of our hope, the ornament of youth, the comfort of age; our support in affliction and adversity, and the solace of that solemn hour, which we must all experience.

—ABIGAIL ADAMS

OUR ANCHOR, OUR HOPE

Abigail Adams understood that the Christian life is not easy. Affliction and adversity come uninvited. Sadness and darkness may fill many of our days. God does not remove those experiences from us; however, when we trust in him, he offers great support and hope.

Like an anchor he holds us firm when the waves threaten. He ornaments our lives, giving beauty and meaning. He brings comfort as we age, for our future is bright and eternal. He supports us in times of affliction and adversity when our own strength fails. And he will be our solace in that final hour when we leave this life and go to him.

What love that he cares so much for us throughout our lives and then wraps his arms around us when our time on earth is finished. Such a wonderful God we have!

Read Hebrews 6:18–20.

> FATHER, LIFE CAN BE HARD, BUT YOU ARE MY
> ANCHOR, MY SUPPORT, MY COMFORT.

When, through the power of the Holy Spirit, we let Jesus reach our dorm floor or neighborhood, he will create a family atmosphere. Jesus will give people a sense of worth. And his love is contagious; people will imitate it.

—REBECCA MANLEY PIPPERT

JUST LIKE FAMILY

We worry sometimes about "evangelism." We want to share our faith but are wary of being too pushy or looking weird.

Jesus says, "Don't worry so much. Just let me come in and do my thing through you!" So you love as Jesus loves. You speak as Jesus would speak. The power of the Holy Spirit working through your life makes people stand up and take notice. "What are you about?" they ask warily.

"I'm all about family," you say, "the family I joined with Jesus."

"Why *that* family?" they wonder.

"Because in this family I have a sense of self worth. I am loved for who I am. I am able to love others."

"Tell me more."

Wherever you are, let Jesus in. He will do the rest.

Read Hebrews 2:11–12.

HOLY ONE, WHAT A PRIVILEGE TO BE PART OF A FAMILY—YOUR FAMILY.

We must learn to seek God's face and not His hand.

—JOYCE MEYER

SEEK HIS FACE

Dad would come back from his business trips and the first thing we'd ask him is, "Did you bring us anything?"

Smiling, Dad would tell us to go and look in his suitcase and there we'd find them, gifts from his trip. It became such a habit that we anticipated Dad's return, not so much to see him, but to see the gifts he brought.

Does that sound at all like your relationship with your heavenly Father?

While God delights in giving good things to us, he does not want to be simply a Giver of gifts; God wants to be the Giver of life. He wants you to seek not his hands full of gifts, but his face full of love and protection and guidance. God desires that you seek him for who he is.

Seek God's face today. That will be enough.

Read Job 33:4.

FATHER, I LOVE YOU FOR WHO YOU ARE,
NOT FOR WHAT YOU GIVE ME.

This love disclosing itself was no cosmic Creator of a mechanistic universe, for the revelation was intimate, personal. . . . God insists on seeing us one by one, each a special case, each inestimably loved for himself.

—CATHERINE MARSHALL

EYE TO EYE . . . WITH GOD

Stars too numerous to count. Fragile butterflies of breathtaking beauty. The laws of gravity and of the seasons. The rotation of the planets. The colors of a rainbow. The intricacies of a rosebud. Surely the Author of all this has a full calendar and a waiting list of at least a few thousand years.

But no. He created us too, and calls us even more beloved than the rest of creation, for we alone are made in his image. He insists on seeing us one by one. He invites us to be his own children, adopted into his family. Personally known by him. *Beloved* by him. We are "inestimably loved," as Catherine Marshall reminds us.

Look at the beautiful love-gifts of the created universe; read God's love letter; feel his delight in you. He desires one-on-one time with you. He's got it set aside. No waiting.

What about you?

Read Hebrews 2:7.

FATHER, THANKS THAT I DON'T HAVE TO WAIT—YOU'RE ALWAYS HERE.

Life appears to me too short to be spent in nursing animosity, or registering wrongs.

—CHARLOTTE BRONTE

WELL DONE

"Well done, good and faithful servant." For the Christian about to step into eternity, no better words can be imagined. Whether the years of life number nine or ninety-nine, someday time will seem short. How are we spending it?

Too many women are passing through the better part of their days wishing for a different life. They nurse animosity against those who have caused their less-than-perfect circumstances. They keep track of wrongs done to them. Life is just too short to waste that way.

Your heavenly Father has granted you a number of days on this earth. Today is one of them. Who knows how many more you have? Let today be focused on worthy things: accomplishing the work God has given you to do, loving others well, appreciating the lovely gifts of God.

Then, at the end, you will hear, "Well done."

Read Matthew 25:13–23.

> *FATHER, HELP ME TO USE MY TODAY AND EVERY DAY WISELY FOR YOU.*

You never know what you might be missing if you grow up too much and stop asking, "Now what?"

—THELMA WELLS

NOW WHAT?

Children are famous for complaining, "There's nothing to do." Send them outside, and suddenly their day unfolds into an exhilarating whirlwind of friends and fun.

Children's lives have a margin in them that allows them to ask, "Now what?" They don't map out their afternoons around who they'll play with and what they'll do. They have room for spontaneity. As adults, however, we tend to schedule our time almost to the minute. No margins. No room for "now what?"

That's too bad, because God needs us to leave a margin in our lives for him. He has people for us to meet. Places for us to go. Love to experience. Laughter to share.

What would happen if once in a while you left the laundry unfolded and left part of your day unfolded as well so you could say to God, "Now what?" Then let him surprise you!

Read Psalm 118:24.

TODAY IS YOURS, LORD. NOW WHAT?

W]e are meant to walk in the light, and we have been groping
[l]ong in the darkness. The creative act helps us to emerge into
[t]he light.

—MADELEINE L'ENGLE

CREATIVITY AND LIGHT

We were created to walk in the light, but too many of us
are groping in the darkness. We hold out our hands in
[t]he murky fog of our lives, feeling unsatisfied, unfulfilled.

[O]ur wonderfully creative God made us to be creative beings.
[S]ome of us have been given great gifts in the areas of art or
[m]usic or writing. Others of us are wonderfully creative as we
[d]ecorate our homes or cook our meals or do our jobs. We may
[f]ind innovative ways to entertain our children or get through
[t]o our teenagers. Even mundane tasks are stirred with interest
[w]hen we try them in a new way.

[D]iscovering and using that creative, God-given energy is the
[k]ey to finding our way out of the fog and emerging into the
[li]ght. We take on a tiny bit of heaven, for the most Creative
[O]ne of all looks down and smiles.

Read Isaiah 40:28.

MAY THE WORK OF MY HANDS BE PLEASING TO YOU,
O GOD, AND HELP BUILD YOUR KINGDOM.

God is not mad at you; He is madly in love with you.

—Victoria Osteen

MADLY IN LOVE

That's it! you think. *I've messed up once too often; God must certainly be mad at me now. The mistakes I've made are unforgivable. It's hopeless. How could God love someone who messes up this much?*

But God is not mad at you; he is madly in love with you. So much so that he sent his only Son to die on the cross so that your sins may be forgiven. You see, God understands your weaknesses; he knows you're not perfect, but he loves you anyway. He is not about to give up on you. When you realize that, you don't need to give up on yourself. Let his love and forgiveness help you overcome the burdens of your past mistakes.

In short, let him love you. He is reaching out to you today. He wants to love you forever.

Read Jeremiah 31:3.

THANK YOU FOR YOUR AMAZING LOVE. I AM
MADLY IN LOVE WITH YOU TOO.

To live circumspectly, within the safe boundaries of either our homes or our churches, ignoring the call to responsibility outside is not to follow the command of Jesus.

—EUGENIA PRICE

STEP OUTSIDE

We could probably do a pretty good job of living purely and kindly and graciously if we just didn't have to deal with one annoying problem—other people. *They* are the ones, out there in our world, who cause us so much frustration and anger and temptation. If not for them, well, we'd be pretty good indeed. We'd "live circumspectly," as Eugenia Price put it.

Safe in our churches and our homes, we can put up the walls and keep those pesky "sinners" out. Problem is, that's not what Jesus told us to do.

New life in Christ makes it possible to shape a nurturing home and a peaceful church family. And new life in Christ compels us to step outside of our homes and churches in order to invite others to know the peace found only in him.

We are called outside—where sinners desperately need a Savior.

Read Isaiah 52:7.

> TEACH ME HOW TO STEP OUTSIDE,
> LORD, WHERE PEOPLE NEED YOU.

God is in the business of giving moments of sunlight, warmth, and joy during the storms as well as speaking a final "Peace" to them.

—CAROLE MAYHALL

THE STORMS

Looking out the living room window, you watch the storm clouds gather in the west. Trees wave wildly in the wind. Big dollop-like raindrops splatter the window.

Then, a brief break in the overcast sky gives you a glimpse of sunlight. An unexpected knock on your door brings a wet, windblown friend with a thermos of hot coffee. The dramatic hues in the turbulent sky catch your eye like the colors of a treasured painting. The storm has a certain beauty all its own.

We often talk about how God will "work it all together for good," as if he only gets involved in our life storms at the end when he puts all the pieces together. Dear sister, he is there *during* the storm, always with you no matter how cold and wet and windy it gets. Watch for those unexpected moments of sunlight, warmth, and joy along the way.

Read Mark 4:35–40.

GOD, HELP ME TO EXPERIENCE YOUR
BRIGHTNESS IN STORMY WEATHER.

Perhaps among a host of other reasons, I think God often ordains a wait because He purely enjoys the togetherness of it.

—BETH MOORE

WAITING WITH GOD

She remembers the words "Good news! You're pregnant" as if they were spoken yesterday. For years to come, she'll speak of the morning sickness, the weight gain, the baby's first kick. Those memories will cement the bond between her and her child for a lifetime.

God longs for you to have a similar life-altering bond with him. And sometimes, he ordains a time of waiting in order to accomplish it. Think about it—when do you spend the most time in prayer, talking with your heavenly Father? Most likely it's while you're waiting for an answer to a need.

God loves that kind of attention! He loves it when you spend time with him.

So hold on. God will deliver you. And after he does, at every opportune moment, you'll speak of his mercies, his provision, his protection. And you'll cherish the memories you made with him while you waited.

Read Psalm 27:8.

LORD GOD, BLESS OUR TIMES
TOGETHER. I WILL WAIT WITH YOU.

As long as there's a God, there's a choice. . . . No matter what life hands us, we still have choice. We can't always choose our circumstances . . . but we can choose our response to them.

—JANETTE OK

ONE CHOICE

When we were young, what seemed like complicated choices were really quite simple. Chocolate or vanilla ice cream with the chocolate cake? A red bike or a blue bike? Lunch from home or from the school cafeteria? Other choices reflected our right-or-wrong beliefs. Cheating on a test. Gossiping about a friend. Being a bad sport.

As adults, however, our choices become more serious. Who will we marry? What kind of job training do we need? Where should we live? Other, more troubling issues could follow: What do we do about an unhappy marriage? How do we handle a life-threatening illness? How can we pay the bills when we've lost our job?

We can't always choose our circumstances. We don't always control life's events. But we *can* choose how to respond when facing those circumstances, those life events. As Jeanette says, as long as there's a God, there's a choice.

Read Proverbs 16:16.

GOD, MAY MY CHOICES BRING
HONOR AND GLORY TO YOUR NAME.

SEPTEMBER

Once we give an inch, God will take a mile. He'll take a million miles. He'll soar on the wings of the wind from heaven to here to show you who He is, to embrace you with His love.

—JONI EARECKSON TADA

AN INCH

When we hear the phrase "Give 'em an inch and they'll take a mile," it usually isn't a good thing. Too often we've been taken advantage of. No matter how much we offer of our time or energy, it seems that people always expect more. Give an inch and they want a mile.

But what happens when we give God an inch? When we open the door and invite him in, he enters not just to visit, but to move in, to take up residence, to take *over.*

Beloved, that's a good thing. That means he is willing to go with you everywhere. He's there in the joys, the struggles, the darkest nights, and the brightest mornings. He is willing to go that extra mile not only *for* you, but *with* you.

Only then can he show you who he is and embrace you with his love.

Read Psalm 18:10–16.

THANK YOU, LORD, FOR THE BLESSINGS YOU POUR OVER ME MILE AFTER MILE.

Those who were able to forgive their enemies were able to return to the outside world and rebuild their lives, no matter what the physical scars. Those who nursed their bitterness remained invalids. It was as simple and as horrible as that.

—CORRIE TEN BOOM

REBUILDING AFTER LOSS

Bitterness and unforgiveness don't hurt the unforgiven ones; they hurt the one who refuses to forgive. Persecuted by the Nazis who also killed many of her loved ones, Corrie ten Boom later learned that God could grant forgiveness for the worst of her tormentors. In the years after the war, she cared for others who, like her, had been imprisoned in the concentration camps, and she discovered that the ones who could forgive were free; those who didn't were still captives.

Whatever loss you have experienced—betrayal, financial crisis, suffering—you need God's power to move on. To start over, to forgive what may need forgiven, takes God's strength. Forgiveness does not mean you don't hurt or don't care; it simply means you want to move forward and rebuild. To refuse to forgive leaves you stuck in your bitterness.

God has better plans for you.

Read Matthew 6:12–13.

FATHER, FOR YOUR SAKE, GRANT ME THE STRENGTH TO FORGIVE THOSE WHO HAVE WRONGED ME.

Simple, sincere people seldom speak much of their piety; it shows itself in acts, rather than in words, and has more influence than homilies or protestations.

—LOUISA MAY ALCOTT

WALK THE WALK

Actions speak louder than words—or so the old saying goes. That's why humble people never have to trumpet their humility. It clearly comes through in every interaction they have.

Since many of us value conviction backed up by action, we cringe when someone "talks the talk" but fails to "walk the walk." Some of Jesus' most biting remarks had to do with behavior of this sort. He easily saw through the veil of hypocrisy the Pharisees drew around themselves and cautioned his followers to avoid behaving in kind.

You want to live for Jesus—then *live* for Jesus. You don't need to talk about it or draw attention to it. You live for him because you love him. You walk the walk because you know it pleases him. Your actions back up your words even when people don't notice.

And God, who sees in secret, will reward you.

Read Matthew 6:17–18.

FATHER GOD, I WANT TO BE GENUINE IN WORD AND DEED.

He [God] wants us to call, to cry, to sing to Him.

—CYNTHIA HEALD

BE HONEST

God wants a relationship with us. That thought alone should cause us to stop in astonishment. "God? Wants to talk with *me*?" He does. Every day, every moment, in any way you might need to talk at the time.

You might call—loudly—in a time of crisis, knowing he will hear and come to your aid. You may cry—softly—over pain and sorrow because you need his peace, his hand of comfort, someone to dry your tears. You may sing—off-key perhaps, but sing nonetheless—simply because praise is on your heart and the best way to express it is with a song you've committed to memory.

Come to God with everything you are and have. Share each victory, sadness, and fear with him. Don't hold back or pretend; live honestly in his presence.

Call, cry, sing. It doesn't matter. Just communicate with your God. He wants to hear from you.

Read Micah 7:7.

FATHER, GIVE ME THE COURAGE TO LIVE
HONESTLY WITH YOU ALL DAY.

We are very well aware that man cannot create in the absolute sense in which we understand the word when we apply it to God. We say that "He made the world out of nothing," but we cannot ourselves make anything out of nothing.

—DOROTHY SAYER

SOMETHING OUT OF NOTHING

We marvel at an artist's ability to create a memorable, soul-stirring piece of art. Consider the last painting, novel, or song that thrilled or inspired you. A work of that kind is pretty unforgettable.

Many artists paint, write, or sing about what they see—the sights that inspired them to create in the first place. And these sights were first created by God. Only he can make a sunset, a robin, a baby's smile, or stormy ocean depths.

The creative act is an act of appreciation for the God who truly made something out of nothing. When we create, God takes our hands and helps us make something out of a blank white page, a canvas, a lump of clay, silent strings on an instrument.

He then uses this act of creation to make something else—a changed life, starting with your own.

Read Exodus 35:30–35.

I CREATE BECAUSE YOU ARE THE CREATOR.

Although we may not acknowledge and confess the sin, there will be judgment for it.

—ANNE GRAHAM LOTZ

PROMISED FORGIVENESS

It may sound crazy, but there are lots of women who don't get mammograms or have regular health checkups, even if they find a lump or aren't feeling well. Not because they're lazy or ignorant but because they'd rather deny the affliction than face it. Once we have a diagnosis, a treatment plan, and a prognosis, there is no turning back. We have to deal with it.

This can also be true of sin. *If we ignore it, maybe it will go away; and if it goes away, maybe it won't be a problem.* Bad news—everyone in the Bible who tried this approach proved this wishful theory wrong. Even when we manage to forget about sin and "move on" without confessing and correcting, we have only set ourselves up for the natural consequences.

Face sin head-on. God promises to forgive, to cleanse, and to heal your wounded spirit.

Read 1 John 1:9.

SEARCH ME AND BRING TO MIND UNCONFESSED SIN. MAKE ME PURE AGAIN.

It's not really important when I choose to meet God every day. What really matters is that I show up regularly. . . . Consistency, after all, doesn't mean perfection; it simply means refusing to give up.

—JOANNA WEAVER

SHOWING UP

As Christian women, we know that our daily time with God is important. We might have tried different scenarios—early morning, late at night, on the train to work, over lunch. As life changes for us, so do our schedules. Yet one thing must be on our calendar daily—a quiet time with God.

It doesn't matter *when* we choose to meet with him. It doesn't matter that while we used to be able to get up at five o'clock in the morning, the sleepless nights with a new baby have precluded that. Change the time to fit your phase of life, but then stick with it as best you can. If you miss a day, meet him the next. Consistency doesn't mean perfection; it just means refusing to give up.

Your time with him is precious. You feel loved, you gain joy, you come away refreshed and reinvigorated. And who doesn't need that?

Read Luke 10:38–40.

FATHER, THANK YOU THAT YOU ALLOW ME—
AND CALL ME—TO MEET WITH YOU.

If you are what you should be, you will set the whole world ablaze.

—CATHERINE OF SIENA

FIRE OF JOY

Have you ever asked someone, "How are you?" and received a long, sad tale of injustices? After such a response, you probably thought twice before inquiring of that person again. You may have even avoided the person so as not to hear their depressing daily report.

Yet how different it is when someone responds to your question with a cheerful outlook on life. Their confident and undoubting mind-set—regardless of what is going on—has the ability to lift your spirits.

These are the kind of people Jesus needs in this world. If we are what we should be, we are positive, uplifting, encouraging, hopeful people of faith. With that kind of attitude, we can, as Catherine of Siena suggests, set the world ablaze with the fire of our joyful hearts—bringing warmth and light to everyone we meet.

Read Psalm 68:3.

LET ME SET MY WORLD ABLAZE WITH
THE FIRE OF MY JOY TODAY!

His ultimate plan for our lives has very little to do with our circumstances. Those are just the tools he uses to transform us into a vessel he can use.

—DONNA PARTOW

UNDER THE CIRCUMSTANCES

If we belong to Christ, the victory is already ours. But why does life often feel more like a loss than a win? Why do our circumstances seem to roll over us like ocean waves, threatening to sink our little boats?

Our circumstances seem to define us, but God would have us think just the opposite. He calls us to define ourselves as his children who are being transformed into people he can use. The circumstances are just tools to give us humility, compassion, understanding, grace, and other attributes that will help make us the people he wants us to be.

You may feel like you're sinking, like the waves are too strong for your little boat. But God is building a ship that can cross even the roughest seas safely.

You are never "under the circumstances"; you are sailing *through* the circumstances . . . with God.

Read Psalm 69:14–18.

TRANSFORM ME, LORD, SO THAT I AM A VESSEL YOU CAN USE.

A prayerful heart and an obedient heart will learn, very slowly, and not without sorrow, to stake everything on God himself.

—ELISABETH ELLIOT

STAKING EVERYTHING ON HIM

The missionary wives' husbands were missing. Even as the women listened to the short-wave radio for news regarding their safety, they prayerfully carried on with household tasks and the mission work God had assigned to them.

Soon Elisabeth Elliot and the other women would discover they were widows. And they learned "very slowly, and not without sorrow, to stake everything on God himself."

Often sorrow is the teacher that takes our prayerful, obedient hearts and draws them ever closer to God himself. People disappoint, jobs fail, disaster and tragedy strike. The life we've been accustomed to disappears, and the pain feels like an avalanche crashing down around us.

It is in those times that we must learn to stake everything on the One who cannot change, on the One who keeps his promises, on the One who loved us enough to die for us.

God will take good care of your heart.

Read Psalm 108:1.

AS I PRAY AND OBEY, LORD, HELP ME
TO STAKE EVERYTHING ON YOU.

Whatever comes, God will give me the strength to deal with it.

—LISA BEAMER

GOD'S STRENGTH

"Whatever comes." Can we really trust God that much?

No one is ever prepared for the unexpected twists and turns of life: hurt, betrayal, sorrow, job loss, financial difficulty, the sudden death of a loved one. No, the unexpected comes when we *least* expect it and, more often than not, it challenges our faith.

But God is here, seeing our tears, knowing our fears, and truly feeling our pain. Whatever comes, we won't go through it alone. Every "whatever" is in God's hands and, as Lisa Beamer discovered on 9/11, God will give us the strength to deal with it. He will hold us up when we want to fall; he will wipe away our tears; he will hold us tight and calm our fears.

When "whatever" comes your way, give it to God.

You *can* trust him that much.

Read Philippians 1:27.

WHATEVER COMES, LORD, I TRUST YOU TO WALK
ME THROUGH IT—TODAY AND EVERY DAY.

How great is the good which God works in a soul when He gives it a disposition to pray in earnest.

—TERESA OF AVILA

EARNEST PRAYER

Prayer is a magnificent gift. Prayer allows you, a mere human being, direct access to your heavenly Father.

Prayer before meals is nice, but think of how little time it takes to do that: fifteen seconds times three meals per day. If our prayer life consists of praying only before meals, then we are spending less than one minute per day engaged in one of the most precious blessings of the Christian life!

Don't be afraid to pray—God isn't expecting fancy words or high theology. He is expecting to hear your praises, concerns, and requests. Talk to him like you would a dear friend. The more time you spend in earnest prayer, the more time you will want to spend each and every day.

You'll find that your time with God in earnest prayer is the greatest gift you have ever received. And the good he works in your soul will change your life.

Read Colossians 4:2.

THANK YOUR FOR THIS PRECIOUS GIFT OF
BEING ABLE TO PRAY TO YOU.

If God wants you in the place you are right now, then there are no greener pastures.

—STORMIE OMARTIAN

THE BEST PLACE

Sometimes we wonder if we are where God wants us. Circumstances seem to go from bad to worse. We struggle. We look across the nearby fence to greener pastures and sigh. If only God would send us over there.

Problem is, sometimes the pasture isn't greener over the septic tank. In other words, what looks greener from where you sit right now may not be the best place for you.

Consider what Stormie Omartian suggests: If God wants you where you are right now, there are no greener pastures—there is no better place for you to be. You may be in a solitary place with God as your only companion. You may be on a journey to freedom from a besetting sin. You may be among the unemployed, or in a hospital bed.

Wherever you are right now, Jesus knows your needs. And he has you right where he wants you. Trust his reputation for taking care of his sheep.

Read Ezekiel 34:14.

LORD, I'M SO GLAD YOU ARE MY SHEPHERD.
I WILL TRUST IN YOU TODAY.

We have it backward. Our being must precede our doing and consuming if we are to grow up into all the fullness of Christ.

—JANE RUBIETTA

JUST BE

So much of our self-worth is wrapped up in the amount of activity we can perform in any given day. We don our Superwoman costumes and fly out the door hoping to multitask our way to true fulfillment.

And so often we conduct our spiritual lives in the same way. Do. Do. Do. We want to feel some sense of accomplishment, so we don our SuperChristianWoman costumes in order to work our way to spiritual growth.

Jane Rubietta says we have it backward. We need to BE first. We can be involved in church activities, which are good, but have we stopped to ask God if that's what we *should* do? Our very busyness often keeps us from the time we need to be a friend of God.

By studying his Word, we seek conviction, direction, and teaching by the Holy Spirit. With our renewed minds, our actions follow.

Read Philippians 3:8–9.

JESUS, HELP ME BE SO THAT I CAN
DO AS YOU WOULD HAVE ME DO.

*When she heard the words, "Our Father," she closed her eyes
. . . and joined her voice softly with the rest. Somehow it seemed
to connect her safety with "our Father," and she felt a stronger
faith than ever in her prayer.*

—GRACE LIVINGSTON HILL

OUR FATHER

What kind of father did you know from childhood? Was he the silent dad who watched you grow up from the sidelines? Maybe he was a dad who you were never able to please. Or was he the type who delighted in you no matter what? Maybe he was the absent dad, never there when you needed him most.

Memories of our earthly fathers tend toward either treasured moments or painful scars. No matter what your paternal experience has been, your heavenly Father invites you with open arms to climb onto his lap and call him "Daddy."

He is a Father who is always near at hand, who is always ready to listen, who offers us the wisest advice, and who loves us dearly and patiently.

Come to him, child. Your Father loves you.

Read Romans 8:15.

FATHER, DADDY, THANK YOU FOR YOUR
CONSTANT PRESENCE AND LOVE.

I realized that out of my future somewhere might be other sorrows. . . . But there was also the sure knowledge that I need never meet any future difficulty alone, that help from a loving God would ever be available.

—CATHERINE MARSHALL

EVER AVAILABLE

How reliable is our Lord! Every time we have our heart wounded, find ourselves stranded, or face great difficulty, God is there to bandage us, soothe us, and help us find our way. He is a faithful Father—we know that. But what we may not realize is that through each painful experience God is building his credibility with us for our future difficulties.

Just like a child learns that her mom will be there when she falls off the bike or gets bullied at school, our heavenly Father is there for us. We learn through our daily challenges that God can be trusted, not only with little skirmishes, but also with the great big battles.

This is the assurance that Catherine Marshall draws from for strength to step forward into the future. Although more sorrows may be ahead for us, we can be confident God will be with us every step of the way. His help is ever available.

Read Isaiah 66:13.

TRUSTWORTHY SAVIOR, TEACH ME TO RELAX IN MY SITUATIONS KNOWING YOU ARE IN CHARGE.

Prayer is not overcoming God's reluctance. It is laying hold of His willingness.

—JULIAN OF NORWICH

HE IS WILLING

God is just waiting to bless us. But too often we bring our prayers to him like attorneys preparing to present a case. We feel we need to *convince* God in order to overcome his reluctance.

Just the opposite. Prayer is laying hold of God's willingness. His plan for each one of us is as different as our fingerprints; therefore, his answers and blessings will be according to our specific needs in alignment with his will.

Praying for blessing isn't a selfish act; it is asking God to infuse your life with everything he has always wanted to give you but was only waiting for you to request.

God is not reluctant to give you what you need. He is eager for you to receive his gifts with gratitude. You need only be willing.

He can't wait to see what you'll do with those gifts!

Read James 4:2.

I PRAY FOR YOUR BLESSINGS ON MY LIFE, LORD,
THAT I MIGHT USE THEM FOR YOU.

If you're generous with other people, they will be generous with you, and that alone will bring you unspeakable joy. Joy starts inside yourself. You can't expect to get it from somebody else first.

—LUCI SWINDOLL

FROM WITHIN

Walking down the street, you encounter a child who is obviously hungry and thirsty. Do you wait for the child to pluck a daisy from a nearby garden or offer you some other token of affection before you extend a helping hand? Of course not. This child's need compels you toward generosity. The reward comes in the form of a relieved and grateful smile beaming up at you. At that moment, a feeling of delight and satisfaction envelops you.

There are times when a *feeling* of joy eludes us and the reality is that we'd be stuck in joylessness if we waited for someone else to deliver it. On these difficult days our best guarantee of recapturing joy is to first bring it to someone else.

You desire joy? It's already there inside you—a gift from the Holy Spirit. Go spread it around. You'll discover that joy was there all along.

Read Nehemiah 8:10.

FILL ME WITH YOUR JOY, LORD, AND
HELP ME SHARE IT WITH OTHERS.

What strikes me now is that in the many ways Mother built our relationship, she illustrated the way God deals with us as children. God knows and loves us completely. As was true of Mother, God loves us when he corrects us.

—RUTH BELL GRAHAM

A PARENT'S DISCIPLINE

As any mother knows, discipline is one of the toughest aspects of love. Although seldom appreciated when administered, discipline is the seed that produces the flower of good character. Rare is the person of integrity who hasn't experienced discipline of some sort. It is an important teaching tool.

When it comes to discipline, God is the expert. He can't be persuaded or sweet-talked out of correcting his children. If discipline is called for, he patiently measures it out and persists until his children learn the lessons they were meant to learn. He endures the grumbling or sullen anger his correction sometimes inspires, knowing the good that will result if only his child will listen and learn.

God loves us when he corrects us. If he didn't care, he wouldn't bother. He wants us to be the very best we can be—and sometimes we just need a little help along the way.

Read Proverbs 3:11–12.

THANK YOU, LORD, THAT YOU CARE ENOUGH TO DISCIPLINE ME.

None of us should be like anyone else. Each of us should be the facet of the Lord that He intends us to be.

—JOYCE MEYER

SPARKLE

A diamond is forever," making it the perfect gem for an engagement ring meant to symbolize "I choose you forever." With facets cut carefully by a diamond cutter, each stone has its own unique quality. The suitor finds a stone that sparkles just the way he wants it and a setting that complements it perfectly. This is what he will place on his beloved's finger. It is chosen just for her.

Dear sister, you are like a facet in a priceless diamond. You have a glimmer all your own. The Lord "cut" you perfectly, like no other. He has called you to sparkle in *your* family, in *your* church, in *your* workplace, in *your* neighborhood. If you don't do it, no one will.

Don't compare yourself to anyone else. You are the only "you" God created. Sparkle right where you are.

Read Song of Songs 7:10.

LET ME SPARKLE FOR YOU TODAY, LORD.

Even when our heart is cold and our mind is dim, prayer is still possible to us. "Our wills are ours, to make them Thine."

—EVELYN UNDERHILL

THE STRENGTH OF WEAKNESS

She grew up in a strong Christian family and had carried her parents' values into her adult life. Though she was a caring, loving person, she'd never fully surrendered her life to Christ. "It took a serious marital crisis to show me that I'd been living a 'Christian life' in my own strength," she says. "In the process, my heart had become cold and hard. I had lost the joy. I had lost the will to serve. I needed to find a way to get back to God."

We have been created by God to draw close to him, but we so often find our hearts cold and our minds dim. As Evelyn Underhill explains, even in those circumstances, prayer is still possible to us. We turn over our will to him so that he can make it his own.

He desires our surrender, our prayers, and our love, not our efforts.

Read Romans 6:16.

MY SAVIOR AND LORD, I SURRENDER
MY "STRENGTH" TO YOU TODAY.

God's not safe in the sense that we have him in a box, predictable and measured. We don't get to control how God operates. No magical formula assures the way God works.

—SHEILA WALSH

OUT OF THE BOX

Our God is the Creator of all that ever has or will exist. We can't put him in a box. We don't get to determine how he operates. We might *wish* to; we certainly would *like* to be able to tell God exactly how to run the world, but that's not our role. We are the created ones.

That's precisely why we will never fully understand everything that happens in our world and in our lives. We wish some magical formula would make sense of it all, but God, who sees the beginning from the end, often surprises us. His answers go beyond what we even could imagine. His blessings are more than we could request. His love is more than we can take in.

If God were safe and predictable, then he would not be worth worshiping.

Be glad your God is not safe, but that he *does* love you.

Read Isaiah 40:18–22.

I NEVER WANT TO PUT YOU IN A BOX. SHOW
YOURSELF BIG IN MY LIFE.

The sooner we quit worrying about doing our part, the sooner we can start rejoicing in the fact that God is doing his part.

—JODIE BERND

HE IS WORKING

God is always at work. He never stops repairing, recovering, and restoring his creation. He never takes a day off; never just decides to take a break. Imagine if he did! The planets would spin out of their orbits, the seas would overflow their boundaries, the stars would fall from the sky.

We need not worry. God has it all under control. What a joy to know that he invites us to participate with him in sharing his story in this world. He doesn't *need* us, but he *invites* us to join him in the work. And even that task is ultimately up to him—only he can prepare a heart to hear the message, only his Spirit can convict a wayward soul.

So don't worry, dear one. Do your part; God will do his. Take him up on the invitation and leave the results to him.

Read Philippians 1:6.

THANK YOU FOR INVITING ME TO JOIN YOU
IN YOUR WORK IN THE WORLD.

You'll never ever satisfy everybody. Someone will always have something negative to say. It's unfortunate. But we're all called to a unique ministry. We're called to be salt and light in our own way.

—YOLANDA ADAMS

SALT AND LIGHT

When Jesus spoke the command to be salt and light, he didn't tell his followers exactly *how* to be either one. The *how* is up to the Holy Spirit, who leads each individual in a unique way. Yet sometimes we get caught up in thinking that there's one "right" way to perform certain ministry tasks. Jesus never expected his followers to emulate each other like cookies on a sheet. Each walk with Christ is meant to be unique.

Salt makes a dull life palatable. Light takes away the darkness. In both cases, we are called to touch our world in ways that bring life and light to those around us. And we won't satisfy everyone. The question we ask ourselves always is, "Does what I'm doing please Jesus?"

He's your ultimate audience. Spread your salt and light. He will take care of the rest.

Read Matthew 5:13–16.

LORD, HELP ME TO BRING SALT AND LIGHT
INTO MY LITTLE WORLD TODAY.

He will never allow Satan to discourage you without a plan to lead to victory! Consider this carefully: We may not always follow Christ to victory, but He is always leading!

—BETH MOOR

FOLLOW THE LEADER

Remember the funhouse mazes at the county fair? You and your friends would go in together for the sole purpose of trying to scare one another. Part of the fun was the uncertainty around every corner. You groped the walls to get a sense of direction and proceeded with caution, fearful of what may lie ahead. In the end you knew you'd all escape, laughing at your fear.

Unfortunately life's not really like that. We don't like the uncertainty. We don't like being afraid. We can't see what's around the next curve and we feel lost and vulnerable. The enemy could be waiting to snatch us at the least wrong turn.

Fortunately, however, our Rescuer is waiting for our cry. He will lead to safety and victory. He rushes in to push the enemy aside and lead us out of the darkness.

Our job? Follow!

Read John 12:26.

LORD, I DON'T WANT TO MEANDER FEARFULLY
IN THE DARK. HELP ME FOLLOW YOU.

In all ranks of life the human heart yearns for the beautiful; and the beautiful things that God makes are his gift to all alike.

—HARRIET BEECHER STOWE

TRUE BEAUTY

What is beautiful to you? A baby's smile? The roar of a waterfall? The smell and taste of fresh blueberry pie?

We tend to think of nature as God-made, and everything else as man-made. But ultimately God is the Creator of everything—the new life that smiles up at you, the mountain chasm over which the waterfall pours, the blueberry that gives the delicious taste to the pie. And then he created human beings with gifts and abilities and senses to enjoy all of that beauty.

God could have created a black-and-white, two-dimensional world with no sounds or tastes or smells. Instead, he gave limitless colors to flowers in the forest and fish deep beneath the ocean's surface. He gave us trees blowing in the wind and, yes, even the smell of blueberry pie.

All for you. He loves it when you enjoy the beauty he created.

Read 1 Timothy 4:4–5.

> LORD, THANK YOU FOR THE BEAUTY
> THAT SURROUNDS ME EACH DAY.

The Christ-life in us, developed and set free, will go by its very nature reaching out and spending itself wherever there is want, in love and longing for the bare places and the far-off.

—ISABELLA LILIAS TROTTER

THE NATURE OF LOVE

By its very nature a river will flow from its source, at times meandering downstream, at other times running at full torrent. As it cuts through the centers of thriving cities or wends its way through desolate prairie, the river is ever drawn toward its ultimate destination—the ocean.

As Christ-followers, we are like the river. Finding our source in Jesus, we allow his love, comfort, peace, and joy to flow outward from us to others we meet on our life journey. Whether it is our neighbor across the street or a hungry child in a war-torn country across the globe, we are called to exemplify Christ by pouring our very selves into the lives of others. The Christ-life in us will cause us to reach out and seek those in need.

The love of Christ in us will spend itself until ultimately we reach our final destination with him.

Read Philippians 2:1–2.

HELP ME, LORD JESUS, TO SPREAD AND LAVISH YOUR
LOVE WHEREVER MY LIFE PATH TAKES ME.

The One who created you, who formed you—body, soul, and spirit—is not only your creator, He is also your sustainer.

—KAY ARTHUR

YOUR SUSTAINER

God created you . . . take a moment to breathe in that very thought. You're not an accident, not a chance of nature, not a result of evolutionary slime. No, you were expressly *created*. God chose every part of you, every physical and emotional detail, every gift and talent, and put the package together to be delivered into the world at a precise time in history, at a precise place, into a precise family.

But beyond that, he sustains you. He doesn't leave you to fend for yourself. He wants to take those details, those gifts and talents—that whole package—and use it for his glory. He wants to keep you strong and vibrant. He wants to draw you ever closer to him, the source of life.

When you feel worn down, ask your Sustainer to refresh, revive, and renew you. It will be his pleasure.

Read Psalm 119:116–117.

I'M FEELING A LITTLE WORN OUT, FATHER. I NEED YOU TO REVIVE ME.

It's all very well to read about sorrows and imagine yourself living through them heroically, but it's not so nice when you really come to have them, is it?

—LUCY MAUD MONTGOMERY

HERO

There comes a time for each of us when life calls our bluff. We can easily parrot the promises we know from Scripture—that God won't give us something we can't handle, that he will work all things together for good, that our faith grows best in the times of testing. Then suddenly we are bowled over by a betrayal that we never saw coming, a tragedy that takes our breath away, a sorrow that won't let go. All that we had imagined of our strong and heroic faith under fire evaporates. We find that trust is hard work indeed.

Sadly, we often fail to live up to our own ideals, which is why we need someone else who can bridge the gap between who we are and who we long to be. Someone to live his life through us.

That someone is Jesus. He will live heroically through you.

Read Galatians 2:20.

LIVE THROUGH ME IN THIS DIFFICULT TIME, LORD. YOU ARE MY HERO.

To receive any deep, inward profit from the Scripture you must . . . plunge into the very depths of the words you read until revelation, like a sweet aroma, breaks out upon you.

—MADAME GUYON

HIS WORD

The Bible can seem like a very scary book. We crack open the pages and hope to read something we can understand, let alone gain some insight and encouragement for life today.

Madame Guyon would say, dive in. Plunge to the very depths of the words. Let them surround you, wash over you. Because it is living and active, God's Word makes its way into your heart. Like the sweet aroma rising from freshly baked bread, the revelation will rise out of the pages. It will shine a light into your darkness.

Light exposes everything, good and bad. When you can see, you can clean away the cobwebs in your life. God's Word will describe how God's holiness can pour over you and rid your life of unhealthy relationships and destructive addictions. The brilliance of his Word burns away the shadows.

It all starts when you open your Bible.

Read Hebrews 4:12.

I'M DIVING INTO YOUR WORD, LORD. I WANT TO LEARN MORE ABOUT YOU.

OCTOBER

The Lord loves you, and He has you on His mind. He's working in your life whether you can see Him or not.

—TERRI BLACKSTOC

ON HIS MIND

We think often about the ones we love. Imagine that our God actually spends time thinking about us!

What an amazing realization: the Maker of the heavens and the Earth, who can count the stars and sees the inner workings of cells, has each of us on his mind! He cares about that pressing problem. He knows our needs today, and the ones we will face tomorrow. He sees our deepest desires. He loves us with an everlasting love.

And, beyond that, he is at work in our lives. Busy making us stronger and deeper. Busy guiding and fulfilling promises. We may not see it or sense it (and at times we may even think just the opposite), but he is there.

Savor that promise. Drink in that knowledge. You are on God's mind. He is at work in you. He loves you that much.

Read Isaiah 41:10.

---

*THANK YOU, FATHER, FOR THINKING ABOUT ME,
FOR BEING MY GOD, FOR LOVING ME.*

I wonder at my recovery, wonder that the very eagerness of my desire to live, to have time for atonement to my God and to you all, did not kill me at once.

—JANE AUSTEN

A NARROW ESCAPE

The desire to live is never more marked than when we look death in the face: a diagnosis of a deadly disease, a devastating car accident, a narrow escape from danger. Suddenly living, even with all of its trials and problems, becomes very beautiful indeed.

What if we lived each day with that intense desire to live—really live? What if we said the loving words to our family that we are often too busy to say (or they are too busy to hear)? What if we finally shared our faith with our co-worker? What if we really listened to our grandparents tell us their life stories?

The desire to live is placed in the human heart by our Creator. We will one day go to him and it will be a glad day indeed, but in the meantime, let's live with all the gusto we can.

Life is short. Make today matter.

Read Proverbs 27:1.

> I WANT TO MAKE TODAY MATTER. LET ME
> LIVE IT TO THE FULL FOR YOU.

When you and I desire God's best for us but become annoyed when He steps in to change the course of our lives, we rebel against the very thing we prayed for.

—PRISCILLA SHIRER

REBELS WITHOUT A CAUSE

No, not that way! Let me show you how I want it done."

Can you imagine saying these words to God? It seems silly when we read them, but how often are we guilty of thinking that way, of trying to direct God's actions? We pray with an agenda—"Lord, please help me find a job, heal my friend, pay my bills"—all valid, deep concerns. God promises that he is working his best for us, so we naturally assume that his understanding of "best" matches our perception of what would be best for us.

When we make assumptions about how God should work, when we get annoyed that he's not following "the plan," we actually end up rebelling against what we asked for.

If we really want God's will and God's best, then we need to trust him enough to let him do it his way.

Read Psalm 77:13.

LORD, HELP ME TO TRUST YOUR PLANS FOR ME,
EVEN WHEN THEY DON'T MAKE SENSE.

For all those dark times, here's a word of hope: God meets us where we are. Even if we aren't looking his direction, he is always looking in ours.

—LIZ CURTIS HIGGS

CANDLELIGHT

Where are you? Did you choose this place? In the dark night of your soul, you are immersed in darkness as black as ink. You can't see your own hand in front of your face. You grope your way through, but you feel lost, as if in a black hole. You walk with your arms out, slowly turning around. Your legs bump into something, a table. You feel the cloth and . . . a stick? Wait, it's a candle. And matches. The tiny light fills the room, bringing warmth and peace.

Now you can see.

And God was there all the time. In the darkness, he was there. You didn't feel him; you didn't see him. But now you know that he was there all along.

No darkness is so deep that God is not there. Hold onto that hope, beloved. Light the candle and see.

Read John 8:12.

GOD, I TRUST THAT EVEN IN MY DARKNESS, YOU ARE WITH ME.

As you visualize the glorious world our Lord created, may you be reminded that His greatest and most beloved creation is you.

—BRENDA NIXON

PICK OF THE CROP

Stroll through an apple orchard. Watch the sun dance off the tree leaves. Breathe in the aroma of ripening fruit. Reach out and pick an apple. Bite in and enjoy sweet, juicy goodness. It's amazing that our Lord attends to such detail simply for the sake of red apples.

Yet we know that everything God created is attended to and surrounded by such detailed care. So just imagine the loving precision he puts into creating us, his favored creation. Every detail of our lives is watched over. He makes sure that nothing happens to us that is beyond what we can handle. Nothing that comes into our lives surprises him.

Like the apple trees in the orchard, God is watching over you—spiritually watering, weeding, and pruning so you grow beautifully.

You are God's most beloved creation. You are the pick of his crop.

Read Ephesians 2:10.

---

*I'M GRATEFUL TO BE YOUR MOST BELOVED CREATION.
I DRAW NOURISHMENT FROM YOU.*

Happiness is not dependent on happenings, but on relationships in the happenings.

—CORRIE TEN BOOM

JOY WITH OTHERS

If you are looking for happiness, you won't find it by yourself. Think about it. Celebrating a graduation, the birth of a child, or a new job loses some of its cheer unless you can share it with someone. Joy fills our hearts when we are connected to others. Sharing our experiences—whether it's attending a wedding or baking cookies—makes all the difference.

God knows this. From the beginning, he created a partner for Adam because he knew that man by himself was not good. We are created for community, to be with others, to share in the joys, the struggles, the successes, and the disappointments with those around us.

You want to find happiness? Look for it no further than a long walk with a spouse, a cup of coffee with a good friend, a book shared with a child, the fellowship of worshiping with other believers, or a quiet moment of thankfulness with your Creator.

Read Hebrews 10:25.

LORD, THANK YOU FOR THE MANY PEOPLE YOU HAVE BROUGHT INTO MY LIFE WHO BRING ME JOY.

Because it begins with a personal God, Christianity provides a consistent, unified worldview that holds true both in the natural realm and in the moral, spiritual realm.

—NANCY PEARCEY

THE CENTER

Everything we do, we do in relationship to God. We use his good gifts wisely or carelessly. We love our fellow humans, made in his image, or we use them for our own ends. We take care of his creation and follow his principles, or we choose to disregard his leading.

God is not just for Sunday mornings; he is the center of our lives. He is the reason we exist and the One who tells us how we were made, how we should live.

With God as the center, everything else in life falls into place. He provides us a consistent, unified worldview that makes sense in our physical lives and in our moral and spiritual lives. Nothing is left out. God has the whole package covered. When we make him and his Word our center and focus, he will provide every answer we need.

Read Colossians 1:15–16.

GOD, MAY I LIVE TODAY WITH YOU
AS THE CENTER OF EVERYTHING.

But He will not reveal Himself openly and communicate His glories and bestow His treasures save on those who He knows greatly desire Him, for these are His true friends.

—TERESA OF AVILA

A TRUSTED FRIEND

A true friend is always there for you. You know she will go out of her way to spend time with you—she's never too busy. She may be far-flung or next door, but you can count on her for honest advice, wise counsel, and a whole lot of laughter. You have built memories with her. You trust her. You love her.

Our Savior wants that friendship with us. He loves to hear our voice. He is never too busy for us—never preoccupied, never bored. We can count on him for honest advice, wise counsel, and yes, even laughter and joy as we experience the life he has for us. We trust him. We love him.

And only those who have that kind of friendship will hear of his glories and receive his treasures. Only when we greatly desire him will we be his true friends.

Read John 15:15.

I WANT TO BE YOUR TRUE FRIEND, JESUS.
I GREATLY DESIRE YOU.

A diamond is never released to the marketplace until the person assigned to polish it can see the image of his own face reflected in the jewel.

—ELIZABETH GEORGE

ROUGH DIAMONDS

Sometimes we feel like diamonds in the rough. We know we have great value—at least we're trying to learn that as we sit at the feet of the Master—but we still feel like we're just not quite sparkling for him. We desire to be more beautiful for Christ, but we too often find ourselves scratched and clouded by pain, grief, difficult circumstances, or failures.

Beloved, Jesus is polishing. Like a master gem-cutter, he sees what is beneath the rough exterior—the priceless beauty just waiting to be displayed. He carefully works to bring out the fine details just as he desires. Sometimes the very pain, grief, difficulties, and failures that you think are keeping you from sparkling are actually his polishing tools. The rough edges are chiseled away, the facets cut, and the surface polished.

Jesus will continue polishing until he sees his reflection in you.

Read 1 Corinthians 15:49.

*O GOD, HELP ME TO SURRENDER TO YOUR POLISHING.
I WANT TO REFLECT YOUR GLORY.*

*welcome each new day with a hopeful expectancy that I, too,
will rise above the ordinary. For I am not content to live a
merely "normal" life or settle for an average existence. No, I am
destined for more—much, much more.*

—MELODY CARLSON

EXTRAORDINARY

Chocolate cake is ordinary. Chocolate fudge cake topped
with ganache, strawberries, and dark chocolate shavings is
extraordinary. While each begins with the same basic recipe of
flour, sugar, and eggs, one rises above the ordinary because of
the extra work involved in its creation.

Likewise, your life can be the average, everyday existence, or
it can be so much more. The only difference is in how much
you are willing to dedicate to making your life extraordinary.
Because you are born again, you already rise above the
ordinary. But what are you doing with your salvation? Is it
simply a "fire insurance policy," or are you striving to know
God's will for you?

Every day is a new opportunity to rise above. God has great
plans for you. Find them. Fulfill them. Be extraordinary for him.

Read Ephesians 1:18.

> I WANT TO LIVE TO PLEASE YOU, GOD. I WANT
> TO BE YOUR EXTRAORDINARY SERVANT!

May this be our prayer, "I do not want to turn my eyes from you, O God. There I want them to stay and not move no matter what happens to me, within or without."

—SAINT CATHERINE OF GENO[A]

A FIXED GAZE

Some hurts in life cause us to run and hide. We feel too wounded to make eye contact with anyone, preferring to withdraw instead. Even gazing toward God can seem as painful as gazing at the sun. We can't do it for long, especially if we fear that he does not care.

What we need instead is the unblinking stare of a trusting child looking up at her loving Father. The desire to keep our eyes on God is usually born out of a desperate need. This need is at its fullest when we realize our weakness, our frailty. It is then that we go to him, for we realize he is the only safe place to go.

A fixed gaze takes discipline and a determination to stay focused on God despite the distractions. Most of all, it takes faith and the knowledge that God's gaze is fixed on you too.

Read Isaiah 26:3.

LORD, WHEN I'M MOST TEMPTED TO TURN AWAY FROM
YOU, HELP ME TRUST THAT YOU STILL CARE.

Millions of stars glittered against its black backdrop. Was this what Abraham saw when God made His promise? Stars so brilliant and numerous no one could doubt His omnipotence?

—DEEANNE GIST

PROMISE IN THE STARS

It's humbling to gaze into the inky blackness of night at the infinite pinpricks of twinkling lights. You feel small. The vastness of the heavens adorned with spectacular white jewels surrounds you, and in that solitary moment you grasp a glimmer of light in your own world of darkness: God is unfathomably big. And if such a God makes promises, he can surely keep them.

As the Lord impressed upon Abraham with his vivid celestial show, he also promises to love you, redeem you, and prosper you for your faithfulness. It's written in the stars across the sky, after all—his beautiful reminder that if he calls the stars by name, you can be assured that you are immeasurably more precious to him. Remember as you stand diminutive, smack in the middle of God's big canvas for your life, that he has painted his love for you all across the heavens.

Read Isaiah 40:25–27.

GOD, THANK YOU FOR DOTTING REMINDERS OF YOUR
PROMISES AND LIGHT ACROSS MY BLACK NIGHT.

People don't want to merely read stories or watch stories or even tell stories. They want to live stories. There is in each of us an innate desire to have a role to play—a major part in the saga that is life.

—LUCINDA SECREST MCDOWEL

LIVE THE STORY

Meaning. Purpose. This is the heart cry of many who long for their lives to count for something. On the days when life seems at its most mundane, we desperately long for more—more excitement, more *meaning*. We wish we could live those stories we've only read about—stories of useful lives well spent and victories won. This longing reminds us that we were created with a purpose—"a role to play," as Lucinda states.

You are part of the greatest story ever told. It began at creation when God first expressed his love by creating a world. It reached its culmination when God offered his Son to die for our sins. His life imbues ours with a vein of purpose only dreamed of before. Through faith and the power of the Holy Spirit, we live out that purpose.

If you trust Jesus, your life *is* the greatest story you'll ever live.

Read Ecclesiastes 5:20.

GOD, I WANT TO LIVE YOUR STORY,
THE GREATEST STORY EVER.

Out into the same old life you go today as ever, but down underneath you can be nourished by the everlasting streams of God.

—L. B. COWMAN

FAITH'S UNDERCURRENT

Oh that we could fully grasp the truth in Cowman's words. She's telling us that there are streams of refreshment down deep in our lives—streams that feed our souls, give meaning to our "same old life," that give us all the nourishment we need to not only infuse our tasks with joy but also to spread joy to others.

How do you tap into God's everlasting streams? Drink from his Word. Bring your thirsty soul to him. Soak in his love as you lean against his chest and discuss your day ahead. Invite him to splash his love into every moment.

Everlasting streams never run dry. It doesn't matter that you feel like you're in a dry desert, or that the wilderness ahead looks tough. You bring his streams along with you, from deep within your soul, welling up to give you all that you need.

Drink deeply.

Read Isaiah 35:6.

HEAVENLY FATHER, SATURATE MY MIND, HEART AND EMOTIONS WITH YOUR REFRESHMENT.

Love God and He will enable you to love others even when they disappoint you.

—FRANCINE RIVER

HE IS OUR EXAMPLE

We've all been let down by someone. Whether a date stood us up or a friend betrayed our confidence, it hurt. The disappointments we endure can run the gamut from a minor inconvenience to a life-altering event.

But we have to keep one thing in mind—people are human. We are all imperfect and capable of letting someone down, be it our family, our friends, or even God. Thankfully, because God is perfect, he can enable us to love others and forgive them when they disappoint us. How can he do such a thing? Because he loves and forgives *us*, no matter how many times we let him down.

God's love and forgiveness are a brilliant reminder of how we can love others, even when they disappoint us.

He is our example. He will give us the strength to do what we cannot do on our own.

Read Matthew 6:14–15.

LORD, TEACH ME TO LOVE PEOPLE AS YOU HAVE LOVED ME, EVEN WHEN I DISAPPOINT YOU.

Pleasures and treasures on earth may be sought after and not found, but only God comes with the guarantee that He will be found.

—JONI EARECKSON TADA

YOUR TREASURE

Are you satisfied? What are you looking for? What pleasures and treasures hang out at the edges of your mind? Granted, you may indeed find and experience some of them; others will never come to be. We make our "bucket lists" knowing full well that we may not live long enough to check off every item, or we may not have the means to make some of those wishes come true.

There simply are no guarantees.

Or are there?

Joni describes one pleasure, one treasure, that comes with a guarantee that we will find it. The treasure map is found in God's Word. The treasure itself is sitting there waiting to be discovered, not hidden from view. It's big enough for everyone to share—no one will miss out.

The treasure? God himself. Yours for the asking.

Read Matthew 7:7.

I HAVE FOUND YOU, LORD, AND I WILL NEVER LET YOU GO!

I offer you my life / from this moment / and for whenever you wish me to lay it down / for your glory.

—SAINT CATHERINE OF SIENA

LIFE OFFERING

God wants nothing less than everything. He wants not just a part of us, not just our Sunday lives, not just the "good" parts, but every part, every moment, every cell, every thought, every desire. His. All his.

When we willingly offer ourselves completely and thoroughly to him, we gain true freedom. We are set free from the bonds of our sinful natures. We are given a life plan that will bring glory to God. We have a purpose. We have meaning. We *matter.*

When we let God have it all, we will learn that where our strength ends, his begins. We will help others. We will build the kingdom. And, beyond our wildest imagining, we will bring glory to our Creator all the way up until the moment when we lay down this life and enter the next.

All for his glory.

Read Romans 6:13.

TAKE MY LIFE, LORD, EVERY PART. I WANT IT ALL TO BRING GLORY TO YOU.

A wise man once said to me, "Joyce, God has given you the ear of many. Stay broken and only speak when spoken through."

—JOYCE MEYER

STAY BROKEN

When something breaks and can't be repaired, we throw it out, deeming it useless. And after someone fails, we might label him or her as "broken" or "useless" also. Yet God takes our brokenness and makes us useful for him.

When we're broken, we're teachable. We stop long enough to listen. We realize maybe we didn't have all the answers and we made a mess of things. We're a little more willing to take advice, to stop where we're headed and go a different direction.

And more than that, when we're broken, we're reachable. God can reach down through the walls we put up, point out our sins, and finally get us to realize our desperate need for him. That kind of brokenness will make us useful for God. It allows him to speak through us. It keeps us humble.

Be willing to stay broken. God can work his miracles through you.

Read Psalm 34:18.

I KNOW I'M BROKEN, LORD. I TRUST THAT YOU
WILL USE ME ANYWAY FOR YOUR GLORY.

I want you to be concerned about your next door neighbor. Do you know your next door neighbor?

—Mother Teresa

LOVE YOUR NEIGHBOR

The neighbor next door—how well do you know that person? Ever had a conversation? Ever offered to help? Ever had a chance to show love?

Mother Teresa was making the point that too many of us don't even know our next-door neighbors. In our highly private, media-saturated, compartmentalized lives, where does the neighbor fit in? When do we take the time to talk over the back fence and show that we care? How often have people come and gone from your neighborhood and you realize you never even got to know them?

It doesn't take much. A hello. Grabbing a moment out of our highly scheduled lives to stop for a chat. Showing we care in ways that say, "I'm here for you should you ever need me." To know that our neighbors care about us is a soft blanket of comfort in an increasingly chilly world.

Read Matthew 22:39.

SHOW ME WAYS TO LOVE MY NEIGHBORS TODAY, LORD.

If you live long enough, you're bound to encounter some rough storms. No one is immune to tragedy in this life. The house is the same, the storm is the same, but what makes the difference is the foundation.

—LISA BEAMER

YOUR FOUNDATION

A seaside home with pilings driven deep into the sand might withstand a tropical storm. A brick Midwest farmhouse secured to concrete pads hidden deep beneath the ground can avoid being scattered for miles by a tornado. Both homes have secure foundations.

The house on the beach, the house in "tornado alley"—both will eventually encounter a rough storm. So will we. Not one of us is immune from difficulty in this life. Not one of us will get to the end without a few bumps and bruises along the way. Those of us who will survive—who will stand strong—are those with the solid foundation. And that foundation is our faith in Jesus Christ.

Storms will come, beloved. When your foundation is secure, so are you. The winds may whip and the waves may spray, but you will stand strong.

Read Matthew 7:24–25.

MY SECURE FOUNDATION IS YOU, JESUS. I NEED YOU ALWAYS.

The place which Jesus takes in our soul he will nevermore vacate, for in us is his home of homes, and it is the greatest delight for him to dwell there.

—JULIAN OF NORWICH

PURE DELIGHT

When was the last time you felt the emotion of sheer delight? An unexpected snowfall? A smile from a chubby newborn?

Delight. When God looks at us, his eyes sparkle. He willingly takes up residence in our lives, delighting to dwell with us. He will never leave us no matter our spiritual or physical condition. He sees something in us that we cannot. He sees the eternal and we only the temporal. He's in it for the long haul. He delights in the long journey of life. He promises never to vacate. He's here to stay.

Pure delight. God loves you so much that he looks around at the angels, points at you, and says, "Can you *believe* how wonderful my child is?" The God of the universe smiles at the very thought of you.

Take delight in who you are, who he created you to be.

Read Psalm 149:4–5.

THANK YOU FOR DELIGHTING IN ME!

Dedicate yourself to make Him your focus. Let all your other loves flow out of that.

—ANNE ORTLUND

LET YOUR LOVE FLOW

What is inside us will eventually come out. If we focus on fear, then fearful thoughts and controlling actions will result. If we focus on worry, it will show on our face and in our shortened fuses. If we focus on bitterness, we will dry up inside and the joy of life will dissipate.

If we focus on Christ, however, we look at the One who came to give us the fruit of his Spirit. We focus on the One who loves us with an everlasting love, who came to give us life to the full, who offers us peace and joy. And what is inside will indeed come out. We will treat others as we would want to be treated. We will be able to love even the unlovely.

Our love can flow from the Source—the One who is love personified—when we focus on him.

Read 1 John 4:16.

LORD, I WANT TO FOCUS ON YOU SO THAT MY
LOVE FLOWS FROM THE SOURCE OF LOVE.

Are we going to go through those so-few years with limited time for our family and friends, with unseeing eyes for the beauties around us, concentrating on accumulating money and things when we have to leave them all behind anyway?

—CATHERINE MARSHALL

SAVOR THE MOMENT

What sort of beauty causes you to stop for a moment and gaze? Do you marvel at the colors of a sunset or the vivid hues of fall? The smell in the air after a rainstorm? The sound of wind in the trees?

What about the people in your life? Are you eager for moments with your children, your parents, even far-flung relatives? Do your friends get the best of your time?

Or are you too busy for all of it, planning to appreciate it "later"—once you have all the money and time and stuff you need? Honestly, will that moment ever come?

Time is short, dear sister. A beautiful world full of loving people is waiting. Your friends, your family, even the creation outside your door would like a moment of your time.

Pause. Savor. Enjoy. It is a gift from God.

Read 1 Timothy 6:17.

GOD, GIVE ME EYES TO SEE THE BEAUTIFUL
GIFTS YOU HAVE GIVEN ME.

To "see God in nature," to attain a radiant consciousness of the "otherness" of natural things, is the simplest and commonest form of illumination.

—EVELYN UNDERHILL

SLOW DOWN

We've all heard the phrase, "Stop and smell the roses." This clichéd advice carries a picturesque invitation to shift your day into a lower gear and notice the beauty around you.

What happens in your soul when you choose to s-l-o-w down and drink in the vivid colors of a sunset? Or when you allow yourself to be wrapped in the soft warmth of a fire in the fireplace? Or when you breathe in the intoxicating scent of crisp fall air?

To give your attention to the beauty of creation is, as Evelyn Underhill notes, a way to devote your attention to its Creator. Noticing the exquisite gifts God has placed in the world around you can become your simple expression of worship. Even if your schedule today is packed with tasks, stop and enjoy the beauty around you—and as you do, honor the One who made it for you.

Read Psalm 97:6.

I AM BREATHING THE SCENT OF THE ROSES YOU MADE TODAY, MY CREATOR!

My prayers are frequent and fervent . . . to do which is right, first in the sight of God, then in the view of my family, and lastly in that of the Society to which I belong.

—ELIZABETH FRY

PRIORITIES

Burned out. Stressed. Drained. Exhausted. How many of us have used one of these words to describe our current emotional setting? One cause of this overload can be letting ourselves take on more than we can handle, more than we should, more than what God is asking of us.

Sometimes when we think our priorities are okay with God, we are shocked to discover that everything has been askew. No wonder we feel so tired! If we are doing what is right first in the sight of God, we will never burn out. But when we add tasks and responsibilities on top of what he requires of us—no matter how noble or religious they may be—our priorities slip out of order.

Fervently pray, along with Elizabeth Fry, that God would set your priorities. He will line them up and show you his will for you—his very best for you.

Read Psalm 68:9.

LORD, I WANT TO DO FIRST WHAT IS RIGHT IN YOUR SIGHT.

God is not primarily concerned about age. He's looking for a willing, teachable spirit as He readies us for service.

—BETH MOORE

PERFECT AGE

The Lord, who is the same yesterday and today, continues to look for anyone whose heart is completely his. He's not worried about your age. *You* may feel like you're too young or too old to be useful to God, but number of years is not a factor with him.

What is he looking for? Above all, he desires that a servant have a willing, teachable spirit.

God can use a woman who is so in love with him and so constantly in communication with him that she is always asking to be shown, to be taught. She wants to learn and then to put that learning into practice. She wants to please him.

Age is just a number. God wants your spirit. If you're willing and teachable, you will never be without an opportunity to serve.

And there is so much to do for his kingdom!

Read Ephesians 4:1.

LORD, I WANT TO BE WILLING AND TEACHABLE
SO THAT I CAN SERVE YOU WELL.

Once you begin being naughty, it is easier to go and on and on, and sooner or later something dreadful happens.

—LAURA INGALLS WILDER

BE ALERT

A stab of jealousy, a flash of unbridled anger, an encouraging nod that signals the permission to gossip, a little white lie, a little bit of flirting. These may seem benign, but be warned. The enemy of our souls is like a devouring lion. He is always stealthily stalking his prey, searching for signs of weakness, waiting for an opportunity to pounce. Satan's goal is to rip open our lives and destroy the sweet fellowship we have with our heavenly Father. And it can start, as the Ma in Wilder's novel knew, "once you begin being naughty."

But we are on to Satan. We've been beguiled once too often. What he offers turns to ashes in our hands.

Our heavenly Father calls us to self-control and alertness. He knows that with his help, we can stand. With him, we are always safe.

Read 1 Peter 5:8–9.

LORD, GIVE ME SELF-CONTROL AND ALERTNESS
TODAY SO THAT I MAY STAY STRONG FOR YOU.

Going through a waiting period doesn't mean there is nothing happening, because when you are waiting on the Lord, He is always moving in your life.

—STORMIE OMARTIAN

SWINGING AND WAITING

A little girl swings back and forth. She's all alone. Her mom told her to go outside and stay there. "I'll call you when we're ready," her mom said.

Although time seems to stand still, the little girl doesn't mind the wait. She isn't bothered that her siblings are still in the house. She doesn't care that her daddy hasn't come out to give her a push on the swing. Because she knows what they're doing—they're busy preparing for her birthday party. With every moment, her excitement grows as she listens for her mother's call.

Are you experiencing a time of waiting? Does it seem as though the party has started without you? If so, remember this: God is at work in your time of waiting. He's always doing something in your life.

And you can be sure he's planning something better than a birthday party.

Read Isaiah 64:4.

> LORD, HELP ME TO WAIT ON YOU
> WITH CHILDLIKE EXCITEMENT.

Father, may all your dreams come true. I don't want to get in the way or hinder You from fulfilling any of the plans You had for me when You dreamed me into being.

—ROBIN JONES GUNN

HIS PLAN, OUR PERFECTION

Everyone who dreams big knows the disappointment of a life that falls short of those dreams. The higher we pin our hopes, the more devastating when they come crashing down. Sadly, to safeguard ourselves, we tend to keep our hopes low, or we may stop dreaming altogether.

Aren't you glad God doesn't give up on his dreams for us? The Bible says God's ultimate dream, his predetermined plan, is for us to be made like Christ—that we take on the image of our older brother.

That was God's plan when he dreamed of you. When He called your name, he said, "I want her to be just like Jesus. I have some great things for her to do."

Let's not get in our own way by hindering God's plans for us. He dreamed big. So should we. Working together with God, all of those dreams can come true.

Read Romans 8:29.

WORK ON MY HEART, JESUS. I WANT TO BE LIKE YOU.

God is more interested in developing our character than He is in manipulating our circumstances to make us happy.

—CYNTHIA HEALD

PURSUIT OF HAPPINESS

W hatever makes you happy." That's the message that bombards us from the world. If we didn't know any better, we'd think that being happy should be our goal and the basis of all our decision making.

God calls us to be different, however. Not that we can't be happy—far from it. But happiness is not the ultimate goal for our lives. We always seek to follow God in and through our circumstances. We aren't all consumed with happiness because we know there's something greater, something deeper.

We can't control our circumstances in order to assure happiness. And God won't do it either. Bad things happen, and through those tough times God wants to develop our character.

Beloved, God loves you, and he has promised unspeakable joy if you follow him. And on the way, he is committed to developing your character—which has an eternal value beyond compare.

Read Psalm 19:8.

> FATHER, HELP ME TO WANT YOU MORE THAN
> THE HAPPINESS THE WORLD OFFERS.

It is a profound irony that the Son of God visited this planet and one of the chief complaints against him was that he was not religious enough.

—REBECCA MANLEY PIPPERT

EXPECTATIONS

We are eager to say how others should act and quick to put a label on them. Rarely does anyone measure up to another person's standards. Jesus didn't.

He came as the Son of God, did miracles, walked on water, taught as no one had ever taught before--and the religious leaders came after him because he didn't keep the Sabbath . . . he didn't keep all the myriad laws they had added . . . he didn't fit the mold.

We just might not meet everyone's expectations. Some will call us too religious; some will say we aren't religious enough. Jesus knew he had completed all that God gave him to do, and that he had pleased his Father in doing so.

It's not about being religious; it's about being exactly who God created us to be and doing what he created us to do. That's all that is asked of us.

Read John 17:4.

HELP ME STAY FOCUSED ON YOUR EXPECTATIONS, LORD. THAT'S ALL THAT MATTERS.

NOVEMBER

Heaven is a prepared place for prepared people.

—CORRIE TEN BOOM

THE KINGDOM OF HEAVEN

Heaven is like an exotic foreign country. We won't be able to find our way if we don't have a guide. We prepare for the journey ahead by studying the Word of God.

We would not be able to understand this place unless we first learn to speak the language. We prepare ourselves for heaven by learning the language of praise and thanksgiving.

We surely must learn the customs and manners of this beautiful land ahead. We prepare to go before God by practicing virtue and living lives of holiness.

To truly enjoy this place, we desire a companion. Jesus offers to walk with us.

To be prepared for the greatest of feasts, we must be purified from the inside out. Our purity of heart and mind should radiate to others, calling them to be prepared as well.

This is the way to ready ourselves for our journey home.

Read Hebrews 11:16.

HEAVENLY FATHER, BURN AWAY MY EARTHLY DESIRES
SO I AM READY WHEN JESUS COMES AGAIN.

When your trial comes, then, put it right into the will of God, and climb into that will as a little child climbs into its mother's arms.

—HANNAH WHITALL SMITH

SAFE IN THE FATHER'S ARMS

What do we do with the questions that seem to have no answers? How do we explain something that makes no sense at all? Where do we turn for help?

Trials come. They hurt. They cause stress and concern. It helps to know that none of those trials have crept in unnoticed by God. Not one happens outside of his will. That's a difficult truth for us to understand. But as a child trusts her mom to comfort her when life hurts, so God calls us into his loving arms.

God lovingly ordains all things for our good, the blessings and the burdens. Each trial is designed by him to develop the image of his Son in us. In our sufferings, he draws us closer to him.

As Hannah Whitall Smith writes, put your trial "right into the will of God." Draw close. You'll find comfort in his embrace.

Read Hebrews 10:36.

DEAR LORD, WRAP ME IN YOUR EMBRACE TODAY.

It is only when we hide that we are living in rebellion. Perhaps not the kind of rebellion that kicks up its heels at authority, but rebellion against the glorious gift of the outrageous love of God.

—SHEILA WALSH

NO PLACE TO HIDE

Hiding from God takes many forms. We can hide in busyness and in overcommitment. We can hide by doing good things, convincing ourselves that we are in God's will. We set ourselves on doing things, but these may not be God's things.

Hiding means rebelling. When we hide from God, in whatever manner we do it, we're saying that we don't want to hear from him. Why? Well, he might make us adjust our plans or change our direction or even make us sit and listen to him.

The truth is, we can't hide from God. And it is also true that in that rebellion—in all that crazy busyness—we're actually missing out on the outrageous love of God. For his love knows just what we need, just how to fill our hearts, just how to give us joy.

There is no reason to hide. Come into the light.

Read Psalm 40:10.

HELP ME COME OUT OF HIDING. I WANT TO LIVE MY LIFE FOR YOU—AND WITH YOU.

How many there are . . . who imagine that because Jesus paid it all, they need pay nothing, forgetting that the prime object of their salvation was that they should follow in the footsteps of Jesus Christ in bringing back a lost world to God.

—LOTTIE MOON

IN HIS STEPS

Jesus paid it all. His death brought salvation to a world without hope. His resurrection assured us of eternal life. The astounding gift given freely to us brings us into God's family.

But are we merely to sit down and enjoy the fact that our eternity is set, that we're going to heaven and have no more worries? Not according to Lottie Moon, missionary to China in the late nineteenth century. The prime object of salvation is not to sit and be happy to be saved. Instead, we are to follow in the footsteps of Jesus, reaching out to a lost world that also needs to know the saving grace God offers.

Jesus intended for us to use our salvation as an active, living, breathing part of our lives that we eagerly and enthusiastically share with others.

Many in your world are lost. They need to meet your Savior.

Read Romans 10:14.

JESUS, SHOW ME WHO NEEDS AN INTRODUCTION TO YOU.

Whether things are good or bad, happy or sad, difficult or easy, you're in the middle of a God-ordained adventure that changes day by day—sometimes second by second.

—Thelma Wells

GRAND ADVENTURE

Every day we venture into the unknown. Every day appears to us as a blank slate (although, of course, God has already painted it). We step out and begin the adventure. What awaits? Isn't it wonderful to know, beyond the shadow of a doubt, that everything that happens to us today has already passed through God's hands? Nothing takes him by surprise. The joys and sorrows are part of the grand adventure of life.

And life changes moment by moment. The events of a split second can send us into joy or sorrow. It's all part of the adventure.

We could face life with fear, anger, bitterness. We could choose to see each day as a sorry journey to nowhere. But why do that when God says, "Join me!" How much better to look at life as a vast uncharted territory to explore, looking to see what God-ordained surprises await us!

Read 1 Corinthians 1:8–9.

LORD, LET'S GO! I'M READY FOR TODAY'S ADVENTURE.

Fear and unhappiness chase each other round and round in a circle.

—ELIZABETH GOUDGE

ROUND AND ROUND

You've seen the poor dog that just can't catch his tail. The harder he chases it, the faster it moves away. It's a dizzying cycle that continues round and round and round—unless someone steps in with a juicy bone, leaving both dog and tail happy with the outcome.

Fear and unhappiness are a lot like that. They can feed off each other in a vicious, unending spiral within your life. Your fear makes you unhappy; your unhappiness makes you fearful. But God can step in to obliterate both unhappiness and fear.

He has so much more for you than running in circles. He wants to rescue you by lifting you out of the chaos and into his still and comforting presence.

The cycle stops here if you let him step in.

Read Isaiah 41:13.

ENTER MY CHAOS, LORD, AND RESCUE ME FROM THE
VICIOUS CYCLE OF FEAR AND UNHAPPINESS.

Each person must live their life as a model for others.

—Rosa Parks

A MODEL LIFE

Sometimes we think we have to live our lives as society tells us to live. It's easy to be drawn in by advertisements promising health, wealth, and adoring friends if we would just act a certain way, dress in these particular fashions, and use the latest buzzwords.

The trouble with living your life as society dictates is that you'll be just like everyone else! You'd be a role model of . . . well . . . nothing special.

Here's an idea: Why not make a point of living your life as the Bible directs? Looking to Jesus as your role model will certainly make you stand out from the crowd! And when you stand out as one who "walks the walk" of the Christian, others will want to follow. How you live your life will speak volumes about your faith, even when you don't have a chance to say a word.

Read Ephesians 5:1.

---

*I WANT TO LIVE MY LIFE WELL, LORD, SO
OTHERS WILL WANT TO KNOW YOU.*

God will bring us to a place in which we must step out of hiding and take a chance on being hurt again.

—JOYCE MEYER

OUT OF HIDING

If you've ever been injured in an accident, whether it was swooshing down a ski slope, standing on a ladder for a home improvement project, or driving along an icy road, you know the memory of that trauma can persist for a long time. The torn ligament, bruises, or damaged vehicle will heal or be repaired, but the lingering fear remains. We don't ski again. We don't use a ladder. We don't drive in bad weather.

God knows our fear. He understands our hurt. He also knows, however, that when we let ourselves be paralyzed, we lose the opportunity to live the full life he intends for us.

As Joyce Meyer says, he may bring you to a place where you need to set aside your fear and step out. Will you be hurt again? Maybe. Will you be able to handle whatever comes?

Yes. Because he goes with you.

Read Deuteronomy 31:8.

TAKE MY HAND, LORD, AND PULL ME FROM
MY HIDING PLACE OF FEAR.

The finest bread hath the least bran, the purest honey the least wax, and the sincerest Christian the least self-love.

—ANNE BRADSTREET

SINCERELY

Quality always matters. It is timeless. From Anne Bradstreet's seventeenth-century world she describes the defining qualities of bread and honey—and sincere Christ followers. And the quality of a Christian, both then and now, has not changed—a sincere believer has the least self-love.

This rubs against our "me-first" culture. Many people live as though their actions happen in a vacuum. They do what they want to do, and their self-love leaves devastation in their wake.

Christians are not immune. While a healthy self-image is certainly important, it is unhealthy to love ourselves more than we love God, more than we love our family, or more than we love our closest friends. Our Savior wants to be first. If we love him more than we love ourselves—really, truly, sincerely—then loving others will come naturally.

Self-love will drive others away; God-love will bring others closer to you, and to God through your example.

Read 1 Peter 1:22.

> BANISH ANY SELF-LOVE SO THAT I CAN BE
> SINCERE IN MY WALK WITH YOU.

Your life is no exception to God's delight in arranging coincidences.

—JONI EARECKSON TADA

JUST A COINCIDENCE?

What a coincidence! Your car broke down right near the service station owned by your new friend's husband—you know, the husband you've been praying for at Bible study. The one who is down on all Christians because he thinks they're hypocrites.

What a coincidence! That answer to your concern came just at the right moment. You know, right before you gave up and gave in.

What a coincidence! You got the money just in time to pay the bill that would have been past due in another day.

What a coincidence! Really? Just a coincidence?

God takes great delight in arranging coincidences. You can be a witness to that friend's husband as you bring in your broken-down car. Each "coincidence" is a touch of God, allowing you to sit back with a smile and see how much he cares.

It's never just a coincidence. It's God's fingerprint.

Read Psalm 139:3.

> THANK YOU FOR THE "COINCIDENCES" THAT
> YOU PUT IN PLACE FOR ME.

A Christian mind is impossible without the discipline of refusal. Part of having a Christian mind is saying no to ungodly influences.

—BARBARA HUGHES

JUST SAY NO!

Maybe you've been here: the house is still, the world asleep, but your mind won't shut off. In the quietness you hear your Loved One's voice, "Spend this time with me." So you slip out of bed. With hot cocoa in one hand and Bible in the other, you settle in, ready to meet with God. You bow your head and thank him for these moments—but then it happens: your mind wanders off.

Our thoughts often take us to places we don't want to go, and once they begin the wayward journey, making a U-turn is pretty difficult. It's sad but true—our own thoughts can be the most ungodly of all influences.

Perhaps we should take Barbara Hughes's advice and begin the discipline of refusal by saying "no" to ungodly thoughts. From there, saying no to the ungodly influences that surround us is that much easier.

Read Philippians 4:8.

LORD GOD, PLEASE FILL MY MIND WITH THOUGHTS OF YOU.

We are made for larger ends than Earth can encompass. Oh, let us be true to our exalted destiny.

—CATHERINE BRAMWELL BOOTH

DESTINED FOR GREATNESS

God created the first human beings so he could walk and talk with his creation in the Garden of Eden. We were meant to share in God's attributes--his life, personality, truth, wisdom, love, holiness, and justice. In fact, we were created in his own image!

It was not God's will that any should perish, but the first sin in the garden set into motion a tragic series of events that removed many humans from their exalted destiny.

As a born-again Christian, you are well aware of your destiny. You are a joint-heir with Jesus Christ! As a child of God, you are entitled to a peaceful heart while here on earth and a place in heaven when you are released from the bonds of this life.

As a follower of Christ, you are created for larger ends than earth can encompass. Yours is an exalted destiny!

Read Romans 8:17.

THANK YOU THAT I AM MADE FOR GREATNESS IN YOU! I WILL BE TRUE TO MY DESTINY.

It isn't "more" he requires of us. In fact, it may be less.

—JOANNA WEAVER

ONLY ONE THING IS NEEDED

Sometimes less is more. A little less stuff in the house, with only a few precious knickknacks in place, gives your home a peaceful air. A little less salt in the stew, with a variety of well-chosen spices instead, brings out the flavor of the meat and vegetables.

Sometimes with Jesus, less is more as well. A little less running around in random acts of service; a little more time to sit at Jesus' feet to learn where and how he wants you to serve. A little less worrying and fretting; a little more time to bring the worries and fears to the Savior.

Jesus simply asks us to sit at his feet and listen. Sitting there shows that we want to know him, to follow him, to experience his love.

The more we have of him, the less we need of anything else.

Read Matthew 6:33.

JESUS, I AM SITTING AT YOUR FEET. I AM LISTENING.

The habit of discernment is a quality of attentiveness to God that is so intimate that over time we develop an intuitive sense of God's heart and purpose in any given moment. We become familiar with God's voice.

—RUTH HALEY BARTON

LISTEN

If you have been married or have been around a certain person for any length of time, you get to know that person well—what he or she is going to say; the response to any given situation, even if he or she has had a bad day. You know without hearing the words. You have developed an intuitive knowledge and understanding.

This is the intimate knowledge and relationship that our heavenly Father desires with us. He wants us to know his voice so closely that we will sense, as Ruth Barton says, his "heart and purpose in any given moment." This is discernment—the ability to understand what God wants as singled out from all of the other voices clamoring for our attention.

To discern his voice is to listen attentively and intimately.

Shhh. Can you hear him?

Read Psalm 119:125.

DEAR FATHER, HELP ME TO DISCERN YOUR VOICE SO
I WILL KNOW YOUR GOOD AND PERFECT WILL.

Faith is for that which lies on the other side of reason. Faith is what makes life bearable, with all its tragedies and ambiguities and sudden, startling joys.

—MADELEINE L'ENGLE

FAITH ALONE

Everything you do in this life requires a measure of faith. When you turn the key in your car's ignition, you have faith it will start. When you step onto an elevator, you have faith it will take you to the next floor.

Sadly, there are many things and people in which we place our faith, only to be let down. But there is one Person in whom we can place our faith and know with certainty that he will never let us down. When life seems out of control, he is in control. When tragedies come, he is there not only to comfort, but to bring good out of the ashes. When friends betray us, he will never leave us nor forsake us. And when we achieve moments of pure joy, we know that he is celebrating right along with us.

Faith gives meaning to our lives.

Read Romans 5:1–2.

MY FAITH IS IN YOU, JESUS,
FOR YOU ALONE GIVE MY LIFE MEANING.

Miracles require bold faith, a submissive spirit, and honest prayer.

—VIRELLE KIDDER

MIRACLES FOR YOU

God can do anything. He constructed an awe-inspired, intricate world out of nothing. He breathed life into mankind. He designed a plan of salvation so we are forgiven and joint heirs with Christ. And besides those awe-inspiring acts, he also performs "routine" miracles—little events like the morning dew, the sunrise and sunset that encircle each day, and the beauty and regularity of changing seasons. The handiwork we admire is effortless to an indefinable God.

Maybe today you're in need of nothing short of a miracle. God knows that and he has the resources in place. Your job? Bold faith that God will care for you. A submissive spirit that allows God to work in his way, in his time. Honest prayer that doesn't dance around the point but tells God exactly what's going on—no holds barred.

God is in the miracle-working business. Are you ready for what he's about to give?

Read Psalm 40:5.

IN MY WALK WITH YOU, LORD, HELP ME
TO ANTICIPATE YOUR MIRACLE.

I know that every soul cannot be alike. There must be different kinds so that each of the perfections of God can be specially honored. To me, He has revealed His infinite mercy.

—THERESE OF LISIEUX

GOD-REFLECTIONS

The attributes of God are innumerable. Among his many characteristics, we know the Creator is merciful, holy, wise, righteous, all-good, all-knowing, faithful, and loving. According to Therese of Lisieux, we are uniquely created so each soul can reflect one of God's characteristics for the world.

Are you strong in prayer or strong in service? You may be gifted with wisdom and patience or an understanding of justice. Maybe you are kind and compassionate to those less fortunate; maybe you are known for your deep faith. All of these facets come together in the body of Christ to reflect his presence.

Therese's message reminds us to humbly appreciate our differences without passing judgment or setting one gift over another. Each of us reflects God's glory. Each of us carries a tiny, glowing lamp. Only by uniting our gifts do we shine God's light so that he can transform the world—one soul at a time.

Read Philippians 2:14–16.

FATHER, GUIDE US TO WORK TOGETHER, AVOIDING JUDGMENTS AND CELEBRATING YOUR LIGHT IN OTHERS.

All my sufferings, by admirable management of omnipotent Goodness, have concurred to promote my spiritual and eternal good.

—SUSANNA WESLEY

SOVEREIGN SUFFERINGS

Do Susanna Wesley's words resonate with you? She was a mother of nineteen children. Some of her children made her proud—and some didn't. She lost her home twice—to arsonists. And once, her husband went on a preaching tour for almost a year, leaving her to fend for herself with the children. Yet, somewhere along the way, she learned to accept God's sovereignty and to believe in his "omnipotent goodness."

What about you? Is your home or marriage in jeopardy? Are you struggling with your children in some way? Has another person's malice touched your life? Then look to the strength of women like Susanna Wesley who know just how you feel. Heed their wisdom and hold fast to the hand of the One who's managing your suffering for your eternal good.

His all-powerful goodness watches over you.

Read 1 Peter 4:12–13.

SOVEREIGN LORD, THANK YOU THAT YOUR OMNIPOTENT GOODNESS WATCHES OVER MY LIFE.

Associate with others who are walking in the right way. . . .
Those who have drawn close to God have the ability to bring
us closer to him, for in a sense they take us with them.

—TERESA OF AVILA

GOOD COMPANIONS

We inevitably become like those with whom we associate. We ought to choose our friends carefully—that hasn't changed since Teresa of Avila wrote these words in the sixteenth century.

Who are the people you allow closest to you? To whom do you go when you need to talk, when you seek advice in one of life's dilemmas?

We should choose as our close friends those who are "walking in the right way"; that is, people who are alongside us on the path of desiring to please Jesus. We can walk along together because we agree. We can trust their advice, for it is dipped in the honey of God's Word. Their wisdom is gleaned from years of walking with him. In short, they draw us closer to God as well.

And we should be the same kind of friend to others. We need each other to make our way through life.

Read Amos 3:3.

SAVIOR, HELP ME CAREFULLY CHOOSE FRIENDS
WHO WILL DRAW ME CLOSER TO YOU.

Tomorrow is a new day with no mistakes in it.

—LUCY MAUD MONTGOMERY

NEW EVERY MORNING

A new day. A blank slate. No mistakes. An opportunity to start over.

That is the definition of grace.

Each day we do our best, but so often we slip up. If a great computer in the sky were tracking our every misstep, we would be overwhelmed and hopeless. The data would be our undoing. But even if that computer did exist, grace means that each night it would crash and all the data would be wiped out. All those mistakes—gone, forgiven, covered by the blood of Christ. Start again tomorrow, dear one. It's a new day.

Cling to the miracle of grace. Grace is the unmerited favor and mercy of God. Grace is the gift of second, third, and fiftieth chances. Every day there is a fresh supply, and it is sufficient to keep you moving forward, seeking to live for the Lord.

Great is his faithfulness.

Read Lamentations 3:22–23.

YOUR COMPASSIONS NEVER FAIL.
THEY ARE NEW EVERY MORNING.

I can never have perfect rest or true happiness, until, that is, I am so attached to him that there can be no created thing between my God and me.

—JULIAN OF NORWICH

STAY ATTACHED

Perfect, heartwarming, refreshing rest and happiness. A quiet elation that fills the soul to overflowing. Yet such rest and happiness seem as elusive as the fountain of youth.

Or are they? Julian of Norwich had the secret to both: Remain attached to God—so close that nothing comes between you and him.

The branch of a vine has only to remain attached to gain nutrients from the vine. So it is with those who trust the Savior. We gain what we need and even what we desire through our attachment to the Savior. He did the work and offers us the benefits through our relationship with him.

Rest and joy are within your grasp. But you can't claim either if your hands are already full. Empty your hands and lift them to the One who can give you perfect rest and true happiness.

Read John 15:7–8.

SAVIOR, GIVE ME THE COURAGE TO LET GO OF ANYONE
OR ANYTHING THAT COMES BETWEEN US.

You may grow so to follow His voice that even your thoughts will be brought "into captivity" to the obedience of Christ. This bondage is perfect freedom, for we desire, He and we, only one and the same thing.

—ISABELLA LILIAS TROTTER

CAPTIVE THOUGHTS

Maybe you have a quiet time with God every morning. You participate in a women's Bible study at church, and you might even teach Sunday school. From all outward appearances, you have your spiritual life on track.

But what about your thought life? Where does your mind tend to go when driving home from work or doing mindless chores at home? Are your thoughts focused on anxieties and worries? Resentments or slights? Do you delve into unwholesome fantasies about what your life could have been?

Conquering our spiritual outward trappings is not enough. Our thoughts must also be taken captive and obedient to Christ. His lordship and authority need to penetrate deeply into every aspect of our lives, including the very thoughts we have. Then our desires and his desires will be the same—and that gives us true freedom!

Read 2 Corinthians 10:5.

TAKE MY THOUGHTS, LORD, SO THAT EVEN
THEY ARE PLEASING TO YOU.

We bear the consequences for what we have done to ourselves, and for the sin that rules this world. Jesus forgave the thief, but he didn't take him down off the cross.

—FRANCINE RIVERS

THE TRUTH OF CONSEQUENCES

Sin has consequences. We may try to look the other way, to rationalize, to pretend it isn't so, but the fact is that if we put our hand on the hot burner of the stove, we will get burned.

And when faced with such consequences, how many folks turn around and get mad at God? They see their difficult situation and wonder why God allowed it to happen—when, in reality, they put the consequences in motion by their own bad choices.

Even then, Jesus brings forgiveness. Those problems we bring on ourselves are not somehow exempt; we can bring them to Jesus and know that he will forgive. Even the thief on the cross was promised Paradise. The consequences however? Those may continue to play out and we must ask God to help redeem those as well.

And you know what? He will.

Read Luke 23:29–43.

FORGIVE ME, LORD, FOR MY SINS. REDEEM THE
CONSEQUENCES FOR YOUR GLORY.

When we serve others, our feet slide into Jesus' sandals. He who came not to be served but to serve showed us the route to happiness. Finding him, we find meaning and learn to love others with his kind of servant love.

—JANE RUBIETTA

HIS SANDALS

To understand another person, we are told to "walk a mile in her shoes." To understand how Jesus lived and served, we would do well to slide our feet into his dusty sandals.

In those sandals we learn how to respond to others as he did, with patience and compassion. We learn to serve others outside our circle of friends—even when they don't recognize or thank us. We learn how to serve even when it means suffering.

His sandals are one-size-fits-all and will not wear out. We might feel unworthy of walking in shoes belonging to the Son of God, but we are commissioned to do so. After all, Jesus returned to heaven and left us here to continue his work.

The route to happiness is walked in the sandals of the Savior. Try them on. You'll find that they fit perfectly.

Read 1 Peter 2:21.

JESUS, TEACH ME TO WALK IN YOUR SANDALS.

Faithfulness today is the best preparation for the demands of tomorrow.

—ELISABETH ELLIO

STEPPING FORWARD

The tasks of each day cry out for our full attention and concentration, but how easily we distract ourselves! We worry about the mysteries of tomorrow. We dwell on the mistakes of yesterday. We procrastinate about what must be done today.

God says, "Trust me." When anxiety and worry glue your feet to the floor, break the adhesive with prayer. God's arms are open to you. Run to them. If fretting, questions, and doubt are ricocheting off the walls toward you, ward them off with God's Word.

We don't know what tomorrow will look like; we don't know where God will send us. We do know that he offers us his strength and wisdom for the work of today. Reach for it. Let his strength become your strength to accomplish what is needed today, and in that, prepare yourself for tomorrow.

Read Isaiah 43:18–19.

TAKE MY YESTERDAYS AND TOMORROWS, LORD. GIVE ME STRENGTH TO BE FAITHFUL THIS DAY.

Suddenly I realized that the missing ingredient in my prayers had been "with thanksgiving." So I put down my Bible and spent time worshiping Him for who He is and what He is. This covers more territory than any one mortal can comprehend.

—RUTH BELL GRAHAM

PRAYING WITH THANKSGIVING

"And Father, please help . . . and give me . . ." How often do we talk to God the way a spoiled child makes requests of his mother in a toy store—"I want this, and this, and this," without even a thank you, and seldom an "I love you"?

For most of us, our already-met needs (and wants) far exceed the list of things we still desire. Like spoiled children, we simply tend to forget about the gifts we have already received and complain about the things we still want. But more than any earthly gift is the presence of God himself, our Creator, Savior, Comforter, Friend. He willingly listens to our urgent petitions at midnight, forgives over and over again, and calls us his own.

When we begin with thanksgiving, we will have far more territory to cover than we can even begin to comprehend..

Read Psalm 100.

THANK YOU, FATHER, FOR ALL OF THESE BLESSINGS . . .

Instead of talking to God only about our problems, we need to talk to Him about Him . . . then we can begin to mention the problem.

—JOYCE MEYER

GOD-FOCUSED

Problems mount. Anxiety closes in. Sensing your desperation, a well-meaning friend advises, "Well, all you can do now is pray." It's your last resort—you've done everything you possibly could. Now it's up to God. Sound familiar?

Praying, however, is not only the first thing we should do; it's also the best way to put our problems in perspective.

When we come to God in prayer, we need to shift the focus of our prayers from our troubles to the One who can handle them. Remember his vastness and steadfastness. His infinite wisdom and almighty power. His unquenchable love for us. His willingness to bridge the gap between his holiness and our sin with his very own beloved Son.

As you offer up praise and awestruck wonder at who God is—at how *big* he is—problems pale in comparison and shrink in his majestic shadow.

Read Psalm 147:3–5.

GOD, YOU ARE SO MUCH BIGGER THAN
ANYTHING I FACE HERE ON EARTH.

The determined fixing of our will upon God, and pressing toward him steadily and without deflection; this is the very center and the art of prayer.

—EVELYN UNDERHILL

KEEP PRESSING

When we think about losing weight or accomplishing some other goal, we long for the determination that sees goals through to their completion. After all, a goal anchored to the will is usually accomplished, isn't it? But we must first have the belief that the goal *can* be accomplished.

This is the kind of attitude that Evelyn Underhill mentions in regard to prayer. The "determined fixing of our will" means we can't be shaken off by discouragement, silence, or answers long in coming. We just keep making a beeline to the Father, pressing steadily toward the throne of grace.

When we're desperate enough, our needs and those of others drive us to keep seeking, keep knocking without deterrence. A steady cry for help or mercy is never ignored.

Read Matthew 7:8.

FATHER, I WILL KEEP COMING TO YOU UNTIL YOU ANSWER, BECAUSE I KNOW THAT YOU WILL.

Serenity is that inner peace that comes with the certainties of knowing in whom you believe, what you believe, who you are, and where you're going.

—GIGI GRAHAM TCHIVIDJIAN

SERENITY

Serenity is a cup of hot tea on a cold day. A toasty comforter. A peaceful interlude. We long for such moments because they are few and far between.

What if you could have serenity all day every day? What if every moment could be described as "inner peace"? Is it possible?

True serenity comes when you have some certainties in life, when you have the big questions answered. Serenity means being settled in your soul about Who you believe in and what you believe about him. You believe that your sins are washed away because Jesus is your Savior. You know Jesus loves you in spite of your human frailty. You know you are his beloved daughter, created to serve him where he has placed you. You know your eternal destination is heaven.

With these certainties, you can settle in to serenity. And nothing can take that away from you.

Read 1 John 5:13.

> *THANK YOU FOR SETTLING THE BIG QUESTIONS AND GIVING ME SERENITY.*

When I get to heaven, the first face that shall ever gladden my sight will be that of my Savior.

—FANNY CROSBY

WE WILL SEE

As a young girl Fanny Crosby began to lose her sight. When a doctor attempted to help her, he damaged her sight further. Eventually, Fanny became completely blind. But she knew her blindness was not forever. She would one day arrive in heaven and her sight would be restored. The first face she would see? Her Savior.

When we arrive in heaven, we will see as we have never seen. The many questions that plague us will be answered in a moment. We will look on the face of our Savior and suddenly everything will have been worth it—the trials, the times we put our faith ahead of our feelings, the times we obeyed even when we didn't feel like it.

On that day we will see—*really see*—the One in whom we placed our faith. And he will be glad to see us as well!

Read 1 John 3:2.

ONE DAY I WILL SEE YOU, LORD. TODAY, I TRUST YOU.

DECEMBER

Because God is firm and steady, you can put your weight on Him.

—Cynthia Heald

SHIFT YOUR WEIGHT

To put your weight on something requires transferring trust from one thing to another. We don't walk out on a frozen pond unless we know for sure the ice can hold our weight. If we see the lines below our feet begin to spread or hear the unmistakable crackle of ice breaking, we know we are in the wrong place at the wrong time.

Putting our full weight on God demands absolute trust in him. Too often, however, we're afraid that he just won't hold us. We fear the crackle of a situation out of our control. We shift our weight back onto ourselves.

God says, "Trust me." We never need to worry that he can't handle it, that we are too much trouble, that we would be in the wrong place at the wrong time. Trusting in him is always our best choice, for he is firm and steady.

Read Deuteronomy 33:12.

O, FATHER, I LONG TO PUT MY FULL WEIGHT ONTO YOU.

Be still, be still, and know that He is God; / be calm, be trustful; work, and watch, and pray, / till from the throes of this last anguish rise / the light and gladness of that better day.

—HARRIET BEECHER STOWE

BE STILL

Be still. That's not easy to do when the boss hands you a pink slip, or your husband says he wants a divorce. When difficulties hit, our immediate response is to take action, try to regain control, and fix whatever is broken. We become anxious, sleepless, and at times, even frantic.

And God calls us to be still? How, exactly, is that supposed to work?

God isn't calling us to inaction. But in the midst of our troubles, he is calling us to pause before we hit the panic button, to listen before we talk, to quiet our racing hearts before we give in to despair.

When we do find time to be still before the Lord, and wait patiently for him, we discover untapped resources with which to cope and hidden strengths with which to carry on. That's because God now is in control, guiding us, caring for us, and moving us toward a better day.

Be still. It's the perfect antidote to worry.

Read Exodus 14:14.

LORD, I WANT TO TRUST YOU AND
GIVE MY WORRIES OVER TO YOU.

Where am I exactly? Already, at this moment, I am IN HIM. And underneath me are His eternal arms.

—CORRIE TEN BOOM

LIFE IN CHRIST

Where are you right now? Maybe you're sitting in an overstuffed chair watching the snow fall silently to the earth. Maybe you're in a hospital bed wondering what tomorrow holds. Maybe you're waiting for your phone to ring—and desperately hoping for good news.

Wherever you are right now, you are also IN HIM. On the eve of Jesus' arrest, he prayed that as he and the Father are one, so we, his followers, would be united to them. He wanted us to be one with him, drawn close, inseparable. Even in a Nazi prison camp, Corrie knew that whatever was happening outside and around her, she was safe in Jesus. His eternal arms held her tight.

Wherever you are, whatever is happening in your life at this very moment, you are IN HIM. And underneath you are his eternal arms. He will not let you go.

Read John 17:21.

LORD, THANK YOU THAT WHEREVER I AM,
I WILL ALWAYS BE IN YOU.

It's so important to be able to say, I am not primarily a worker for God; I am first and foremost a lover of God. This is who I am.

—LINDA DILLOW

TAKE MY HEART

Every single thing we do takes on a positive tone when we're doing it for love. Whether we're searching for that perfect gift or mowing the lawn; whether we're cooking Sunday dinner or cleaning out the garage; whether we're reading a story to someone or writing a letter—if our motivation is love, we find joy in the endeavor. Demonstrating our love for someone we're madly in love with is our privilege and pleasure.

It's the same in our relationship with God. When we serve him for no other reason than because we love him, our service becomes our delight, rather than our duty. As Linda Dillow explains, we need to be able to say that we are first and foremost lovers of God. And out of our love, we serve.

Then every task we do becomes a joy.

Read Joshua 22:5.

TAKE MY HEART, O GOD, AND FILL IT WITH LOVE FOR YOU.

He could not have shown you greater love than by giving his life for you (John 15:13). You can hardly resist being drawn by love, then, unless you foolishly refuse to be drawn.

—SAINT CATHERINE OF SIENA

NO GREATER LOVE

An unexpected bouquet of flowers. A backrub. A chore done to enable you to rest. When someone proves his or her love through action, that gets your attention, doesn't it? Actions speak louder than words. That's why, as Catherine explains, there is no greater act of love than Jesus' death on the cross. What more could he have offered beyond his own life?

While Jesus' death has the power to draw all people to him, this offer of love still has to be accepted by each person. And some resist, seeing only strings attached to the gift. Still others react out of cynicism or pain, unsure they can trust without being hurt once more.

Has this love drawn you? Have you opened your heart and received it? There is no greater love in all the world than the love Jesus has for you.

Read John 15:13.

JESUS, I ACCEPT YOUR LOVE AND OFFER YOU MINE IN RETURN.

God's way of working . . . is to get possession of the inside of us, to take the control and management of our will, and to work it for us. Then obedience is easy and a delight, and service becomes perfect freedom.

—HANNAH WHITALL SMITH

A PRACTICED HAND

Some activities require the guidance of a practiced hand—one that takes hold of yours and leads you to make the proper response. This is helpful in the first awkwardness of learning to play an instrument, drive a car, or learning a complicated dance. But when life hits the skids, we feel so out of our depth that we have no clue what to do. We long for someone to take control of the situation and act on our behalf if necessary.

God guides us from the inside out, starting with our will, as Hannah explains. As we trust him, the Holy Spirit moves our hands, our mouths, our feet. Our responses become his. But instead of being robots or puppets, ironically we have more freedom than we had when we acted on our own.

Need a hand? Take his.

Read Psalm 25:9.

WHEN I DON'T KNOW WHAT TO DO, HELP ME
TRUST THAT YOU WILL GUIDE ME.

[W]omen were first at the Cradle and last at the Cross. They had never known a man like this Man. . . . A prophet and teacher who never nagged at them, never flattered or coaxed or patronized.

—DOROTHY SAYERS

THE PERFECT MAN

We look for perfection—and are disappointed. The reality is that the men in our lives are far from perfect. They cannot be perfect for us any more than we can be perfect for them. So we would be wise to stop expecting it.

We should look instead at the One who defines perfection, the only human being ever to live a flawless life. Many people at the time didn't see it, but a few did—the women who surrounded him as a baby, birthing him, protecting him, rejoicing in him; those who surrounded him on the cross, weeping and agonizing over his unjust death.

They had found the perfect man—he didn't nag or flatter or coax or patronize. He loved. He showed them their value. He taught them. He made them his disciples.

And they went out and changed the world.

Read John 19:25.

YOU ARE PERFECT, MY JESUS. THANK YOU FOR PERFECTLY LOVING ME.

The fruit of silence is PRAYER. The fruit of prayer is FAITH.
The fruit of faith is LOVE. The fruit of love is SERVICE.
The fruit of service is PEACE.

—MOTHER TERESA

BEGIN WITH SILENCE

Tending to the needs of the sick, the suffering, and the dying, Mother Teresa shared the light of Christ with the world. She practiced five simple steps in her life, steps that lead to peace. Each step builds upon the previous step, and so step one is vital—the need for us to find a place of silence in order to commune with God.

Silence allows us to open our hearts to God, who longs for us to turn to him. This is followed by prayer, where we share our concerns with God. Prayer leads to faith, which wells up in our hearts as confident trust in our Savior. This reassurance allows us to embrace others with kindness and to serve them. That kind of service brings peace. Like falling back onto a sumptuous featherbed, God's peace enfolds us and brings us in silence back to him, to begin the cycle again.

Read Isaiah 32:17.

LORD, IN SILENCE I COME TO YOU TO HEAR
AND TO SERVE AND TO FIND PEACE.

Sometimes God wraps His glory in hard circumstances or ugly obstacles or painful difficulties, and it just never occurs to us that within those life-shaking events is a fresh revelation of Him.

—ANNE GRAHAM LOTZ

THIS IS OUR GOD

Matt and Shelley experienced the tragedy every parent dreads. Their precious daughter, Malayne, came into this world with a myriad of problems. She clung to life for eleven days. Within moments of hearing her mommy sing "Jesus Loves Me," Malayne met him face to face.

This is what Shelley later said: "When God requires us to go through something we before thought unendurable, he gives of himself to a degree which is nothing short of miraculous. He was right there! In my face, by my side, surrounding me. It was overwhelming. If I had to do it all over again, I would—if it meant feeling and experiencing the palpable presence of Jesus once again."

God revealed himself to Matt and Shelley during what should have been their darkest days. They found him to be all their aching hearts required.

That is the Jesus we serve. That is the Jesus we love.

Read Psalm 139:5.

LORD, I PRAISE YOU, THE MIGHTY GOD WHO
REACHES DOWN TO LIFT UP HIS CHILDREN.

I think he [Mister Rogers] made me less narrow-minded, more tolerant, and more in awe of what's mysterious about our faith. I think I thought I had my faith all figured out, and he reintroduced mystery.

—AMY HOLLINGSWORTH

CELEBRATE THE MYSTERY

The mysterious part of Christianity is many times ignored. We don't understand it, so we choose not to think on it. How did a virgin have a baby? What was God doing before he made the earth? How did Jesus turn water to wine? The questions make us uncomfortable, as if our inability to answer them puts our faith on shaky ground.

We can't answer many of those questions—and we ought to be glad of that. What is the point of faith if everything can be explained, if we have all the answers, if there is no mystery left? God delights in our questions and he will give us whatever information we truly need. Beyond that, we should simply be in awe of him.

Let your questions lead you straight back to God himself, and to your knees in worship of his greatness. Celebrate the mystery!

Read Hebrews 11:1.

I STAND IN AWE OF YOU, LORD, AND THE MYSTERY OF YOUR LOVE FOR ME.

Because of who he is, when Jesus touches anything, there is blessing.

—REBECCA MANLEY PIPPERT

MASTER OF MULTIPLICATION

In the little boy's hands it was simply five loaves of bread and two fish. In God's hands that same one-boy picnic fed over five thousand people, with twelve baskets of leftovers!

We don't feel like we have very much to offer. Our resources are limited. Our talents are few (and not really all that great). Our time is full.

Like the disciples, the world says, "That's not enough to make any difference to anyone." Jesus says, "Give it to me." Then he blesses it and sends it out to change the world—maybe just for a little bit, maybe just for a few people. But those few people in that moment in time feel the touch of God.

You see, God hasn't changed. He loves it when his children hand over what they have so that he can go to work making miracles happen.

Read John 6:1–13.

---

*I'M GLAD SIZE DOESN'T MATTER TO YOU, LORD.
LITTLE BECOMES MUCH IN YOUR HANDS.*

Love is enough. . . . When there's nothing left to give the Lord, then you have to look at what you have. Your soul. Yourself. And that is the only gift He wants from His children.

—BODIE THOENE

THE BEST GIFT OF ALL

We've all made them, requested or not—our Christmas wish list. As children we weren't concerned about the prices or availability of the items on our list, so we could let our imaginations run wild.

If God were to make a wish list, what do you think he'd want from us? Our gifts of money or time? Maybe he really would like to see more acts of service. Anything we consider difficult—maybe *that's* what God wants from us.

Or maybe we're in difficult straits right now and we have no time or money or strength to give anything. What can we possibly give?

Bodie Thoene tells us. Ourselves. That's what God wants.

You are the best and most valuable gift of all.

Read Deuteronomy 6:5.

I GIVE MYSELF AND MY LOVE TO YOU. IT'S ALL I HAVE.

Despite everything that had happened, God's fingerprints were everywhere.

—KAREN KINGSBURY

THE FINGERPRINTS OF GOD

Our fingerprints are unique to us. Like snowflakes, no two sets of fingerprints are the same. We can't help but leave our fingerprints on everything we touch. The phone. The computer keyboard. Doorknobs. Papers. Books. We know our fingerprints are there, but we can't see those little invisible ridges that unmistakably say, "I was here."

God's fingerprints are like that. Although he is always present, always aware of our circumstances, and always hearing our prayers, at times we wonder. When situations spin out of control or head in tragic directions, we feel that God has left us.

At some point we will look back at that time and, despite all that happened, recognize God's fingerprints everywhere. A word of encouragement, a flash of insight, a situation cared for in a way we had not imagined.

God's fingerprints are everywhere in your life. That's how much he cares.

Read Deuteronomy 2:7.

I THANK YOU, GOD, FOR WATCHING OVER ME AND LEADING ME EVEN WHEN I CAN'T SEE YOU.

God is doing in each one of our lives something expressly different than He is doing in another's. He will give us the unique grace to bear our unique cross.

—JONI EARECKSON TADA

GRACE FOR THE JOURNEY

The versatile dough from a sugar cookie recipe can be transformed into as many beautiful shapes and designs as we can imagine and create. No two creations are exactly alike.

The same is true for us. We are not cookie-cutter people. God is doing something in our lives that is expressly different than what he is doing in the lives of our sisters, our friends, our neighbors. He is shaping us and our journeys, and no two journeys are exactly alike.

We often wish our journey was easier, our cross lighter. If we start comparing, we may decide that the cross we bear seems heavy and cumbersome compared to someone else's. *If only we could trade places!*

Instead God says, "Let me work in you."

The cross you bear is yours alone, but he will give you the unique grace to bear it. And one day you will lay it at his feet.

Read Psalm 138:8.

FULFILL YOUR PURPOSE FOR ME, LORD.
HELP ME TO GRASP YOUR GRACE.

God is the Divine Quilter. How lovingly he gathers up the scraps and remnants and leftovers of my experiences, my brokenness, and my joy. With the skillful needlework of grace, he stitches it all together to make a wonderful whole.

—LUCINDA SECREST McDOWELL

STITCHED TOGETHER

You don't have to be a quilter to appreciate the hard work and artistry of a handmade quilt—a lifetime of memories held in each stitch, each piece of fabric lovingly chosen.

Our lives are like a patchwork quilt. On the days when we believe we are a mess or at best, a "crazy quilt," God thinks differently. Somehow he fits each event of our lives—even the senseless ones or the painful ones we wish to forget—into a display of surpassing beauty. Faith in Jesus is the thread that runs throughout the handiwork. This thread not only holds everything together, it makes our quilt priceless.

Perhaps in heaven we'll finally realize why that thread of brokenness we believed so ugly was the perfect complement to the thread of joy. For now we can rest content that God, the Divine Quilter, is creating a masterpiece.

Read Colossians 1:17.

LORD GOD, I TRUST THAT YOU HOLD THE THREADS OF MY LIFE SECURELY IN YOUR HAND.

If, then, you sometimes fall, do not lose heart. Even more, do not cease striving to make progress from it, for even out of your fall God will bring some good.

—TERESA OF AVILA

AFTER A FALL

Falls and failures *hurt*. With some hurts, we bear the emotional and sometimes physical scars for a long time. We are often left to feel that we no longer have any value to God—after all, we've let him down. We could retreat and lick our wounds. We could find a way to blame someone else. We might just decide to never try again.

By simply living our lives we will fail once in awhile, Teresa explains. But even if we're at the ground zero of failure and feeling utterly humiliated, we're not to give in to discouragement. God knows our hearts, and he certainly knows that failing is not the end of our usability as believers. He can bring good out of the mess we sometimes make of our lives.

Don't lose heart. God can bring good out of any failure. You simply need to trust him.

Read Matthew 26:41.

IF I FALL, LORD, LIFT ME UP SO THAT I MIGHT CONTINUE TO SERVE YOU.

It is a constant exercise of faith for me to relinquish my children into God's hands. He is a loving Father, who loves them more deeply than I ever could.

—INGRID TROBISCH

WELCOMING "FIRSTS"

If you're a parent, you remember your child's firsts: first word, first day of school, first time driving, first job. Those events are major milestones marking your child's journey toward independence. The fact that there are "firsts" also means that there are "lasts": the last time crawling once walking is discovered, the last day of elementary school, the last time as an unmarried kid hanging out for Christmas vacation.

Parenting is about releasing your children to step into each "first" God has planned for them, knowing that all the while you are preparing them to leave you. Your job is to work yourself out of a job—and it's bittersweet at best. As you surrender your children to God each day, you'll find the grace to welcome each "first" and "last" in your children's lives—and in your own.

After all, he loves them even more than you do. Imagine that!

Read 3 John 4.

I SURRENDER MY CHILD(REN) TO YOU TODAY, FATHER.

A wandering period can be a very real time of prayer, trust, and faith in God—that He will provide, protect and guide us into the exact place He wants to put us for our greatest development and outreach.

—LUCI SWINDOLL

WONDER AS I WANDER

There are times in our spiritual lives when we're not sure where we're headed or if God is even listening. Such spiritual dryness often comes after an event of great spiritual triumph or a spiritual "high" (ironically). Sometimes it comes after a painful defeat. Either way, we feel alone in a vast wilderness with no oasis in sight. We wander. We don't know which direction to turn.

If you're facing such a wandering period right now, beloved, don't despair. You aren't lost, or alone, or cast aside. This is a faith-building time. Like any muscle, faith is built up through hard work and discipline. Taking faith steps exercises that muscle. Continue to talk to God, even if you're not sure he's listening. Continue to trust that he will provide, protect, and guide—even if no evidence presents itself.

God is there even as you wander. He will bring you back. Soon.

Read Psalm 107:4–9.

LORD, WHEN I CAN'T SENSE YOUR PRESENCE, HELP ME SEE YOU THROUGH THE EYES OF FAITH.

It is not on our forgiveness any more than on our goodness that the world's healing hinges, but on His.

—CORRIE TEN BOOM

PEACE ON EARTH

As we near the Christmas season, we sing carols that describe the hope of peace on earth. Corrie ten Boom, living through the heinous evil of the concentration camps in World War II, deeply understood the depravity of the human soul without Christ. Healing for the world will not come through human goodness or even our ability to forgive others. We are fallible, imperfect, and, without Christ, unable to truly display those noble characteristics. And even if we *can* act with forgiveness and goodness, who's to say everyone else on the planet is willing and able?

Healing will only occur because of Christ's forgiveness and goodness. Only he can change hearts. Only he can take the darkness and bring light. Only he can heal the sickness of sin. Only he can offer us his righteousness.

Peace on earth? It begins right in your own heart.

Read Malachi 4:2.

PEACE ON EARTH BEGINS WITH ME, IN MY HEART, TODAY. LORD, GIVE ME YOUR PEACE.

Only the Lord forgets sin. Only God can take it and send it as far away as the East is from the West. Man remembers. Man recounts. Man condemns.

—FRANCINE RIVERS

WIPING THE SLATE

Some people won't let it go. You know the ones. They like reminding you of times you've messed up in the past. Maybe they've said they forgive you, but the next time a disagreement erupts, a historical timeline of offenses is unpacked, shaken about, and aired out—again.

People may do that, but God doesn't. The Word says that when we repent of our sins, they're gone! They have been removed as far as the East is from the West—in other words, they're in a void, can't be found. The slate is clean because God doesn't maintain records of sins confessed with a contrite and repentant heart.

People may periodically try to usher you through your Hall of Shame, pointing out errors and losses, but you don't have to tread the archives with them. If you've cleared your record with the Lord, no one else's scorecard matters.

Read Psalm 103:7–12.

GOD, THANKS FOR FORGETTING MY SINS. HELP ME GIVE THAT GRACE TO OTHERS.

Most people believe that God loves them when they can feel they deserve it. Problems arise when they feel that they do not deserve God's love but desperately need it.

—JOYCE MEYER

LOVE BROKE THROUGH

She was caught. She never meant for it to happen. How could things get so far? It was useless trying to cover herself as they dragged her into the streets. What can you wear to hide from the leering eyes of men and the contemptuous looks from women? How do you hide from yourself?

She had risked it all for him, but he left her to bear the shame alone. Suddenly it didn't matter. Death would be a welcome escape from this unbearable guilt.

And that's when Love stepped in. Love in the flesh came to her defense. Love sent all of her accusers home. Love looked in her eyes and said, "Neither do I condemn you."

Love picks us up, clothes us in righteousness, and gives us the strength to leave our sin behind. Love always steps in just when we need him the most.

Read John 8:1–11.

WHILE I WAS STILL A SINNER,
YOU DIED FOR ME. THANK YOU.

Oh, the fullness, pleasure, sheer excitement of knowing God on earth!

—ELISABETH ELLIOT

SHEER JOY!

In the classic Dickens tale *A Christmas Carol*, Scrooge is a stingy old man obsessed with making money. One night, in a dream, he's shown the horrible future that will be his unless he changes his selfish ways. Delighted for the second chance, Scrooge bounds out of bed and makes amends with his family and employees. After giving his clerk a long-overdue raise, he exclaims, "I'm so happy. I just can't help it!"

Do you long for that kind of happiness? Does it seem as if joy is always just beyond your grasp? Have you searched but can't find it?

The truth is, it's right in front of you, around you, within you. When you know God during your sojourn on this earth, life has fullness, pleasure, sheer excitement. Ask God to renew such joy in you so that you will be so overflowing you just can't help it!

Read Psalm 16:11.

LORD, PLEASE OVERFLOW MY HEART
WITH THE JOY OF KNOWING YOU.

He could have roared on top of a mountain, but he whispered in the voice of a baby. He could have ordered our obedience; instead he calls for our hearts.

—SHEILA WALSH

CHOOSE HIM

From the farthest galaxies to the tiniest microscopic creature—God is the creator of all. We exist because he allowed us to.

As such, does he not have the right to demand our love and obedience? Indeed, he had every right to roar from the top of the mountain and demand that we obey him *or else*. Instead, he decided to let us choose. Instead of yelling at us from a mountain, he whispered at us in the voice of a baby—his Son—born to save us. Instead of ordering us to obey, he woos us to love.

We choose to respond because we see eyes brimming with tenderness. We willingly comply because our souls are captivated by his grace. We obey because it shows that we love the one who lavishes love on us.

God wants you to *choose* him today. That's how much he loves you.

Read Joshua 24:15.

THANK YOU, LORD, FOR LOVING ME.
YOU'VE CAPTURED MY HEART.

All the privilege I claim for my own sex (it is not a very enviable one; you need not covet it), is that of loving longest, when existence or when hope is gone.

—JANE AUSTEN

GOD'S EVERLASTING LOVE

We might read and sigh over this description found in the novel *Persuasion*. Anne Elliot's heart-wrenching statement shows her at her most persuasive and vulnerable. As Anne describes, a woman goes on loving, even after the hope of having that love returned is gone.

While many of us can relate to the resiliency of love, only God can lay claim to the title of "the one who loves the longest." His love is fueled by faithfulness. He can no more stop loving than he can stop being faithful. He loves—often beyond hope—even those who continually reject him.

That love came in the form of a baby. That love allowed for death on a cruel cross. That love goes on from now into eternity. That love is ours for the asking. That love is offered to us.

That love is yours.

Read 1 Chronicles 16:34.

FATHER, THANK YOU FOR GIVING ME YOUR EVERLASTING LOVE.

She had never heard anything so beautiful. She couldn't remember ever hearing the complete story before as it was given in the scripture. . . . A little baby born in a stable was God's Son.

—JANETTE OKE

THE BEST STORY OF ALL

It's a familiar story. A young Hebrew teenager is told by an angel that she has been chosen by God to bear a very special child. Her fiancé threatens to cancel the wedding. The same angel interrupts his plan. She visits her relative Elizabeth, who is much older and also pregnant. She returns to Nazareth to wait for her child's birth, only to be required to make the ninety-mile journey to Bethlehem close to her due date. With no room in the inn, she gives birth in a manger and uses an animal feeding trough as a bassinette.

A strange story? Yes. A story full of surprises? Yes. A story that affects us today? Another yes! This little baby—Jesus—was a gift to all humankind. Our Healer. Our Savior. Our Lord.

No story is more beautiful, more astounding, more life-changing. The little baby born in a stable was God's Son.

Read Luke 2:4–7.

THANK YOU, GOD, FOR THE WONDERFUL
GIFT OF YOUR SON, JESUS.

Think of having a whole penny for your very own. Think of having a cup and a cake and a stick of candy and a penny. There had never been such a Christmas.

—LAURA INGALLS WILDER

THE LITTLE THINGS

What small pleasures do you remember from your childhood Christmases? What small item came to you in the toe of a stocking that you still remember to this day?

The contents of the Christmas stocking in Wilder's story seem pitifully little to us today—a cup, a small cake, a stick of candy, and a penny. Yet in a life that had few material possessions, those were wonders, and she marveled at her riches.

What small but important riches has God given you? What "little" gifts came into your life this past year, almost overlooked because they were—well—expected? What grace did God give to you and your family? It might appear like no more than a "whole penny" to some folks, but to you, it is a precious gift from God.

Think back across your year, beloved, and thank God for his gifts to you.

Read Matthew 7:11.

THANK YOU, FATHER, FOR THE SMALL GIFTS YOU
HAVE GIVEN ME IN THIS PAST YEAR.

He hideth my soul in the cleft of the rock / that shadows a dry, thirsty land; / He hideth my life with the depths of His love, / and covers me there with His hand.

—FANNY CROSBY

HE'S GOT YOU COVERED

What images come to mind when you hear the word "cover"? Snow blanketing the ground? A beautiful homemade quilt resting on a bed? A shawl to throw around cold shoulders? Perhaps a police officer backing up her partner, armed and ready?

A common expression we like to hear is "I've got you covered." But it doesn't have anything to do with snow, blankets, shawls, or guns. It's a positive statement assuring us that someone is alongside, offering protection, safety, encouragement, support.

Beloved, realize this today: God has you covered. When you're stuck in a dark place, thirsty for someone who cares, drowning in despair—God is with you. He covers you with his hands of hope, protection, support. Rest in his all-encompassing love today.

Read Psalm 18:2.

I THANK YOU, GOD, FOR YOUR LOVE AND PROTECTION.

God gives us his light in an instant, allowing us to know all that we need to know. No more is given to us than is necessary in his plan to lead us to perfection.

—SAINT CATHERINE OF GENOA

A LITTLE LIGHT, PLEASE

When we're lost or confused, we want to know now—*right* now—how to find our way toward our destination or toward understanding. No one likes that feeling of helpless floundering about, especially in dark places!

Isn't it great to know that God freely gives us the understanding we crave? However, as Catherine explains, he doesn't show us every step of the path. He gives us just enough light to take the next step in his plan. Sometimes we grow frustrated with this process, impatient to know the whole story all at once. Yet if he told us everything about every bend in the road, we would never pray or realize our dependence on him.

Just enough light. That's all you really need.

Read 2 Peter 1:19.

HOLY SPIRIT, PLEASE GIVE ME THE UNDERSTANDING I NEED FOR THE SITUATION I'M FACING NOW.

Eden is always behind us—Paradise always before.

—LUCY MAUD MONTGOMERY

IN THE REARVIEW MIRROR

Eden was nice for awhile, wasn't it? Leisurely strolls, peaceful companionship with marvelous animals, fragrant flora that offered tasty fruit. Then came that forbidden fruit. It was so enticing that . . . well, you know the rest of the story. We tend to blame Eve, but doesn't this same scenario play out repeatedly in our own lives? We think, *Oh, this is just one little thing that won't hurt anyone.* Before we know it, sin has crept into Paradise.

Regardless of the temptations we've yielded to, God still yearns for us to walk with him. He wants it so much that he extends amazing grace through his Son, whose blood covers sin and makes us holy all over again. He longs to restore us and bring us back into relationship with him.

Accept that mercy. Rejoice in the grace. Put Eden in your rearview mirror as you speed enthusiastically toward Paradise.

Read 1 Corinthians 9:24.

HELP ME ESCAPE EDEN—THE PLACE OF MY SIN— AND RACE TO PARADISE WITH YOU.

The adventure of living has not really begun until we begin to stand on our faith legs and claim—for ourselves (and all that concerns us)—the resources of our God.

—CATHERINE MARSHALL

ADVENTUROUS LIVING

Recall those first days after high school or college when you moved away from your parents' house into a new place. It was exciting because of all the unknowns, but also a bit scary because you didn't have all the resources figured out.

What a wonderful way to begin your faith journey! You don't have resources of your own, you don't know what the future holds, you aren't sure how you're going to get from point A to point B.

And that's exactly how God likes it. When you stand only on faith and trust in the resources of God, *that's* when the adventure begins.

If life doesn't still feel like an adventure, maybe you need to do something that stretches your faith. The life of a believer—*your life*—should be filled with excitement as you continually stand on your faith legs and claim God's resources.

Read Psalm 143:10.

LORD, I WANT TO TRY OUT MY FAITH
LEGS AND WALK WITH YOU.

I challenge you to grow wiser, even as you let go of the potentiality of youth. Put meaning into the rings of your life tree. Mellow. Sweeten. Lighten. Strengthen. Deepen.

—VALERIE BELL

GROW STRONG

The years in a tree's life are recorded in the rings. The circles tell its life story, including years of plenty and drought. Count the rings and you'll know how long the tree stood and grew toward heaven.

We count our years with birthday candles and gray hairs. But like trees, each passing year puts its mark on our lives. We too have lived through times of plenty and of drought. We have enjoyed the sunshine and gentle rains, and we have been battered by storms and maybe even struck by lightning.

Continue to grow in the coming year, dear one. Continue to mellow as you understand that no situation lasts forever; to sweeten, knowing that everyone can use a little kindness from you; to lighten, for you can help to bear another's burden; to strengthen as you offer your strength to others; to deepen in your love for him.

Read Psalm 1:1–3.

I WANT MY LIFE TO TELL A BEAUTIFUL STORY OF YOUR FAITHFULNESS.

JANUARY

1 Smith, Hannah Whitall. *The God of All Comfort* (Chicago: Moody Press, 1956), 31.

2 Lotz, Anne Graham. *My Heart's Cry* (Nashville: W Publishing, 2002), 27.

3 Guyon, Madame. *Song of the Songs of Solomon.* Christian Classics Ethereal Library (http://www.ccel.org/ccel/guyon/song.vi.html).

4 Feinberg, Margaret. *The Sacred Echo* (Grand Rapids: Zondervan, 2008), 89.

5 De Waal, Esther. *Lost in Wonder* (Collegeville, MN: Liturgical Press, 2003), 42.

6 Elliot, Elisabeth. *Quest for Love* (Grand Rapids: Revell 1998), 213.

7 Cymbala, Carol. *He's Been Faithful: Trusting God to Do What Only He Can Do* (Grand Rapids: Zondervan, 2001), 59.

8 Bronte, Charlotte. *Jane Eyre* (London: Folio Society, 1996 ed.), 58.

9 Gateley, Edwina. *A Mystical Heart* (New York: The Crossroad Publishing Co., 1998), 72–73.

10 Pippert, Rebecca Manley. *Hope Has Its Reasons: The Search to Satisfy Our Deepest Longings* (Downers Grove, IL: InterVarsity Press, 2001), 106.

11 Sayers, Dorothy. *Creed or Chaos?* (Manchester, NH: Sophia Institute Press, 1974), 63.

12 Schaeffer, Edith. *The Art of Life,* compiled and edited by Louis Gifford Parkhurst, Jr. (Wheaton, IL: Crossway Books, 1987), 82.

13 Tada, Joni Eareckson. *Heaven: Your Real Home* (Grand Rapids: Zondervan, 1995), 177.

14 Omartian, Stormie. *The Power of a Praying Woman* (Eugene, OR: Harvest House, 2002), 97.

15 Catherine of Siena. *The Dialogue of Saint Catherine of Siena.* http://www.ccel.org/ccel/catherine/dialog.iv.ii.iv.html.

16 Barton, Ruth Haley. *Sacred Rhythms: Arranging Our Lives for Spiritual Transformation* (Downers Grove, IL: InterVarsity Press, 2006), 116.

17 O'Connor, Flannery. *Mystery and Manners* (New York: Farrar, Straus and Cudahy, 1961), 159.

18 Marshall, Catherine. *Something More* (New York: McGraw-Hill Book Co., 1974), 22.

19 Arthur, Kay. *Lord, Teach Me to Pray in 28 Days* (Eugene, OR: Harvest House Publishers, 1982/2008), 50.

20 DeMoss Nancy Leigh. *Brokenness* (Chicago: Moody, 2002), 84.

21 TerKeurst, Lysa. *What Happens When Women Walk in Faith: Trusting God Takes You to Amazing Places* (Eugene, OR: Harvest House Publishers, 2005), 15.

22 Payne, Leanne. *Listening Prayer* (Grand Rapids: Baker Book House, 1994), 189.

23 Silvious, Jan. *Fool-proofing Your Life* (Colorado Springs: Waterbrook Press, 1998), 126.

24 Wilder, Laura Ingalls. *Little Town on the Prairie* (New York: HarperCollins, 1941), 89.

25 Johnson, Barbara. *Pack Up Your Gloomees in a Great Big Box, Then Sit on the Lid and Laugh!* (Nashville: Word Publishing, 1993), 19.

26 ten Boom, Corrie. *The Hiding Place.* (Minneapolis: World Wide Publications, 1971), 195.

27 Shirer, Priscilla. *And We Are Changed: Encounters with a Transforming God* (Chicago: Moody Publishers, 2003), 23.

28 Teresa of Avila. *The Interior Castle* (or *The Mansions*). Christian Classics Ethereal Library (http://www.ccel.org/ccel/teresa/castle2.v.i.html).

29 Stowe, Harriet Beecher. "Uncle Tom's Cabin" in *Three Novels* (New York: Penguin Putnam, 1982), 100–101.

30 Swindoll, Luci. *Wide My World, Narrow My Bed* (Portland: Multnomah Press, 1982), 35.

31 Adams, Michelle Medlock and Gena Maselli. *Daily Wisdom for Working Women* (Uhrichsville, OH: Barbour Publishing, 2004), June 28.

FEBRUARY

1 Moore, Beth. *Believing God* (Nashville: Broadman & Holman Publishers, 2004), 191.

2 Guyon, Madame. http://www.giga-usa.com/quotes/authors/mme_guyon_a001.htm.

3 Christenson, Evelyn. *"Lord, Change Me!"* (Wheaton, IL: Victor Books, 1977), 103.

4 Gaither, Gloria. *We Have This Moment* (Waco, TX: Word Books, 1988), 17.

5 Burnham, Gracia, with Dean Merrill. *In the Presence of My Enemies* (Wheaton, IL: Tyndale House Publishers, 2003), 142.

6 Julian of Norwich. *Revelations of Divine Love.* Quoted at http://www.readprint.com/author-1713/Julian-of-Norwich-books.

7 Neff, Miriam. *From One Widow to Another: Conversations on the New You* (Chicago: Moody Publishers, 2009), 142.

8 Karon, Jan. *Home to Holly Springs* (New York: Viking/Penguin, 2007), 339.

9 Feinberg, Margaret. *The Sacred Echo* (Grand Rapids: Zondervan, 2008), 37.

10 Keller, Helen. *The Story of My Life* (New York: W.W. Norton, restored classic, 1903/2003), 93.

11 Crosby, Fanny. www.Christianhistory.net.

12 Carmichael, Amy. http://dailychristianquote.com, Sept 25, 2001.

13 Briscoe, Jill. *Thank You for Being a Friend* (Chicago: Moody Publishers, 1999), 171.

14 Eldredge, Stasi. *Captivating: Unveiling the Mystery of a Woman's Soul* (Nashville: Thomas Nelson Publishers, 2005), 112.

15 Bradstreet, Anne. *Works in Prose and Verse* (Charlestown, MA: Abram E. Cutter, 1867), 8.

16 Young, Sarah. *Jesus Calling: Enjoying Peace in His Presence* (Nashville: Thomas Nelson, 2004), xii.

17 Burnett, Frances Hodgson. *A Little Princess* (Boston: David R. Godine, 1989), 108.

18 Mother Teresa. http://thinkexist.com/quotes/mother_teresa/2.html.

19 Demuth, Mary. *Ordinary Mom, Extraordinary God* (Eugene, OR: Harvest House Publishers, 2005), 94.

20 Hurnard, Hannah. *Hinds' Feet on High Places* (Wheaton, IL: Living Books, 1975), 27.

21 Alcott, Louisa May. *Little Women* (Wheaton, IL: Tyndale House, 1997 reprint), 434.

22 Underhill, Evelyn. Grace Adolphsen Brame, ed. *The Ways of the Spirit* (New York: Crossroad, 1993), 123.

23 Rubietta, Jane. *Come Along: The Journey in to a More Intimate Faith* (Colorado Springs: Waterbrook Press, 2008), 89.

24 Sayers, Dorothy. *Creed or Chaos?* (Manchester, NH: Sophia Institute Press, 1974), 44.

25 Bolton, Martha. *Cooking with Hot Flashes and Other Ways to Make Middle Age Profitable* (Minneapolis: Bethany House, 2004), 152.

26 Akers, Michelle with Gregg Lewis. *The Game and the Glory—An Autobiography* (Grand Rapids: Zondervan, 2000), 228.

27 Brestin, Dee. *The Friendships of Women* (Wheaton, IL: Victor Books, 1988), 20.

28 Higgs, Liz Curtis. *Rise and Shine* (Nashville: Thomas Nelson, 2002), 103.

MARCH

1 Elliot, Elisabeth. *Loneliness* (Nashville: Oliver-Nelson Books, A Division of Thomas Nelson Publishers, 1988), 50.

2 "Dream Big: The Henrietta Mears Story," *Christianity Today,* June 21, 1993, 41.

3 Tada, Joni Eareckson. *Heaven* (Grand Rapids: Zondervan, 1995), 98.

4 Catherine of Genoa. *Life and Doctrine of Saint Catherine of Genoa.* http://www.ccel.org/ccel/catherine_g/life.iv.xi.html.

5 Moore, Beth. *A Heart Like His* (Nashville: LifeWay Press, 1996), 124.

6 Lathbury, Mary Artemisia. *Poems* (Minneapolis: The Nunc Licet Press, 1915), 156.

7 L'Engle, Madeleine. *Glimpses of Grace: Daily Thoughts and Reflections* (San Francisco: HarperSan Francisco, 1996), 217.

8 Omartian, Stormie. *The Prayer That Changes Everything* (Eugene, OR: Harvest House Publishers, 2004), 161.

9 Arthur, Kay. *Lord, Is It Warfare? Teach Me to Stand* (Portland, OR: Multnomah, 1991), 206.

10 Price, Eugenia. *God Speaks to Women Today* (Grand Rapids: Zondervan, 1964), 128.

11 Goudge, Elizabeth. *The Dean's Watch* (Mattituck, New York: Ameron House, 1960), 382.

12 George, Elizabeth. *Life Management for Busy Women: Living Out God's Plan with Passion & Purpose* (Growth and Study Guide) (Eugene, OR: Harvest House Publishers, 2002), 101.

13 ten Boom, Corrie. *Amazing Love* (New York: Pillar Books by arrangement with Christian Literature Crusade, London, 1976), 14.

14 Carmichael, Amy. *From Sunrise Land: Letters from Japan* (London: Marshall Brothers, 1895), 60.

15 Nightingale, Florence. *Notes on Nursing* (London: Harrison and Sons, 1859), 15.

16 Higgs, Liz Curtis. *Bad Girls of the Bible* (Colorado Springs: Waterbrook Press, 1999), 26.

17 Teresa of Avila. *Life of St. Teresa of Jesus of the Order of Our Lady of Carmel.* 5th ed. David Lewis, trans. (New York: Benziger Brothers, 1916), 40.

18 Mayhall, Carole. *Help Lord, My Whole Life Hurts* (Colorado Springs: NavPress, 1988), 36.

19 Feldhahn, Shaunti. *For Women Only* (Sisters, OR: Multnomah Publishers, 2004), 178.

20 Meyer, Joyce. *The Battle Belongs to the Lord* (New York: Warner Books, 2002), 81.

21 Mother Veronica Namoyo. *A Memory for Wonder: A True Story* (San Francisco: Ignatius Press, 1993), 180–181.

22 Dillow, Linda. *Calm My Anxious Heart* (Colorado Springs: NavPress, 1998), 32.

23 Spangler, Ann. *The Tender Words of God* (Grand Rapids: Zondervan, 2008), 21.

24 Dravecky, Jan. *A Joy I'd Never Known* (Grand Rapids: Zondervan, 1996), 129.

25 Prentiss, Elizabeth. *Stepping Heavenward* (Amityville, NY: Calvary Press, 1992), 270.

26 DeMoss, Nancy Leigh. *Holiness* (Chicago: Moody Publishers, 2004), 22.

27 Austen, Jane. *Pride and Prejudice* (New York: Barnes & Noble Books, 1993), 10.

28 Crosby, Fanny. *Memories of 80 Years* (Boston: James H. Earle & Co, 1906), 96.

29 Mother Teresa. Quoted from Thinkexist.com.

30 Moore, Beth. *Praying God's Word* (Nashville: B&H Publishing Group, 2009), 91.

31 Trobisch, Ingrid. *The Confident Woman: Finding Quiet Strength in a Turbulent World* (New York: HarperCollins Publishers, 1993), 10.

APRIL

1 Clairmont, Patsy. *Mending Your Heart in a Broken World* (New York: Warner Books, 2001), 5.

2 Guyon, Madame. *Short and Easy Method of Prayer.* Christian Classics Ethereal Library (http://www.ccel.org/ccel/guyon/prayer.xxv.html).

3 Rubietta, Jane. *Come Along* (Colorado Springs: Waterbrook Press, 2008), 126.

4 Peale, Ruth Stafford. *The Adventure of Being a Wife* (Englewood Cliffs, NJ: Prentice-Hall, Inc., 1971), 72.

5 Barnes, Emilie. *Meet Me Where I Am, Lord* (Eugene, OR: Harvest House Publishers, 2006), 184.

6 Bottke, Allison. *God Answers Prayers* (Eugene, OR: Harvest House Publishers, 2005), 147.

7 Lisieux, Therese of. *The Autobiography of St. Therese of Lisieux: The Story of a Soul*, John Beevers, trans. (Garden City, NY: Image Books, Doubleday, 1957, 1963), 101.

8 Lathbury, Mary Artemisia. *Poems* (Minneapolis: The Nunc Licet Press, 1915), 133.

9 Hughes, Barbara. *Disciplines of a Godly Woman* (Wheaton, IL: Crossway Books, 2001), 57.

10 Rice, Anne. *Christ the Lord—Out of Egypt* (New York: Random House, 2005), 308.

11 Parks, Rosa. *Rosa Parks: My Story* (New York: Scholastic Inc., 1992), 187.

12 Marshall, Catherine. *Christy* (New York: McGraw-Hill, 1967), 95.

13 Cowman, L. B. *Streams in the Desert* (Grand Rapids: Zondervan, 1997), 25.

14 Pearcey, Nancy. *Total Truth* (Wheaton, IL: Crossway, 2004), 45.

15 Webb, Joan C. *The Relief of Imperfection* (Ventura, CA: Regal, 2007), 124.

16 Adams, Sarah. "Nearer, My God, to Thee." Quoted from http://nethymnal.org/htm/n/m/nmgtthee.htm.

17 Moore, Beth. *A Heart Like His* (Nashville: LifeWay Press, 1996), 99.

18 Kingsbury, Karen. *A Time to Embrace* (Nashville: Westbow Press, 2002), 303.

19 Bradstreet, Anne. "Verses upon the Burning of Our House, July 18th, 1666" in the *Norton Anthology of Literature by Women* (New York: W. W. Norton & Company, 1985), 72.

20 Jackson, Neta. *The Yada Yada Prayer Group Gets Tough* (Nashville: Thomas Nelson, 2005), 232–234.

21 Goudge, Elizabeth. *The Child From the Sea*. (New York: Coward-McCann, Inc., 1970), 566.

22 DeMoss, Nancy Leigh. *Lies Women Believe* (Chicago: Moody, 2001), 99.

23 Wilkinson, Darlene. *The Prayer of Jabez for Women* (Sisters, OR: Multnomah, 2002), 51.

24 Lotz, Anne Graham. *Heaven* (Nashville: W Publishing, 2001), 30.

25 Alcott, Louisa May. famousquotesandquthors.com/authors/louisa_may_alcott_quotes.html.

26 Underhill, Evelyn. *The Life of the Spirit and the Life of To-day* (New York: E. P. Dutton & Co., 1922), 294.

27 Bethune, Mary McLeod. *Building a Better World* (Bloomington, IN: Indiana University Press, 1991), 142.

28 Copeland, Lori. *Simple Gifts* (Grand Rapids: Zondervan, 2007), 229.

29 Anthony, Susan B. Quoted from thequotationspage.com.

30 Bright, Vonette. *The Greatest Lesson* (San Bernadino, CA: Here's Life Publishers, 1990), 178.

May

1 Partow, Donna. *Becoming the Woman God Wants Me to Be* (Grand Rapids: Revell, 2008), 23.

2 Thomas, Angela. *Do You Think I'm Beautiful?* (Nashville: Thomas Nelson, 2003), 28.

3 Wesley, Susanna. Quoted from www.godtoday.com/famous.htm.

4 Cymbala, Carol. *He's Been Faithful* (Grand Rapids: Zondervan, 2001), 145.

5 Arthur, Kay. *Lord, I'm Torn Between Two Masters* (Sisters, OR: Multnomah, 1996), 221.

6 ten Boom, Corrie. *Amazing Love* (New York: Pillar Books by arrangement with Christian Literature Crusade, London, 1976), 17.

7 Hatcher, Robin Lee. *Ribbon of Years* (Wheaton, IL: Tyndale House, 2001), 183.

8 Higgs, Liz Curtis. *Mad Mary* (Colorado Springs: Waterbrook Press, 2001), 244.

9 Clairmont, Patsy. *Normal Is Just a Setting on Your Dryer* (Colorado Springs: Focus on the Family Publishing, 1993), 98.

10 Briscoe, Jill. *Grace to Go On* (Wheaton, IL: Victor Books, 1989), 88.

11 Jackson, Mahalia. http://www.brainyquote.com/quotes/authors/m/mahalia_jackson.html.

12 Sayers, Dorothy. *Spiritual Writings* (Boston: Cowley Publications, 1993), 93.

13 Elliot, Elisabeth. *Passion and Purity* (Old Tappan, NJ: Fleming H. Revell, 1984), 39.

14 Keller, Helen. *The World I Live In* (New York: The Century Co., 1920), 183–184.

15 DeMoss, Nancy Leigh. *A Place of Quiet Rest* (Chicago: Moody Publishers, 2000), 216.

16 Crosby, Fanny. "Blessed Assurance." Quoted from http://nethymnal.org/htm/b/l/e/blesseda.htm.

17 Heald, Cynthia. *Becoming a Woman of Purpose* (Colorado Springs: NavPress, 1994), 14.

18 Guyon, Madame. *Autobiography of Madame Guyon*, Thomas Taylor Allen, trans. (London: Kegan Paul, Trench, Trubner & Co., Ltd., 1897), 104.

19 Eareckson, Joni and Steve Estes. *A Step Further* (Grand Rapids: Zondervan, 1978), 172.

20 Carmichael, Amy. *Sunrise Land* (London: Marshall Brothers, 1895), 33.

21 Julian of Norwich. *16 Revelations of Divine Love* (London: Kegan Paul, Trench, Trübner & Co., 1902), 57.

22 Kent, Carol. *A New Kind of Normal* (Nashville: Thomas Nelson, 2007), 160.

23 Falsani, Cathleen. Quoted in *The Wittenburg Door*, issue no. 203 (November/December 2006), n.p.

24 Walsh, Sheila. *Outrageous Love* (Nashville: J. Countryman, 2004), 119.

25 L'Engle, Madeleine. *Miracle on 10th Street* (Wheaton, IL: Harold Shaw Publishers, 1998), 76.

26 Stowe, Harriet Beecher. *Footsteps of the Master* (London: Sampson, Low, Marston, Searle, & Rivington, 1877), 202–203.

27 Hurnard, Hannah. *Hinds' Feet on High Places* (Wheaton, IL: Tyndale House, 1975), 259.

28 Rich, Ronda. *What Southern Women Know about Faith* (Grand Rapids: Zondervan, 2009), 24.

29 ten Boom, Corrie. *Tramp for the Lord* (Grand Rapids: Revell, 1974), 97.

30 Arthur, Kay. *Lord, Heal My Hurts* (Sisters, OR: Multnomah, 1988), 199.

31 Rivers, Francine. *The Last Sin Eater* (Waterville, ME: Thorndike Press, 1998), 419.

JUNE

1 Mother Teresa. *Reaching Out in Love*. Compiled by Edward Le Joly and Jaya Chaliha (New York: Continuum, 2000), 98.

2 Shepherd, Sheri Rose. *His Princess: Love Letters from Your King* (Sisters, OR: Multnomah, 2004), 14.

3 Shirer, Priscilla. *And We Are Changed* (Chicago: Moody Publishers, 2003), 59.

4 Dravecky, Jan, with Connie Neal. *A Joy I'd Never Known* (Grand Rapids: Zondervan, 1996), 24.

5 Rice, Helen Steiner. *In the Vineyard of the Lord* (Old Tappan, NJ: Fleming H. Revell Company, 1979), 118.

6 Bolton, Martha. *Cooking with Hot Flashes* (Minneapolis: Bethany House, 2004), 152.

7 Teresa of Avila. *The Interior Castle* (or *The Mansions*). Christian Classics Ethereal Library http://www.ccel.org/ccel/teresa/castle2.xi.iv.html.

8 Niequist, Shauna. *Cold Tangerines* (Grand Rapids: Zondervan, 2007), 15.

9 Marshall, Catherine. *Something More* (New York: McGraw-Hill, 1974), 256–57.

10 Huggett, Joyce. *The Joy of Listening to God* (Downers Grove, IL: InterVarsity Press, 1986), 169.

11 Low, Juliette. http://www.brainyquote.com/quotes/authors/j/juliette_g_low.html.

12 Burnham, Gracia, with Dean Merrill. *In the Presence of My Enemies* (Wheaton, IL: Tyndale House Publishers, 2003), 307.

13 Johnson, Barbara. *I'm So Glad You Told Me What I Didn't Wanna Hear* (Dallas: Word Publishing, 1996), 38.

14 Warren, Kay. *Dangerous Surrender* (Grand Rapids: Zondervan, 2007), 29.

15 Mayhall, Carole. *Help Lord, My Whole Life Hurts* (Colorado Springs: NavPress, 1988), 142.

16 Howe, Julia Ward. *The Walk with God* (New York: E. P. Dutton & Co, 1919), 7.

17 Clairmont, Patsy. *Mending Your Heart in a Broken World* (New York: Warner Books, 2001), 44.

18 LaHaye, Beverly. *The Spirit-Controlled Woman* (Irvine, CA: Harvest House Publishers, 1976), 17.

19 George, Elizabeth. *A Woman After God's Own Heart* (Eugene, OR: Harvest House Publishers, 1997), 40.

20 ten Boom, Corrie. *The Hiding Place* (Minneapolis: World Wide Publications, 1971), 197.

21 Thrupp, Dorothy. *Savior, Like a Shepherd Lead Us.* http://nethymnal.org/htm/s/l/slaslus.htm.

22 Feinberg, Margaret. *The Sacred Echo* (Grand Rapids: Zondervan, 2008), 125.

23 Smith, Hannah Whitall. *The Christian's Secret of a Happy Life* (Old Tappan, NJ: Fleming H. Revell, 1942, 1970), 32.

24 Elliot, Elisabeth. *Discipline* (Old Tappan, NJ: Fleming H. Revell Company, 1982), 137.

25 Schaeffer, Edith. *Lifelines: The Ten Commandments for Today* (Wheaton, IL: Crossway, 1982), 60.

26 Nation, Carrie. Quote from BrainyQuote.com.

27 DeMoss, Nancy Leigh. *A Place of Quiet Rest* (Chicago: Moody Publishers, 2000), 17.

28 L'Engle, Madeleine. *Walking on Water* (Wheaton, IL: Harold Shaw Publishers, 1980), 12.

29 Holmes, Marjorie. *I've Got to Talk to Somebody, God* (Garden City, NY: Doubleday & Co. Inc., 1969), xv.

30 Julian of Norwich. Quoted from http://www.readprint.com/author-1713/Julian-of-Norwich-books.

July

1 Moore, Beth. *Praying God's Word* (Nashville; B&H Publishing Group, 2009), 307.

2 Higgs, Liz Curtis. *Bad Girls of the Bible* (Colorado Springs: Waterbrook Press, 1999), 81.

3 Marshall, Catherine. *Beyond Ourselves* (New York: Avon Books, 1961), 342.

4 Price, Eugenia. *Leave Your Self Alone* (Grand Rapids: Zondervan, 1979), 102.

5 Lotz, Anne Graham. *My Heart's Cry* (Nashville: W Publishing Group, 2002), 3.

6 Rubietta, Jane. *Between Two Gardens* (Minneapolis: Bethany House, 2001), 23.

7 Huggett, Joyce. *The Joy of Listening to God* (Downers Grove, IL: InterVarsity Press, 1986), 124.

8 Briscoe, Jill. *Prayer that Works* (Wheaton, IL: Tyndale House Publishers, 2000), 83.

9 Sherrill, Elizabeth. *All the Way to Heaven* (Grand Rapids: Revell, 2002), 21.

10 Weaver, Joanna. *Having a Mary Heart in a Martha World* (Colorado Springs: Waterbrook Press, 2000), 29.

11 Graham, Ruth Bell. *It's My Turn* (Old Tappan, NJ: Fleming H. Revell, 1982), 75.

12 Clairmont, Patsy. *God Uses Cracked Pots* (Colorado Springs: Focus on the Family Publishing, 1991), 143.

13 ten Boom, Corrie. *The Hiding Place* (Minneapolis: World Wide Publications, 1971), 177.

14 Hurnard, Hannah. *Hinds' Feet on High Places* (Wheaton, IL: Living Books, 1975), 294.

15 Rice, Anne. *Called Out of Darkness* (New York: Alfred A. Knopf, a division of Random House, Inc., 2008), 164.

16 Christenson, Evelyn. *Gaining Through Losing* (Wheaton, IL: Victor Books, 1981), 159.

17 Holmes, Marjorie. *Love and Laughter* (Garden City, NY: Doubleday & Co., 1967), 213.

18 Alcott, Louisa May. *Little Women* (New York: Penguin, 2004), 419.

19 Feinberg, Margaret. *The Sacred Echo* (Grand Rapids: Zondervan, 2008), 183.

20 Moore, Beth. *A Heart Like His* (Nashville: LifeWay Press, 1996), 36.

21 Karon, Jan. *Light from Heaven*. (New York: Viking/Penguin, 2005), 377.

22 Elliot, Elisabeth. *Passion and Purity* (Old Tappan, NJ: Fleming H. Revell, 1984), 60.

23 George, Elizabeth. *A Woman's Call to Prayer* (Eugene, OR: Harvest House Publishers, 2004), 116.

24 Lewis, Beverly. *The Covenant* (Minneapolis: Bethany House Publishers, 2002), 139.

25 DeMoss, Nancy Leigh. *A Place of Quiet Rest* (Chicago: Moody Publishers, 2000), 168.

26 Cymbala, Carol. *He's Been Faithful* (Grand Rapids: Zondervan, 2001), 15.

27 Higgs, Liz Curtis. *Rise and Shine* (Nashville: Thomas Nelson Publishers, 2002), 239.

28 Crosby, Fanny. "All the Way My Savior Leads Me." Quoted from www.cyberhymnal.org.

29 Goudge, Elizabeth. *A Book of Faith* (New York: Coward, McCann & Geoghegan, 1976), xii.

30 Bronte, Charlotte. *Villette* (New York: Barnes & Noble Classics, 2005), 409.

31 Jackson, Mahalia. Quoted from http://www.brainyquote.com/quotes/authors/m/mahalia_jackson.html.

August

1 Marshall, Catherine. *Christy* (New York: McGraw-Hill, 1967), 190–91.

2 Mother Teresa. *No Greater Love* (Novato, CA: New World Library, 1995), 30.

3 Meyer, Joyce. *Never Give Up: Relentless Determination to Overcome Life's Challenges* (New York: FaithWords, 2008), 64.

4 Omartian, Stormie. *The Power of a Praying Woman* (Eugene, OR: Harvest House Publishers, 2004), 46.

5 Moore, Beth. *A Heart Like His* (Nashville: LifeWay Press, 1996), 165.

6 Arthur, Kay. *How to Study Your Bible* (Eugene, OR: Harvest House Publishers, 1994), 5.

7 Rivers, Francine. *The Prophet* (Wheaton, IL: Tyndale House, 2006), 179.

8 Stowe, Harriet Beecher. *Religious Poems: Light after Darkness* (London: Sampson Low, Son and Marston, Ludgate, Hill, 1867), 29.

9 Hurnard, Hannah. *Mountains of Spices* (Wheaton, IL: Tyndale House Publishers, 1977), 46.

10 George, Elizabeth. *A Woman's Walk with God* (Eugene, OR: Harvest House Publishers, 2000), 91.

11 Peterson, Tracie. *A Dream to Call My Own* (Minneapolis: Bethany House, 2009), 278.

12 Higgs, Liz Curtis. *Embrace Grace* (Colorado Springs: WaterBrook Press, 2006), 10.

13 Lotz, Anne Graham, *Heaven: My Father's House* (Nashville: W Publishing Company, A Division of Thomas Nelson, Inc., 2001), n.p.

14 Elliot, Elisabeth. *A Path through Suffering* (Ann Arbor, MI: Vine Books, an imprint of Servant Publications, 1990), 169.

15 DeMoss, Nancy Leigh. *A Place of Quiet Rest* (Chicago: Moody Publishers, 2000), 242.

16 Rich, Ronda. *What Southern Women Know about Faith* (Grand Rapids: Zondervan, 2009), 23.

17 Kent, Carol. *When I Lay My Isaac Down* (Colorado Springs: NavPress, 2004), 186.

18 Nixon, Brenda. *Life's Little Rule Book* (Lancaster, PA: Starburst Publishers, 1999), 71.

19 Pearcey, Nancy. *Total Truth* (Wheaton, IL: Crossway, 2004), 88.

20 Adams, Abigail. *Letters of Mrs. Adams: The Wife of John Adams, Volume 2* (Boston: Charles C. Little and James Brown, 1841), 229.

21 Pippert, Rebecca Manley. *Out of the Salt Shaker & into the World* (Downers Grove, IL: InterVarsity, 1979, 1999), 98.

22 Meyer, Joyce. *Battlefield of the Mind* (New York: Time Warner Book Group, 1995), 123.

23 Marshall, Catherine. *Christy* (New York: McGraw-Hill, 1967), 427.

24 Bronte, Charlotte. *Jane Eyre* (London: Folio Society, 1996 ed.), 60.

25 Wells, Thelma. *The Great Adventure Devotional* (Nashville: W Publishing Group, 2002), 105.

26 L'Engle, Madeleine. *Glimpses of Grace: Daily Thoughts and Reflections* (San Francisco: HarperSan Francisco, 1996), 231.

27 Osteen, Victoria. *Love Your Life* (New York: Free Press, 2008), 212.

28 Price, Eugenia. *The Wider Place* (Grand Rapids, MI: Zondervan, 1966), 172.

29 Mayhall, Carole. *Lord of My Rocking Boat* (Colorado Springs: NavPress, 1981), 119.

30 Moore, Beth. *Get Out of That Pit* (Nashville: Thomas Nelson Publishers, 2007), 146.

31 Oke, Janette. *A Quiet Strength* (Minneapolis: Bethany House, 1999), 176–77.

SEPTEMBER

1 Tada, Joni Eareckson. *When God Weeps* (Grand Rapids: Zondervan, 1997), 157.

2 ten Boom, Corrie. *Tramp for the Lord* (Grand Rapids: Revell, 1974), 55.

3 Alcott, Louisa May. *Little Women* (Wheaton, IL: Tyndale House, 1997), 391.

4 Heald, Cynthia. *Becoming a Woman of Prayer* (Colorado Springs: NavPress, 1996, 2005), 14.

5 Sayers, Dorothy. *Christian Letters to a Post-Christian World* (Grand Rapids: William B. Eerdmans, 1969), 103.

6 Lotz, Anne Graham. *The Glorious Dawn of God's Story* (Dallas: Word Books, 1997), 93.

7 Weaver, Joanna. *Having a Mary Heart in a Martha World* (Colorado Springs: Waterbrook, 2000), 111.

8 Catherine of Siena. *Deep Conversion/Deep Prayer* by Thomas Dubay (San Francisco, CA: Ignatius Press, 2006), 63.

9 Partow, Donna. *Living in Absolute Freedom* (Minneapolis: Bethany House, 2000), 135.

10 Elliot, Elisabeth. *Secure in the Everlasting Arms* (Ann Arbor, MI: Vine Books, an imprint of Servant Publications, 2002), 34.

11 Beamer, Lisa. *Let's Roll!* (Carol Stream, IL: Tyndale House Publishers, 2002), 79.

12 Teresa of Avila. *The Life of Saint Teresa of Jesus* (London: BiblioBazar, 1904, 2006), 123–124.

13 Omartian, Stormie. *Just Enough Light for the Step I'm On* (Eugene, OR: Harvest House Publishers, 2008), 167.

14 Rubietta, Jane. *Resting Place* (Downers Grove, IL: InterVarsity Press, 2005), 32.

15 Hill, Grace Livingston. *The Girl from Montana.* Quoted from http://www.gracelivingstonhill.com/bookshelves/etexts/15274-h.htm.

16 Marshall, Catherine. *To Live Again* (Grand Rapids: Baker, 1985), 75.

17 Julian of Norwich. Quoted from http://womenshistory.about.com/od/quotes/a/julian_norwich.htm.

18 Swindoll, Luci. *Life! Celebrate It: Listen, Learn, Laugh, Love* (Nashville: W Publishing Group, 2009), 187.

19 Graham, Ruth Bell. *A Legacy of Love* (Grand Rapids: Zondervan, 2005), 47.

20 Meyer, Joyce. *Beauty for Ashes* (Nashville: FaithWords, 2003), 124.

21 Underhill, Evelyn. From *The Essentials of Mysticism*, excerpted in *Devotional Classics*, Richard J. Foster and James Bryan Smith, eds. (San Francisco: HarperSanFrancisco, 1993), 115.

22 Walsh, Sheila. *Outrageous Love* (Nashville: J. Countryman, 2004), 56.

23 Berndt, Jodie. *Praying the Scriptures for Your Children* (Grand Rapids: Zondervan, 2001), 23.

24 Adams, Yolanda. Quote from "One Day at a Time" by Andree Farias, posted 1/09/2006 at http://www.christianitytoday.com/music/interviews/2006/yolandaadams-0106.html?start=2).

25 Moore, Beth. *A Heart Like His* (Nashville: LifeWay Press, 1996), 183.

26 Stowe, Harriet Beecher. Quoted from http://www.brainyquote.com/quotes/authors/h/harriet_beecher_stowe.html.

27 Trotter, Isabella Lilas. *Sowing Heavenly Seed,* quoted from http://unveiling.org/Articles/seeds.html.

28 Arthur, Kay. *Lord, Heal My Hurts* (Colorado Springs: WaterBrook Press, 1989, 2000), 26.

29 Montgomery, L. M. *Anne of Green Gables* (New York: Grosset & Dunlap Publishers, 2008), 46.

30 Madame Guyon. From *Experiencing the Depths of Jesus Christ,* excerpted in *Devotional Classics,* Richard J. Foster and James Bryan Smith, eds. (San Francisco: HarperSanFrancisco, 1993), 321.

OCTOBER

1 Blackstock, Terri. *The Gifted* (Nashville: Thomas Nelson, 2002), 101.

2 Austen, Jane. *Sense and Sensibility* (New York: Signet Classics, 1980), 278.

3 Shirer, Priscilla. *He Speaks to Me* (Chicago: Moody Publishers, 2006), 87.

4 Higgs, Liz Curtis. *Embrace Grace* (Colorado Springs: WaterBrook Press, 2006), 22.

5 Nixon, Brenda. *Quiet Reflections of Hope* (Grand Rapids: Revell, 2009), 124.

6 ten Boom, Corrie. *Tramp for the Lord* (New York: Jove Books, 1978), 133.

7 Pearcey, Nancy. *Total Truth* (Wheaton, IL: Crossway, 2004), 219.

8 Teresa of Avila. *The Way of Perfection,* E. Allison Peers, trans. (New York: Doubleday, 1991), 231.

9 George, Elizabeth. *Beautiful in God's Eyes* (Eugene, OR: Harvest House Publishers, 1998), 17.

10 Carlson, Melody. *Finding Alice* (Colorado Springs: Waterbrook, 2003), 105.

11 Catherine of Genoa. From *Life and Teachings,* excerpted in *Devotional Classics,* Richard J. Foster and James Bryan Smith, eds. (San Francisco: HarperSanFrancisco, 1993), 214.

12 Gist, Deeanne. *Deep in the Heart of Trouble* (Minneapolis: Bethany House, 2008), 261.

13 McDowell, Lucinda Secrest. *Role of a Lifetime* (Nashville: B&H Publishing Group, 2008), 7–8.

14 Cowman, L. B. *Springs in the Valley* (Grand Rapids: Zondervan, 1997), 169.

15 Rivers, Francine. *And the Shofar Blew* (Carol Stream, IL: Tyndale, 2003), 132.

16 Tada, Joni Eareckson. *Heaven* (Grand Rapids: Zondervan, 1995), 122.

17 Catherine of Siena. Quoted from http://home.infionline.net/~ddisse/siena.html#anchor330655.

18 Meyer, Joyce. *"Me and My Big Mouth!"* (Nashville: Warner Faith, 1997), 70.

19 Mother Teresa. *No Greater Love* (Novato, CA: New World Library, 1995), 27.

20 Beamer, Lisa. *Let's Roll!* (Wheaton, IL: Tyndale House Publishers, 2002), 304–305.

21 Julian of Norwich. *The Wisdom of Julian of Norwich,* compiled by Monica Furlong (London: Lion Hudson, 1996), 17.

22 Ortlund, Anne. *Fix Your Eyes on Jesus* (Dallas: Word Publishing, 1991), 22.

23 Marshall, Catherine. *Christy* (New York: McGraw-Hill, 1967), 204.

24 Underhill, Evelyn, *Mysticism.* Quoted from http://www.ccel.org/ccel/underhill/mysticism.iv.iv.html.

25 Fry, Elizabeth. *Memoir of the Life of Elizabeth Fry,* by Elizabeth Gurney Fry, Katherine Fry, and Rachel Elizabeth Cresswell (London: John Hatchard and Son, 1848), 110.

26 Moore, Beth. *A Heart Like His* (Nashville: LifeWay Press, 1996), 100.

27 Wilder, Laura Ingalls. *On the Banks of Plum Creek* (New York: HarperCollins Publishers, 1981), 35.

28 Omartian, Stormie. *Just Enough Light for the Step I'm On* (Eugene, OR: Harvest House Publishers, 2008), 109.

29 Gunn, Robin Jones. *Sisterchicks in Sombreros* (Sisters, OR: Multnomah, 2004), 138.

30 Heald, Cynthia. *A Woman's Journey to the Heart of God* (Nashville: Thomas Nelson, 2000), 140.

31 Pippert, Rebecca Manley. *Out of the Salt Shaker & into the World* (Downers Grove, IL: InterVarsity Press, 1979), 40.

NOVEMBER

1 ten Boom, Corrie. *Tramp for the Lord* (New York: Jove Books, 1978), 135.

2 Smith, Hannah Whitall. *The Christian's Secret of a Happy Life* (Westwood, NJ: Barbour, 1985), 240.

3 Walsh, Sheila. *Outrageous Love* (Nashville: J. Countryman, 2004), 17.

4 Moon, Lottie. Quoted from http://www.burnthickory.com/aboutlottiemoon.

5 Wells, Thelma. *The Great Adventure Devotional* (Nashville: W Publishing Group, 2002), 85.

6 Goudge, Elizabeth. *The Child from the Sea* (New York: Coward-McCann, Inc., 1970), 198.

7 Parks, Rosa. Quoted from http://www.brainyquote.com/quotes/authors/r/rosa_parks.html.

8 Meyer, Joyce. *Beauty for Ashes* (New York: Warner Faith, 2003), 59.

9 Bradstreet, Anne. "Meditations Divine and Moral," in *Norton Anthology of Literature by Women* (New York: W. W. Norton & Company, 1985), 69.

10 Tada, Joni Eareckson. *When God Weeps* (Grand Rapids: Zondervan, 1997), 89.

11 Hughes, Barbara. *Disciplines of a Godly Woman* (Wheaton, IL: Crossway, 2001), 69.

12 Booth, Catherine Bramwell. Quoted from http://www.answers.com/topic/catherine-booth.

13 Weaver, Joanna. *Having a Mary Heart in a Martha World* (Colorado Springs: Waterbrook Press, 2000), 5.

14 Barton, Ruth Haley. *Sacred Rhythms* (Downers Grove, IL: InterVarsity Press, 2006), 111.

15 L'Engle, Madeleine. Quoted from http://womenshistory.about.com/od/quotes/a/madeleinelengle.htm.

16 Kidder, Virelle. *Meet Me at the Well* (Chicago: Moody Publishers, 2008), 114.

17 Therese of Lisieux. *The Autobiography of St. Therese of Lisieux: The Story of a Soul*, John Beevers, trans. (Garden City, NY: Image Books, Doubleday, 1963), 110.

18 Wesley, Susanna. From *Susanna Wesley: The Complete Writings, 1711-1712*, quoted in *The Wesley's Amazing Love* in Classic Christian Bible Studies by Carolyn Nystrom, series ed. (Downers Grove, IL: InterVarsity Press, 2002), 50.

19 Teresa of Avila. From *Interior Castle*, excerpted in *Devotional Classics*, Richard J. Foster and James Bryan Smith, eds. (San Francisco: HarperSanFrancisco, 1993), 198.

20 Montgomery, L. M. *Anne of Green Gables* (New York: Grosset & Dunlap Publishers, 2008 printing), 223.

21 Julian of Norwich. From *Revelations of Divine Love*, excerpted in *Devotional Classics*, Richard J. Foster and James Bryan Smith, eds. (San Francisco: HarperSanFrancisco, 1993), 70–71.

22 Trotter, Isabella Lilias. Quoted from http://unveiling.org/Articles/nature8.html.

23 Rivers, Francine. *A Voice in the Wind* (Carol Stream, IL: Tyndale, 1993), 13.

24 Rubietta, Jane. *Resting Place* (Downers Grove, IL: InterVarsity Press, 2005), 159–160.

25 Elliot, Elisabeth. *Secure in the Everlasting Arms* (Ann Arbor, MI: Vine Books, an imprint of Servant Publications, 2002), 39.

26 Ruth Bell Graham, *The Greatest Lesson*. Vonette Bright, ed. (San Bernadino, CA: Here's Life Publishers, 1990), 97.

27 Meyer, Joyce. *The Battle Belongs to the Lord* (New York: Warner Books, 2002), 11.

28 Underhill, Evelyn. From *The Essential of Mysticism*, excerpted in *Devotional Classics*, Richard J. Foster and James Bryan Smith, eds. (San Francisco: HarperSanFrancisco, 1993), 115.

29 Tchividjian, Gigi Graham. *A Quiet Knowing* (Nashville: Thomas Nelson, Inc., 2001), 5.

30 Crosby, Fanny. Quoted in *101 Hymn Stories* by Kenneth W. Osbeck (Grand Rapids: Kregel Publications, 1982), 167.

December

1 Heald, Cynthia. *Becoming a Woman of Faith* (Nashville: Thomas Nelson, 2000), 2.

2 Stowe, Harriet Beecher. *Religious Poems: Light after Darkness* (London: Sampson Low, Son and Marston, Ludgate Hill, Bell and Daldy, York Street, 1867), 45.

3 ten Boom, Corrie. *Amazing Love* (New York: Pillar Books by arrangement with Christian Literature Crusade, London, 1976), 111.

4 Dillow, Linda. *Satisfy My Thirsty Soul* (Colorado Springs: NavPress, 2007), 19.

5 Catherine of Siena. From *The Dialogue*, excerpted in *Devotional Classics*, Richard J. Foster and James Bryan Smith, eds. (San Francisco: HarperSanFrancisco, 1993), 288.

6 Smith, Hannah Whitall. From *The Christian's Secret of a Happy Life*, excerpted in *Devotional Classics*, Richard J. Foster and James Bryan Smith, eds. (San Francisco: HarperSanFrancisco, 1993), 265.

7 Sayers, Dorothy. *Are Women Human?* (Grand Rapids: Eerdmans, 1971), 47.

8 Mother Teresa. *A Simple Path*. Compiled by Lucinda Vardey (New York: Ballantine Books, 1995), 1.

9 Lotz, Anne Graham. *I Saw the Lord* (Grand Rapids: Zondervan, 2006), 79.

10 Hollingsworth, Amy. Quoted from Beliefnet interview with Holly Lebowitz Rossi, "Mister Rogers' Theology of 'Neighbor,'" May 12, 2005.

11 Pippert, Rebecca Manley. *Out of the Salt Shaker & into the World* (Downers Grove, IL: InterVarsity Press, 1979, 1999), 107.

12 Thoene, Bodie. *A Thousand Shall Fall* (Minneapolis: Bethany House, 1992), 387–388.

13 Kingsbury, Karen. *A Time to Embrace* (Nashville: Westbow Press, 2002), 308.

14 Eareckson, Joni Tada and Steve Estes. *A Step Further* (Grand Rapids: Zondervan, 1978), 97.

15 McDowell, Lucinda Secrest. *Quilts from Heaven* (Nashville: B&H Publishing Group, 2007), 5.

16 Teresa of Avila. From *Interior Castle*, excerpted in *Devotional Classics*, Richard J. Foster and James Bryan Smith, eds. (San Francisco: HarperSanFrancisco, 1993), 198.

17 Trobisch, Ingrid. *The Confident Woman: Finding Quiet Strength in a Turbulent World* (New York: HarperCollins Publishers, 1993), 102–103.

18 Swindoll, Luci. *After You've Dressed for Success* (Waco, TX: Word Books, 1987), 30.

19 ten Boom, Corrie. *The Hiding Place* (Minneapolis: World Wide Publications, 1971), 215.

20 Rivers, Francine. *Unspoken* (Wheaton, IL: Tyndale House, 2001), 174.

21 Meyer, Joyce. *Beauty for Ashes* (Nashville: FaithWords, 2003), 42.

22 Elliot, Elisabeth. *Through Gates of Splendor* (New York: Harper & Brothers Publishers, 1957), 255.

23 Walsh, Sheila. *Outrageous Love* (Nashville: J. Countryman, 2004), 30.

24 Austen, Jane. *Persuasion* (New York: Barnes & Noble Books, 1818; B & N edition: 2004), 283.

25 Oke, Janette, *Love Comes Softly* (Minneapolis: Bethany House, 1979), 119.

26 Wilder, Laura Ingalls. *Little House on the Prairie* (New York: HarperCollins, 1935), 250.

27 Crosby, Fanny. "He Hideth My Soul." Quoted from http://nethymnal.org/htm/b/l/e/blesseda.htm.
28 Catherine of Genoa. From *Life and Teachings*, excerpted in *Devotional Classics,* Richard J. Foster and James Bryan Smith, eds. (San Francisco: HarperSanFrancisco, 1993), 214.
29 Montgomery, L. M. *The Golden Road* (New York: McGraw-Hill Ryerson, 1944), 198.
30 Marshall, Catherine. *Beyond Ourselves* (New York: Avon Books, 1961), 92.
31 Bell, Valerie. *A Well-Tended Soul* (Grand Rapids: Zondervan, 2000), 24.

Share Your Thoughts

With the Author: Your comments will be forwarded to the author when you send them to *zauthor@zondervan.com*.

With Zondervan: Submit your review of this book by writing to *zreview@zondervan.com*.

Free Online Resources at

www.zondervan.com

Zondervan AuthorTracker: Be notified whenever your favorite authors publish new books, go on tour, or post an update about what's happening in their lives at www.zondervan.com/authortracker.

Daily Bible Verses and Devotions: Enrich your life with daily Bible verses or devotions that help you start every morning focused on God. Visit www.zondervan.com/newsletters.

Free Email Publications: Sign up for newsletters on Christian living, academic resources, church ministry, fiction, children's resources, and more. Visit www.zondervan.com/newsletters.

Zondervan Bible Search: Find and compare Bible passages in a variety of translations at www.zondervanbiblesearch.com.

Other Benefits: Register yourself to receive online benefits like coupons and special offers, or to participate in research.